INTERNATIONAL JOINT VENTURES: ECONOMIC AND ORGANIZATIONAL PERSPECTIVES

edited by

Kalyan Chatterjee
and
Barbara Gray

Center for Research in Conflict and Negotiation
The Pennsylvania State University
University Park, Pennsylvania, USA

SPRINGER SCIENCE+BUSINESS MEDIA, LLC

Library of Congress Cataloging-in-Publication Data

International joint ventures : economic and organizational perspectives / Kalyan Chatterjee and Barbara Gray.
p. cm.
Papers from April, 1992 symposium on "International Joint Ventures and Strategic Alliances," held by the Center for Research in Conflict and Negotiation, The Pennsylvania State University.
Includes bibliographical references.
ISBN 978-94-017-1946-9 ISBN 978-94-017-1944-5 (eBook)
DOI 10.1007/978-94-017-1944-5
1. Investments, Foreign—Congresses. 2. Joint ventures—Congresses. 3. Strategic Alliances (Business)—Congresses.
I. Chatterjee, Kalyan. II. Gray, Barbara, 1946–
HG4538.I597 1995
338.8'8—DC20 95-19907
CIP

Originally published by Kluwer Academic Publishers in 1995
Softcover reprint of the hardcover 1st edition 1995

Printed on acid-free paper.

CONTENTS

Group Decision and Negotiation, 4: 379–382 (1995)

International Joint Ventures: Economic and Organizational Perspectives

KALYAN CHATTERJEE
Department of Management Science and Information Systems, Center for Research in Conflict and Negotiation, The Pennsylvania State University, 313 Beam Business Administration Building, University Park, PA 16802

BARBARA GRAY
Department of Management and Organization, Center for Research in Conflict and Negotiation, The Pennsylvania State University, 313 Beam Business Administration Building, University Park, PA 16802

In April 1992, the Center for Research in Conflict and Negotiation at The Pennsylvania State University held a symposium on International Joint Ventures and Strategic Alliances. The purpose of the symposium was to take a cross-disciplinary look at economic and managerial issues affecting joint-venture formation, operation, and performance. Executives, policy makers, and scholars from several fields discussed issues ranging from the impact of international trade policy to cross-cultural communication on joint-venture operations. The outcome was a more complete understanding of joint ventures as a mode of entry into domestic and international markets.

The articles in this book represent a subset of those at the symposium and include two discussants' commentaries. While quite different in their orientations and insights, together the articles examine political, economic, and organizational factors affecting joint-venture initiation and performance. In this overview, the contribution of each article is summarized, common themes and major differences among the studies are reviewed, and future research areas are identified.

The economic and strategic analyses of joint ventures, especially research and development, have joint ventures focused on two categories of questions. The first consists of issues of importance to the potential and actual participants in a joint venture, including:

- What are the incentives to *cooperate* in R&D?
- What are the organizational forms that such cooperation can take? These include: information-sharing arrangments among firms, "delegative" R&D, in which one firm does the R&D and licenses its use, and formation of a separate entity to develop a specific process or product, usually with equity participation of the parents.

The second category of question relates to the social effects of joint ventures and adopts the point of view of society as a whole, or its agent, the regulator. For example:

- Do joint ventures increase the speed of new process or product development and the frequency of innovation?
- Do joint ventures eliminate wasteful duplication of research activities? Do they induce the socially efficient degree of correlation in R&D projects?
- What are the effects of cooperation on individual incentives to perform research, and what net effect do joint ventures have on competition in an industry?

The articles in this volume attempt to address some of these questions, using simple theoretical models and conceptual discussions as well as empirical analyses.

Michael Katz primarily addresses the questions in the first category in "Joint Ventures as a Means of Assembling Complementary Inputs," though he also discusses the effects on competition of joint ventures vs. mergers. Katz examines several alternative motivations for forming a joint venture and points out that some of them, such as cost sharing, need to be considered with caution. Why, for instance, is "cost sharing" with the capital market not a preferred strategy for the potential innovator? Why must internal funds be used? The article proposes some answers to these questions. Katz's piece focuses on the monitorability of inputs if a separate entity is formed. "The accounting bright lines" created by a new entity make it easier to verify the contribution made by each participant in a joint venture. In discussing organizational forms for cooperation, the article points out that, as a way of exploring particular synergies, a joint venture has a much smaller potential for anticompetitive effects than an outright merger.

The article by Marjit and Shi is almost entirely devoted to the study of organizational forms for R&D cooperation among competing firms. Three forms are studied: "noncooperative R&D," i.e., independent research and development, "cooperative R&D," i.e., joint ventures, and "delegative R&D," or licensing. Circumstances under which licensing is preferred to joint ventures, from both private and social perspectives are considered. A joint venture is conceived as a cost/input sharing entity. However, it undertakes exactly the same amount of research that an individual firm would if it could afford to.

Gauvin adopts a more global empirical perspective in "Networks of Innovators: Evidence from Canadian Patents," analyzing the incidence of joint patents in Canadian patent data from 1978–1989. He finds that Japanese firms tend to participate more in joint development than do U.S. and Canadian ones. Most alliances are intra-sectional, except among Japanese firms, where interindustry alliances are more frequent. On the efficacy of joint ventures in generating research Gavin notes that U.S firms had the largest share of patents but the least joint development, whereas Japan and Germany were both heavily involved in collaborative development and have both done well economically.

A further perspective on the social benefits from joint ventures is provided by Dennis Yao of the Federal Trade Commission. Yao discusses the nature of antitrust scrutiny of alliances. When integrative efficiencies are created, JV's are analyzed using the "rule of reason" on a case-by-base basis. Yao gives the example of the General Motors/Toyota joint venture where the FTC's consent order limited output and duration, so that GM continued to maintain its line of small cars. In that way, any potential socially deleterious effects were to be attenuated.

The research reported here is part of an active program of work in this area. Following on the original work of Katz (1986), d'Aspremont and Jacquemin (1988), and others, various authors have considered research cooperation as a response to the free-riding incentives produced by spillovers. Grossman and Shapiro (1987) have also briefly considered the issue of joint ventures in the early stages of a multistage R&D race. Such joint ventures may, in fact, enhance competition by enabling the participants in the venture to remain competitive with each other in the remainder of the race. Thus, a growing body of insightful work is being produced, to which the present articles make a worthwhile contribution.

In "Patterns of Strategic Alliances between Rival Firms," Bernard Garrette and Pierre Dussauge develop an empirically based taxonomy of strategic alliances, based on strategic and organizational factors hypothesized to influence the evolution of alliances over time.

They identify three distinct classes of alliances: (1) quasi-concentration alliances, (2) market penetration alliances, and (3) shared supply alliances, differentiated on the basis of two dimensions: competitive stance and symmetry of control. Quasi-concentration alliances tend to be symmetrical and anticompetitive. Market penetration alliances tend to be asymmetric. Shared supply alliances tend to be symmetric and precompetitive.

In "Agency Costs and the Structure and Performance of Domestic and International Joint Ventures," J. Michael Geringer and C. Patrick Woodcock investigate the impact the number of partners and cross-cultural differences have on venture performance. They argue from an agency theory perspective that (1) more partners and (2) goal conflicts induced by cultural differences reduce survival rates. In both cases, performance is expected to decrease because of contract inefficiencies. As the number of principals increases, agents incur increased transaction costs in communicating with the principals, and the potential for disagreement about goals increases. Divergent cultural norms also increase the potential for differing goals among principals and agents. Only partial support for these predictions was found. Two aspects of cultural difference, uncertainty avoidance and individualism, influenced survival rates, while the number of partners did not.

Yan and Gray take a close, intensive look at four joint ventures in "Bargaining Power, Management Control, and Performance in U.S./China Joint Ventures: A Comparative Case Study." They explain why firms adopt different management control structures and the nature of the relationship between control and performance. The study does not find a simple direct relationship between control and performance, but suggests that informal means of control, i.e., mutual trust, common and contractually specified goals, may ameliorate differences in formal control mechanisms and enhance overall performance.

In "Barriers to International Joint Ventures and Strategic Alliances," Kathyrn Rudie Harrigan notes that new motivations for joint-venture formation arise from the need to rationalize productive assets and share capacity with competitors at home while competing abroad. Major barriers to successful alliances arise from the need for homogeneity and interchangeability of parts, products, and personnel across production operations worldwide. Harrigan acknowledges the clash between corporate strategies and government objectives for economic development. Policy makers' desires for their share of "knowledge workers," improved living standards, and antitrust protection conflict with corporate rationalization strategies. Harrigan asserts that developing core competencies should be a key objective for corporate alliance partners (antitrust restrictions notwithstanding). Also, gaining competitive advantage as first-movers or copycats necessitates overcoming the barriers to efficient information transfer among alliance partners.

Vicki Golich elaborates on some of the policy considerations highlighted by Harrigan. In "Transnational Partners in Commercial Class Aircraft Manufacturing: Why and How," Golich brings a political science perspective to the analysis of joint-venture formation in commercial aircraft manufacturing, tracing the evolution of the industry from an open field of competitors through oligopoly to the current focus on alliances. Her analysis reveals the political, economic, and technological factors that have shaped industry-level dynamics and propelled the formation of joint ventures. According to Golich, "the policy outcomes of the political game essentially define the framework of economic activity by affecting the size and operating rules of the marketplace." For example, European firms were more inclined toward collaboration than the Americans after World War II, influenced by national policy. More recently, U.S. national policy has propelled transnational production strategies among U.S. firms. Examples of four global production strategies within the industry are provided. Comparison of the articles reveals some predictable similarities and some unexpected surprises.

Both Golich and Dussauge and Garette classify joint ventures, Golich on the basis of production strategy, and Dussauge and Garette by competitive strategy and asymmetry. The latter suggest that European aerospace alliances fall into the quasi-concentration category, comparable to Golich's horizontal globalization, which is consistent with the argument that national policy shapes firm strategy in that most European governments are unwilling to give up local control of aerospace manufacturing. However, Golich classifies the production strategies of the two major U.S. aerospace firms as primarily asymmetrical (corresponding to market penetration alliances), suggesting that U.S. firms demand even greater control over their alliances than do the Europeans. This raises the question of how inclusion of nationality differences might alter Dussauge and Garette's typology. (Country of origin was included in their study, but only to ensure representativeness, not as a defining variable in the taxonomy.) Harrigan and Golich both point to potential antitrust interference with partners' strategies to cooperate through specialization and market division.

Both Dussauge and Garette and Geringer and Woodcock predicted that as the number of partners in a joint venture increases, the overall stability of the enterprise will decrease. However, neither found strong effects for his variable. The number of partners did not critically differentiate classes of joint ventures.

Taken as a whole, the articles reinforce the importance of studying individual firm experience in strategic alliances within a very complex context of organizational, economic, and political decision making, considering the impact of decisions about investments, resource allocations, formal and informal control structures, and cross-cultural communication on venture performance and longevity. They should consider how industry and national economic and political forces constrain or enlarge the range of options and ultimately affect survival.

We would like to express our appreciation to the following reviewers, who have contributed significantly to the overall quality of this effort: Francis Bloch, Vicki Golich, Norges Handelshoyskole, Sugata Marjit, Richard Moxin, James Sebenius, Martin Soros, Yossef Spiegel, Aimin Yan, and Dennis Yao. We would also like to thank Mr. Hideki Kaihatsu and Fuji-Xerox as well as the Penn State Institute for Policy Research and Evaluation and the Smeal College of Business Administration, for their generous financial support of the symposium. Thanks are also due to the staff at Kluwer Academic Publishers, in particular to the Senior Editor, Marie Stratta, and to Judith Kemp of the GRUP Editorial Office for their forbearance during the long process of getting this book together.

Kalyan Chatterjee and Barbara Gray

References

d'Aspremont, Claude, and A. Jacquemin. (1988). "Cooperative and Noncooperative R&D in Duopoly with Spillovers," *American Economic Review*, December, 78, 1133–1137.

Grossman, G., and C. Shapiro. (1987). "Dynamic R&D Competition," *Economic Journal* 97, 372–387.

Katz, M.L. (1986). "An Analysis of Cooperative Research and Development," *Rand Journal of Economics* 17 (Winter), 527–543.

Group Decision and Negotiation, 4: 383–400 (1995)

Joint Ventures as a Means of Assembling Complementary Inputs

MICHAEL L. KATZ
Haas School of Business, University of California at Berkeley, Berkeley, California 94720

Abstract.

In recent years, economists have devoted considerable attention to mechanisms through which firms can cooperate, particularly in the conduct of R&D. This literature had tended to focus on cooperation's effects in *output* markets. In contrast, the present analysis examines the effects of cooperation on *input* markets. In particular, joint ventures are often said to be motivated by the desire to assemble complementary assets into a package needed to conduct a successful project. Some of the ways in which joint ventures may faciliate the acquisition of needed inputs are explored.

Key Words: complementary assets, cooperative R&D, innovation, joint ventures

1. Introduction

Many potential benefits of interfirm cooperation can be identified, including the more efficient use of complementary assets, the avoidance of wasteful duplication of effort, and risk sharing. These benefits must be weighed against the potential costs. From a firm's perspective, the private costs include the administrative and transactions costs of establishing and managing cooperative relationships and the potential erosion of competitive position by helping one's rivals. From the public perspective, the costs include the erosion of competition itself. Indeed, concern for these social costs lies behind antitrust policy that often limits the degree of interfirm cooperation.

There are reasons to believe that the private and social benefits of cooperation in the conduct of R&D are especially large relative to the costs. In particular, there are several characteristics of R&D that pose obstacles to the efficient operation of a simple price system in which firms interact at arm's length, buying inputs and selling outputs at posted, uniform prices.

One, there is both anecdotal and econometric evidence that *technological spillovers*—whereby the research done by one firm can be utilized by another firm even though the

This article was originally prepared for the Penn State International Symposium on Joint Ventures and Strategic Alliances, April 6–8, 1992. I am grateful to the conference participants, to seminar participants at Duke University and Harvard Business School, and to an anonymous referee for useful comments and suggestions. I would also like to thank my colleague Benjamin Hermalin for his careful reading of an earlier draft and for many insightful discussions of the issues raised here. This material is based on work supported by the National Science Foundation under Award No. SES-9112076.

latter does not receive permission to use the R&D results—can be significant.[1] The difficulty that a firm faces in obtaining payment from firms who benefit from its R&D through spillovers reduces the incentive to conduct R&D.

A second set of problems stems from *rent seeking*. Successful innovation may give rise to the award of a patent or the realization of some other first-mover advantage yielding quasi-rents. As private firms attempt to appropriate these rents, each firm is willing to take costly actions in order to gain profits at other firms' expense. Consequently, firms may engage in overinvestment as they race with one another to win a patent or attempt to improve their positions in bargaining over license terms.[2] Moreover, monopoly pricing of R&D results may lead to inefficient sales levels, while the fact that a firm typically is unable to appropriate all of the gains from the sale of intellectual property may lead to socially insufficient incentives to undertake R&D projects.

A third set of difficulties results from *asymmetric information*. Given the low costs of dissemination relative to discovery, it generally is efficient to have firms disseminate their R&D result widely. But the fact that the dissemination of these results entails the sale of information raises well-known problems of opportunism and asymmetric information that can greatly limit the effectiveness of the market for R&D results and can lead to inefficiently little dissemination of knowledge.

Problems of asymmetric information may also make it difficult to assemble the inputs needed to conduct R&D successfully. One reason that inputs may be hard to trade is that it can be difficult to assess their quality prior to purchase. Indeed, the inputs to an R&D project often include the outputs of earlier R&D projects, so that the asymmetric information problems identified above for selling intellectual property arise here too. Similar problems may arise for other inputs. Research personnel, for example, may possess unique creative talents that are better observed by their current employers than by potential future employers.

The inputs potentially subject to problems of asymmetric information also include financial capital. With most inputs, the problem of asymmetric information is that the buyer of the input is less informed about the quality of the input than is the supplier. In the case of project finance, the problem may be reversed. The firm undertaking the project and demanding financial capital may be better informed about a project's chances of success or about the performance of the personnel working on the project than would be an outside capital supplier. Problems of both moral hazard and adverse selection can make project finance difficult.[3]

It has become popular for members of business, government, and academia to suggest some form of interfirm cooperation as a potential means of overcoming at least some of these difficulties. In the present article, I explore ways in which research joint ventures might improve economic performance. In conducting this exploration, I address three fundamental issues that arise in the study of interfirm cooperation, in general, and research joint ventures, in particular.

The first issue is the choice of an appropriate benchmark. A firm has a variety of options when choosing how to cooperate with other firms. Firms may conduct R&D collectively through a joint venture or a consortium. Alternatively, a single firm may complete an R&D project and then license its findings to others. Or firms may use less formal sharing mechanisms, such as information and know-how trading. Individual papers in the economic literature have tended to focus on a single means of developing and disseminating intellectual property. Thus, there is a "licensing literature," a "know-how trading literature," and a "research joint venture literature." Actual firms, however, face all of these alternatives simultaneously. I believe that one can understand the role of research joint ventures only if one considers the alternatives. For example, research joint ventures are sometimes defended on the grounds that it is inefficient for two firms to perform duplicate research. But would the absence of a joint venture lead to such duplication, or would a single firm conduct the research and license its findings to the other? Clearly, the answer to this question has great bearing on our analysis of the private and social incentives to form a research joint venture. An important question from both the business strategy and public policy standpoints is how firms make choices from among the available *portfolio* of options for R&D cooperation.

To understand the choice among different forms of cooperation, one must understand how the alternative arrangements differ in form and function. This observation leads to a second basic point: a joint venture combines several features at once.

- *A joint venture is a form of ex ante cooperation.* Prior to the project's being undertaken, a joint venture agreement typically spells out the members' commitments and responsibilities for financial and other contributions to the effort. The agreement also typically lays out principles for the dissemination of any results obtained.

- *A joint venture is a form of mutual monitoring.* A joint venture agreement may set up a structure that increases its members' abilities to monitor one another's actions.

- *A joint venture entails the provision of capital or other inputs to the R&D process.* The members of a joint venture typically make up-front contributions of inputs to the project. These contributions may be both a form of commitment and a form of hostage exchange—where each party is contributing assets that will have value only if the partnership is conducted successfully.

- *A joint venture gives partners equity stakes in the outcome.* In speaking of equity interests, I am not limiting myself to equity in the form of shares of stock. Rather, I mean that the parties to the venture all have financial stakes in the ultimate success or failure of the project, and they share the risk of undertaking it.

- *A joint venture has a particular status with governments,* either in terms of the way in which governments enforce agreements among the venture's members, or in terms of how favorably disposed the governments are toward the member firms (e.g., the willingness of a government to grant market access to a foreign firm often rises when it takes on a local venture partner).

In any given setting, some of these features play critical roles, while others are of less importance. In order to assess the private and social desirability of joint ventures, it is important to understand which characteristics matter, and when. Drawing on my first point above, both patent licensing and research joint ventures are means of disseminating R&D results. But they differ dramatically in terms of the timing of agreements. For instance, a joint venture may set up a license fee schedule before any results have even been obtained, while the licensing of patents individually obtained occurs after one party has been granted a monopoly position. Rather than simply state that a research joint venture is necessary for cooperation, we need to understand whether these differences in timing lead to a research joint venture's overcoming problems that a licensing agreement cannot.

A similar point can be made about another potential role of joint ventures. Contractor and Lorange (1988) (among others) emphasize that a joint venture may be a particularly fast way to pull assets together. We might expect these effects to be especially strong when there are benefits associated with the formation of teams of personnel who work well together. But, while this argument is superficially appealing, by itself it does not explain why firms would not simply hire out their workers or other assets as preassembled teams. Again, we need to ask what is special about the structure and operation of a joint venture.

This observation leads to my final basic point. Joint ventures and other forms of cooperation are responses to such problems as asymmetric information, rent seeking, and weak property rights. In analyzing the choice of cooperative mode, one needs to model carefully how different institutional arrangements solve these problems. Here, I think the literature on vertical and lateral integration is instructive. Most of this literature simply assumes that integration gives one party complete control and information regarding all aspects of the combined operations, shedding no light on how or why.[4] In contrast, Grossman and Hart (1986) adopt the extreme view that integration alters neither the set of feasible contracts between the stages of production nor the goals of the self-interested decision makers at the different stages. Their approach has been a fruitful one, because it pushes us to consider more deeply what the fundamental differences between alternative institutions really are.

Turning to joint ventures, to understand fully how a joint venture works, one should not simply assume that a research joint venture eliminates the incentive problems to which it is a response. While at least some of the strategy literature is sensitive to this point, much of the economics literature looks at symmetric models of fairly limited forms of cooperation in which the venture members have largely coincident interests.[5] Informed by experience, one knows that actual ventures can have strong intra-venture conflicts. The theoretical literature should examine models rich enough to capture these conflicts.

In the present article I consider some simple models in which interfirm conflicts arise, whether or not the firms are members of a joint venture. I examine the role of a joint venture in mitigating these conflicts. Critically, I do not *assume* that a joint venture will overcome these problems. Rather, I examine how specific elements of the venture's structure can be designed to provide individual firms with incentives to work in the collective interest. Moreover, in doing so, I compare a joint venture with alternative organizational forms.

If one writes down a matrix whose rows are potential problems and whose columns are features of research joint ventures that potentially solve these problems, one is confronted by rather a lot of cells. The potential problems in the conduct and dissemination of R&D occur in both the market for inputs to R&D and the market for the output generated by successful R&D. To date, economists (e.g., d'Aspremont and Jacquemin 1988; Grossman and Shapiro 1986; Katz 1986; Ordover and Willig 1985) have tended to focus on problems in the output market and on the potential anticompetitive effects of R&D cooperation.[6] In contrast, business decision makers often characterize cooperation as a means of overcoming problems in the markets for R&D inputs. Here, I will focus my attention on some simple formal models exploring the role of research joint ventures in solving input-market problems.

In examining how research joint ventures can overcome these problems, I will limit consideration to the use of equity interests to create incentives and to the use of administrative structures to improve information flows. While the effects of ex ante agreement and commitment—two other features of joint ventures—are no doubt important, they have been studied by others (e.g., Katz 1986, and 1990; Reinganum 1981; Green and Scotchmer 1992). I will take up the interesting issue of hostage exchange briefly in the conclusion.

The remainder of this article is organized as follows. Section 2 lays out a simple model that is then used to compare research joint ventures with other organizational forms as means of assembling the inputs needed to conduct R&D. Section 3 presents some observations regarding the particular case of financial inputs. As will become clear, while the analysis of these two sections is couched in terms of research joint ventures, the issues and findings apply to joint ventures more generally. A brief summary closes the article.

2. A Simple model of asymmetric information about input quality

The model laid out in this section provides a starting point for understanding how a research joint venture can serve as a way to pool assets utilized in the conduct of R&D.

Suppose there is an R&D project, the "pooled project," that requires two assets to complete. The output of this project is x, which is produced according to the "production" function $x = f(q_1, q_2)$, where q_i is the quality of asset i and x is the dollar value of the innovation generated.[7] Normalize quality so that $q_i = 0$ denotes having none of the input assigned to the pooled project. The necessity of having both inputs is captured by the assumption that $f(0, q_2) = 0 = f(q_1, 0)$. Quality has a positive marginal product: $\partial f(q_1, q_2)/\partial q_1 > 0$ for all $q_2 > 0$, and $\partial f(q_1, q_2)/\partial q_2 > 0$ for all $q_1 > 0$. Asset i's cost is a function of its quality and is denoted by $c(q_i)$. Quality is costly: $dc(q_i)/dc_i > 0$. Initially, asset i is owned by firm i.

Several possible interpretations can be given to the inputs and their quality levels. The one to which I will refer most in the exposition is that q_1 and q_2 represent the quality levels of two teams of researchers who are brought together to complete an R&D project. Suppose that the sizes of the research teams are fixed and that each firm has a limited number of high-quality researchers in its total workforce. Then the cost of providing a high-quality team to the pooled project is the opportunity cost of taking these researchers away from other projects.

The assumption that output depends on the average quality of each of two distinct teams is made solely to simplify the notation. More generally, output could be a function of all of the individual skill levels of the personnel involved. In general, one also would want to consider firms who choose the size of the research teams and not solely their composition. My focus here is on quality, to the exclusion of quantity, because one would expect quantity to be more readily verifiable and easier to incorporate into explicit contractual provisions.

An alternative interpretation of this model is that q_i represents firm i's ongoing allocation of the *services* generated by the asset that remain under its control. Under this interpretation, q_i is the fraction of the services from asset i that is allocated to use on the pooled project. This case may arise when there are benefits from assembling assets into teams and a given asset may perform multiple tasks. These assets might include key personnel, or labs that are used for a variety of projects simultaneously, and thus cannot be separated from their parent firms. In such instances, there may be economies of scope and team benefits that would be lost as personnel or other assets were transferred among different firms.

Before examining different institutional arrangements for combining the two assets, it is useful to consider two extreme cases as benchmarks. One benchmark is provided by consideration of what would happen if a single entity chose the quality levels for both teams and did so with the objective of maximizing joint profits. The decision maker would choose the quality levels to:

$$\max_{q_1, q_2} f(q_1, q_2) - c(q_1) - c(q_2). \tag{1}$$

Call the resulting quality levels the first-best levels.

If it were possible for parties to write enforceable contracts directly specifying the quality levels of the two inputs, then we would expect the parties to write contracts calling for the first-best levels. But in many circumstances, it is difficult for an outsider (e.g., the courts) to discern the quality of the inputs actually provided (in the words of contract theory, q_1 and q_2 often are *unverifiable*). Indeed, it may even be difficult to describe or specify the quality levels in a contract. For the remainder of the analysis, I will assume that the quality levels are unverifiable, so that the two firms cannot write enforceable contracts setting quality levels directly.

At the other extreme from unified control or the direct specification of the quality levels, suppose that one party simply sold its asset to the other at price that was independent of the input quality. Under a straight fixed price, the input supplier would always provide the lowest possible quality, since it would choose q_i to maximize $p - c(q_i)$, where p is the transfer price.[8]

The problem faced by the two firms can thus be seen as the following. In the absence of direct contractual clauses specifying the quality levels, the parties must devise institutional or contractual arrangements beyond a simple fixed price that will generate *indirect* incentives to provide inputs of the appropriate quality.

A. A joint venture

Under a joint venture arrangement, each firm provides the input that it initially owns, and the two firms then share the output of the joint venture according to a set sharing rule. Firm i receives $s_i(x)$ when the output of the venture is x. Faced with this sharing rule, firm i chooses q_i to:

$$\max_{q_i} s_i[f(q_1, q_2)] - c(q_i). \tag{2}$$

In an informal analysis of this problem, Buckley and Casson (1988, p. 47) noted that "each firm may be suspicious of the quality of the input supplied by the other firm" but that these fears are lessened by the fact that each firm has an equity stake in the venture and is planning to use the output of the venture. They also note that this cannot be expected to work completely. Examination of program (2) confirms these observations.

As long as $s_i(\cdot)$ is an increasing function, firm i has some incentive to provide quality. But this approach cannot solve the problem completely, as we can see by piggybacking on Holmstrom's (1982) analysis of the team agency problem. In the form in which I have presented it, the joint venturers' decision problem is isomorphic to the team agency problem examined by Holmstrom.

Proposition (Holmstrom): There is no balanced sharing rule (i.e., no sharing rule whose shares total 100%) that yields the first-best quality levels.

The intuition behind this result is most clear when the parties have a joint venture with constant shares. Denote firm i's sharing rate as σ_i, where budget balancing implies $\sigma_1 + \sigma_2 = 1$. Then firm i allocates personnel to equalize marginal *private* productivity and marginal private costs:

$$\sigma_i \, \partial f(q_1, q_2)/\partial q_i = \partial c(q_i)/\partial q_i. \tag{3}$$

Since at any point at least one firm must get less than 100% of the gains at the margin, that firm's incentives to provide quality will be too low.[9] Thus, under the interpretation where the firm also has an independent project of its own, this result says that the firm will tend to allocate better resources to its solely conducted project—on which it earns 100% of the returns—than to the joint venture—on which it earns less than 100% of the returns.

As Holmstrom observed, the problem arises from the budget balancing requirement. It might seem that budget balancing could be broken if the two parents were to put additional money into the venture (say through start-up contributions of cash) or if they implemented a sharing rule whose shares totaled less than 100% over an initial range. Either way, it would then appear feasible to implement a scheme in which, for a range of returns, the sum of the shares exceeded 100% *at the margin*, thus overcoming the dilution of incentives.

In calculating their incentives, however, the parties have to account for what will happen to the funds in the venture if neither partner "earns" them. If the agreement calls for all of the profits to be distributed eventually, then the venture is right back to the balanced budget problem. To avoid this problem, the members must, in effect, commit themselves to "burning money" in some contingencies.

Burning money is problematical for at least two reasons. One, there is a question of whether the self-imposed threat is credible. The parties potentially could rely on their lawyers to burn their money—if there were residual funds, these funds would all be dissipated in a costly legal battle over who should get them. Alternatively, the two firms could contract with a third party, who would agree (in advance) to take any money that was not otherwise earned by the venture members. Either solution leads to the second problem: In a stochastic world, contingencies under which burning money is called for may arise even along the equilibrium path. But then the two firms are simply throwing money away ex ante. Of course, they might demand an ex ante payment from the third party, but then one is getting away from the notion of a joint venture, and the third party is taking on the role of a capitalist of the sort that I will discuss in the next subsection.

B. Arm's-length input sales

Absent purely financial participation by an outsider, a research joint venture cannot support the first-best outcome. It does not, however, follow that a research joint venture is an inefficient organizational form. One must measure the performance of a joint venture against other institutional arrangements for assembling the needed inputs. We already have seen that a joint venture performs better than an arm's-length sale at a fixed price. In this subsection, I will examine the use of more sophisticated forms of arm's-length sales.

A firm may sell either the asset itself or the flow of services that it generates. In doing so, there is an important difference between labor and other inputs. With nonworker inputs, one firm has the right to sell control of its inputs to another firm. But workers retain the rights to make their own decisions. With the exception of the armed forces, the U.S. does not enforce contracts calling for indentured servitude. Since workers cannot be bought and sold like other assets, it is useful to consider the two types of input separately.

Begin by supposing that the two inputs are some physical assets owned by the firms. Then one firm could contract with the other to purchase its input. To abstract from competitive effects (where each of the two firms fights to be the one to assemble the team), assume that only firm 1 is capable of conducting the project, but that to do so it needs to procure the additional input. Thus, the question is how firm 2 can sell its input to firm 1.

A simple fixed-price sales contract results in the minimal quality level being provided. Given this, one would expect firms to consider performance-based pricing to overcome the problems posed by asymmetric information. For instance, a royalty scheme under which the payment to firm 2 depends on the realized value of x would offer a partial solution to these problems in much the same way that a joint venture does.[10]

To press this point further, suppose firm 1 were to purchase the input from firm 2 and were to agree to pay royalties to do so. That is, firm 1 would pay a royalty of $r[f(q_1, q_2)]$ to firm 2 for its input. Firm 1 would choose q_1 to maximize $f(q_1, q_2) - r[f(q_1, q_2)] - c(q_1)$, while firm 2 would choose q_2 to maximize $r[f(q_1, q_2)] - c(q_2)$. At this level of analysis, this situation would be identical to a joint venture. And just as with a research joint venture, budget balancing would present an obstacle to attainment of the first best.

There can, however, be an important difference between an arm's-length sale and pure joint venture: A third party may become involved. Suppose that a third firm hires the two inputs from firms 1 and 2 and pays each firm 100% of the profits *at the margin* (e.g., $r[f(q_1, q_2)] = f(q_1, q_2) - \alpha$, where α is a positive constant). The two input suppliers then have incentives to provide the efficient allocation of researchers to the project. This is the role that Holmstrom suggested for capitalist—as opposed to worker-owned—firms.

Taken literally, this analysis suggests that an arm's-length deal could more effectively overcome problems of asymmetric information than could a joint venture. Of course, this model is a great oversimplification. But if the result is inappropriate, which part of the model has led us astray? One possibility is the assumption that the value of x is publicly verifiable and the information structure is independent of the form of interfirm interaction. One role for a joint venture may be to draw "bright lines" for accounting purposes so that the value of x is not lost in an aggregate measure of the returns from a firm's entire portfolio of projects and activities. The joint venture agreement is likely to set up a separate set of accounts for the joint entity and to spell out the rights of the partners to audit these accounts and to monitor one another's contributions to the venture. When the joint venture has its own facilities, it would seem that this role could be a significant one.

When the joint venture has no fully dedicated facilities or personnel of its own (as is often the case), it is difficult to see what the informational advantages of the venture are. In this case, it appears that the joint venture is very close to an arm's-length sale. Perhaps the difference is that the joint venture structure simply represents a mechanism whereby the parties agree to engage in extensive mutual monitoring, say by exchanging some personnel between their facilities.

Now, suppose that the essential inputs are workers. One can think of hiring workers in two ways. One approach is to induce each worker individually to switch firms. The current employer could however act to retain some or all of its workers, and therein lies a problem. One would expect the firm to keep those workers who were most productive relative to what they have been offered by the outside firm. Thus, as Greenwald (1986) modeled formally, the new employer could face an adverse selection problem which greatly reduces one's ability to hire workers in this fashion.[11]

One might think of using an equity arrangement here too (i.e., profit-sharing with workers). But typically the quality of any one worker makes little difference to overall results of a project. There may be hundreds, or thousands, of workers. To make each worker a residual claimant would require individuals to bear significant amounts of risk. Shareholders also would be required to bear large risks—for every additional dollar the firm earned, shareholders collectively would lose thousands of dollars. While equity arrangements may be appropriate for a few key personnel, these arrangements seem an unlikely solution to the overall problem.

A second approach to hiring labor is to buy an ongoing research lab from another firm and to hope that the employees remain with the lab following the transfer of ownership. I will treat this form of hiring as equivalent to an acquisition; and now I turn to the examination of merger and acquisition as means of assembling R&D inputs.

C. Merger and acquisition

In addition to comparing a joint venture with arm's-length dealing, it is worthwhile to compare a joint venture with full integration or merger. In doing so, it is important to be clear about what constitutes a merger. There are at least two dimensions with which to be concerned. One is how the inputs are transferred. The other is how decisions are made (and who has the information needed to make them) after the merger has taken place.

Suppose that a merger is taken to mean bringing all of the projects and associated assets into a single firm. Under one interpretation of what constitutes a firm, all of the assets of one firm are transferred to the control of the other, and a single (all-knowing) decision maker allocates inputs among the different projects to solve the optimization problem given by expression (1). The first-best obviously is attained under this outcome.

It is far from clear, however, that this is a sensible model of integration. Both before and after a merger, information about the quality of particular researchers resides with particular managers. Both before and after the merger, each manager will take those actions that best serve his or her self-interest. In analyzing joint ventures and arm's-length sales, I implicitly assumed that a manager in firm i acted to maximize the profits of firm i. That is, I assumed that it was in his or her self-interest to do so. When there is a manager who can observe worker quality and must allocate workers among projects, owners of the merged firm should make the manager's compensation depend on the performance of the total portfolio of projects that his or her decisions influence.[12] In this way, the firm can avoid inefficient allocation of workers. Formally, the manager who originally was in firm i would be paid

$$w[f(q_1, q_2) - c(q_i)]. \tag{4}$$

In the multiproject interpretation, this scheme entails the firm's making the manager's compensation depend on the total profits earned by all of the projects for which he or she allocated personnel. Since compensation is a function of this sum, there is no misallocation among projects. In the current setting—with no other problems of moral hazard—even low-powered incentives of this form would attain the first-best.[13]

Why not implement similar compensation schemes under the aegis of a joint venture? First, it would be in each firm's interest to have its manager maximize $s_i[f(q_1, q_2)] - c(q_i)$, not $f(q_1, q_2) - c(q_i)$. Thus, it would be necessary to have the joint venture members reach some sort of collective agreement to use compensation schemes based on total venture revenues, rather than on each member's share. Such an agreement might be an explicit contract or an implicit understanding that each will use this type of managerial incentive scheme as long as the other one does. But either mechanism relies on the assumption that the contract between a firm and its manager is observable to the other firm.

In my opinion, the assumption of contract observability is almost always an inappropriate one. The contract between an executive and his or her firm may largely be an implicit, self-enforcing one. Although the Securities and Exchange Commission requires firms to announce the amount of compensation paid to their top managers, simply knowing the actual payment made to an agent is not the same as knowing the rule by which the compensation was calculated, and thus by itself does not allow one to infer what the agent's incentives are. Even when there is a visible, explicit compensation contract, there might be a secret side agreement that supersedes it. It may well be too costly to write and *enforce* contracts among venture members ruling out such side payments. For instance, monitoring all possible payments made between a manager and his or her firm in response to the manager's performance in one task may be impossible when the manager performs many other tasks as well.

Problems of observability are particularly acute when career concerns are a significant component of incentives. In many joint ventures (e.g., the CFM joint venture formed between GE and SNECMA to produce commercial jet engines), the personnel continue to be employees of the parent companies. These personnel remain in the overall internal labor markets of their respective firms, and a significant component of their compensation may come in the form of future rewards (e.g., promotions) for current performance.

In summary, one advantage of a merger, as compared to a joint venture, is that a merger makes it credible to take a broad-based measure of profit as the performance measure for compensation purposes, while a joint venture may not.

I believe that there is a second important feature of a merger. One way to avoid receiving an *adverse* selection is to avoid getting a *selection*. That is, to hire the entire relevant population or purchase the entire relevant asset class in a merger or acquisition. For example, the acquirer would seek either whole companies, or whole research teams. Of course, the extent of an arm's-length input sale or the design of a joint venture agreement could be set along similar lines (this may, in fact, be what happens with some biotech agreements, where a small firm is fully dedicated to its alliance). I would, however, expect these effects to be strongest in the case of a merger.

So far, an acquisition seems to be an ideal solution (ignoring potential objection by antitrust authorities). But there are costs, as well as benefits. One should not minimize the obstacles proposed by transactions costs. When a joint venture is formed to solve a narrowly defined problem, a merger may be too cumbersome to be a viable alternative. Moreover, a limited acquisition is unlikely to work well when asset i is used to provide services for a variety of activities. While a firm may be able to sell the services of a single asset to several different buyers concurrently (e.g., a specialized machine tool could be used to meet the needs of a number of firms over a given time period), it is difficult to see how the firm would sell the asset itself to several buyers.

There is another shortcoming of acquisitions that, to this point, has been hidden by the analysis. I have examined only how a merger helps solve problems of asymmetric information *after* the deal has been consummated. But the sale itself entails an asymmetric information problem. The parties need to come up with a price for the merger. Evaluating the quality of the acquired firm's overall workforce is relevant even when there are no questions of adverse selection among the firm's workers. Problems can arise when the value of the firm being acquired is better known to its original owner than to the acquirer.

The problem here is very similar to those considered above, with one difference. Before, the quality was subject to choice, and equity arrangements served to provide incentives to provide quality. Here, the quality level is exogenously fixed. Again, we would expect the seller to retain some sort of equity participation in the sold-off division. But here, rather than to provide incentives to act, the role of equity is to make credible claims about the quality of the division being sold.

One way to create this equity is to pay for the acquisition by transferring shares of stock in the acquiring company to the owners of the acquired company.[14] There are several potential problems with such a scheme. First, this may confound the returns earned by the acquired division with the results of many other projects that the acquirer has. If the firm attempts to report the results of different operations separately, there may be concerns about the manipulation of the accounting data. If the results are kept pooled, then the acquired firm will have to form a prediction of the value of the shares it is being paid—one asymmetric information problem may be replaced with another.[15] Moreover, the owners of the acquired firm may find their liquidity limited—attempts to sell their shares in the acquired firm might be taken as a signal of private information that the acquired firm was overpriced.[16]

A cleaner method may be to set up a joint venture. Once again, the advantage of a joint venture over other institutional arrangements is that it creates accounting bright lines. Of course, any such advantage would have to be weighed against the distortions in managerial incentives discussed earlier.

3. Complementary financial assets and risk sharing

Consideration of how to price an acquisition raises issues of project finance more generally. Joint ventures are often portrayed as means by which firms can pool their resources to obtain sufficient capital to finance large R&D projects and to share their risks. Following the approach that I outlined in the introduction, I believe there are two critical questions that must be answered. First, how does a joint venture solve the problems that arise in financing R&D projects? Second, what makes a joint venture a particularly good financial structure in comparison with others? After all, the modern corporation is designed precisely to pool the financing and risk-bearing capacities of a number of investors.

Rather than attempt to provide full answers to these questions here, I will content myself with raising some of what I see as critical points that must be addressed. Because their organization and their access to capital markets can be so different, I will distinguish between large, publicly traded firms and small start-up firms in making my remarks.

A. Small firms

Consider a start-up firm, with a single owner/manager and a single project (e.g., the prototypical biotech or computer firm set up by a scientist with a bright idea). The idea for the project could be the firm's sole asset. As noted earlier, asymmetric information can create several difficulties for project finance. The firm undertaking the project may be better informed about its chances of success than is a potential outside capital supplier, giving rise to potential adverse selection. Or the firm undertaking the project may engage in moral hazard by not working as hard on the project, because it knows that the outside investor's money rather than its own, is at risk. Here, I will focus on the adverse selection problem.

Suppose that the firm's project has some fixed probability of success. This success probability is the measure of the project's "quality." Moreover, suppose that, while the owner/manager knows the project's quality, potential outside investors (venture capitalists, banks, and equity buyers) observe only imperfect signals of the project's quality. In large part, the owner/manager's problem is to "sell" the idea to potential investors. Potential investors will recognize, however, that the owner/manager has incentives to overstate the quality of his/her project in order to obtain financing on favorable terms. A mechanism is needed whereby the owner/manager is given incentives to report his/her assessment of the project's quality truthfully.

Tying the owner/manager's income to project performance is one way to induce truthful revelation—the initial owner of a project with a poor chance of success will be more reluctant to have his/her income tied to the project's performance than will the initial owner of a project with good prospects. As Leland and Pyle (1977) showed, the owner/manager's income can be tied to performance by having a financial structure that entails his/her retaining a significant equity stake in the project.[17]

Entering his/her wholly owned firm into a joint venture with another firm to undertake the project is one way of having the initial owner/manager retain an equity share in the project. But this fact alone cannot explain the use of joint ventures. Issuing debt, or issuing equity and retaining a significant fraction of it, can serve a similar function. What is it that sets a joint venture apart from other means of project finance?

One possible answer is that a joint venture should simply be viewed as an investment made by an investor that is particularly well-informed, another firm that is capable of undertaking the project. While this effect explains why such firms would be financial investors, it does not explain why they would actively engage in the project itself.

A joint venture partner may also play the role of a *large* stockholder that has incentives to engage in extensive monitoring rather than to exhibit the rational apathy of a small shareholder. Note, that since this role is being played by the manager of another firm, this role relies on the shareholders of the partner firm's providing their manager with incentives to undertake this oversight role. These incentives could simply arise from tying the compensation of the manager of the investing firm to the performance of his firm, and thus to the performance of the firm in which it invests. Again, however, this effect explains why one firm might take financial stake in another, but it does not explain why direct project participation is necessary.

Unlike the first two effects, the third one speaks directly to the issue of partner participation. In contrast with a purely financial investment relationship, joint participation in the project may lessen the impacted state of information. A firm participating in the conduct of the project may better be able to monitor the other firm's actions than would an outside investor engaging in purely financial participation. As discussed earlier, the joint venture agreement is likely to spell out the rights of the partners to audit the joint entity and to monitor one another's contributions to it. Presumably, similar sorts of arrangements could be reached between banks and borrowers. When the capital supplier participates in the conduct of the project, however, the firm's own employees will be involved and on-site, and these employees can be given a broad range of incentives to report on the project's progress. While within-firm agency problems will remain, it would be difficult, if not impossible, to provide a similar range of incentives to the employees of another firm.

In analyzing the role of joint venture agreements, one should not rule out the possibility that the investing firm is supplying managerial advice (or some other asset on whose quality it is difficult to contract directly), because it is a particularly well-suited supplier and not because of its role as an investor. Under this interpretation, the joint venture agreement plays two roles. First, it serves as a means of project finance. Second, it generates the proper incentives for the "investor" to provide high-quality managerial or other support along the lines discussed in section 3 above. In this view, project participation by the firm supplying capital is not a response to problems of finance. Rather, the joint equity arrangement between the venture partners is the solution to a two-sided incentive problem—two proverbial birds are being killed with one metaphorical stone.

There is a final explanation for why joint ventures might be an attractive form of finance for a young firm. It may be that the managers in the firm providing the financial capital enjoy being involved with "high-tech" start-ups even if their financial participation is not profitable. In this view, joint ventures are a manifestation of control problems at the investing firms, rather than a solution to asymmetric information about investments.

This last point raises issues concerning the separation of ownership and control more generally, and to these issues I now turn.

B. Large firms

A basic fact of the modern large corporation is that its owners and managers are two largely distinct groups. This fact has at least two implications. First, to the extent that private information resides with the managers, outside investors should be interested in the *managers' compensation* as an incentive or signalling mechanism. Thus, one must ask what, if any, role the firm's *financial structure* plays in solving the asymmetric information problem?[18] One possible answer is that financial structure does not have a significant role to play. Dybvig and Zender (1991) and Hart (1991) give conditions under which financial structure is irrelevant.

There are conditions under which financial structure can be important. One reason that capital structure can matter is provided by the difference in outsiders' ability to observe compensation schemes and capital structure. For reasons which I have already stated, it may be difficult to observe a manager's full compensation scheme directly. One may, however, be able to make inferences about managerial incentives from the firm's capital structure, which is more readily observable.

Ross (1977) analyzed the use of debt as a signal when managers are better informed about a project's likelihood of success than are investors. Taking on a high level of debt will make the firm susceptible to bankruptcy if the project does poorly. Assuming that bankruptcy is costly to the manager (e.g., he/she may lose his/her job, have his/her authority restricted, or suffer disgrace), the willingness to issue debt can thus serve as a signal of the manager's confidence in his/her firm. Interestingly, this analysis suggests that a joint venture arrangement may not be an effective financial structure, because it insulates managers from the possibility of bankruptcy if the project goes poorly.[19] This observation leads to the second implication of the separation of ownership and control.

Joint ventures are said to "spread the risk" among the partners. But reducing the riskiness of a publicly traded firm's profits in this way is not manifestly a benefit. Shareholders can diversify their holdings to include portfolios of companies. So why is there a benefit from having a *firm* diversify? In fact, a long-standing point in finance is that it is better to let shareholders diversify than to have the firms themselves diversify, because the latter reduces the number of pure securities that are traded.

I believe that the answer lies with the separation of ownership and control. Given the separation of ownership and control, managerial attitudes toward risk are relevant to corporate decision making. While the owners likely have widely diversified holdings, there are several reasons why managers typically are unable to diversify away the risks associated with the performance of their companies. First, a manager's reputation (and, hence, his or her future income) may depend on the performance of the one firm that he or she is currently managing, and it is hard to imagine one person managing several different companies in order to diversify this "reputation risk." Moreover, to ensure that a manager has strong incentives to work hard, the owners may want to tie managerial compensation heavily to the performance of the company that he or she manages. But then riskiness of the firm's investment translates into riskiness in the manager's income.

Since most managers probably are risk-averse, their lack of diversification will induce them to make risk-averse investment decisions. Hence, managers may value joint ventures as a means of diversifying the firm. For a given investment, a firm can participate in twice as many projects when it undertakes each as part of a 50–50 joint venture rather than undertaking individual projects itself.[20] If the manager's compensation scheme is a *set* function of some measure of corporate performance, the manager may value diversifying the set of projects over which this measure is calculated. Bankruptcy may be a particularly salient outcome for managers in assessing risks. To the extent that a manager suffers a large personal loss in the event of bankruptcy, he/she will find it valuable to lay off some of the risk of a project that is so large that its failure would drag the entire company into bankruptcy.

The fact that managers gain does not imply that it is efficient to diversify in this way. One must examine whether reducing risk in this manner is an example of managerial utility maximization at the expense of shareholders. What are the potential benefits to shareholders? Diversified shareholders do not benefit directly from a reduction in the riskiness of the firm's profit stream. But not all, or even a significant fraction, of the costs of bankruptcy necessarily fall on the managers. It would appear that diversification through joint ventures to minimize expected bankruptcy costs could generate benefits to investors as well. Before reaching this conclusion, however, one must answer the following question: Why not rely on other forms of financing, such as publicly traded equity or financial intermediaries who engage in direct monitoring?[21] Moreover, as already discussed, at least one strand of the corporate finance literature suggests that bankruptcy plays a disciplining role and thus generates benefits as well as costs.

Even if they do not benefit directly from risk reduction or the reduced probability of bankruptcy, shareholders might gain indirectly. One might suspect that, by lowering the compensation level needed to attract and retain (risk-averse) managers, or by reducing the distortions in managers' investment decisions, a policy of within-firm diversification and risk sharing among firms could be valuable even to already diversified shareholders. This intuition is incomplete and potentially misleading. Before reaching any conclusions, one must examine the optimal compensation scheme and how it varies with the number of projects in which the firm participates. In Hermalin and Katz (1993), we show that diversifying managerial effort does not necessarily reduce the riskiness of the firm's financial returns, that reducing risk *per se* may be of no value in an agency relationship where the principal is risk-neutral and the agent is risk-averse, and that diversification may increase the costs of agency.

It should be abundantly clear that my remarks here only scratch the surface of these issues. I hope, however, that these remarks shed some light on the need to improve our collective understanding of the role of joint ventures as a form of project finance. It is no substitute for analysis simply to assert that joint ventures are needed to share the risks of projects requiring large investments and offering uncertain returns.

4. Conclusions

I have examined how a joint venture creates equity interests and concomitant incentives that can at least partially overcome problems posed by asymmetric information in the markets for R&D inputs. In doing so, I have compared joint ventures with other organizational forms. I found that—purely in terms of incentive creation—a joint venture may not be much different from an arm's-length sale with royalty payments and that a joint venture may be less effective than a full-scale merger. Of course, there are other costs and benefits that must be taken into account when choosing among alternative institutional arrangments. For example, in addition to creating equity interests, a joint venture agreement may create channels for greater information flows among different parties.

A particular feature of joint ventures that merits further exploration is the creation of an ongoing relationship of mutual dependence. When each member contributes assets that become venture-specific (i.e., have comparatively low salvage values outside of the venture), the two parties have a greater mutual interest in the success of the venture. This commonality of interests may reduce the transactions costs and distortions that arise when there are ongoing interactions, such as when technological progress necessitates purchasing multiple generations of a technology over time. A model constructed along the lines of Williamson's (1983) mutual hostages analysis might prove helpful.

Notes

1. For a theoretical analysis of the effects of spillovers, see Spence (1984). For empirical evidence of the significance of R&D spillovers, see Jaffe (1986) and Bernstein and Nadiri (1988).
2. Several models of patent races are surveyed in Reinganum (1989).
3. Note that I have *not* identified the riskiness of R&D projects, which arises from the large upfront costs and the potential for failure, as the source of difficulty in obtaining project finance. While these characteristics of R&D investments give rise to benefits from risk sharing, their presence does not explain why traditional capital markets encounter difficulties sharing the risk.
4. For examples of this approach, see Perry (1989).
5. Two notable exceptions are Bhattacharya et al. (1987)—who consider venture partners who each possess private, productive information—and Darrough and Stoughton (1989)—who consider the division of revenues between partners who each have private information about their costs.
6. Reinganum (1981) allows for R&D cooperation to improve the efficiency of the conduct of R&D, but the sources of these efficiency gains are not explicitly modeled.
7. More generally, one might expect the value of x to depend on the number of firms receiving the innovation. x can be thought of as the value to a monopoly seller, and I will ignore the fact that the value of an innovation may well depend on the market structure and the nature of the innovating organization.
8. I am abstracting from considerations of repeat play and reputation effects. The repeat purchase mechanism and the formation of reputations could provide incentives to provide more than the minimal amount of quality (for general discussions of reputations supporting quality provision, see Klein and Leffler 1981 and Shapiro 1983).
9. Of course, given the deterministic relationship between output and the quality of the inputs in this model, a firm can infer the input quality that its partner has provided, and the firms might be able to sustain cooperation if they were in a repeat-play situation. It would be a simple matter to add in noise, however, making cooperation difficult even with repeat play. And, of course, even with no noise, the forces of repeat play are not always strong enough to sustain cooperation.
10. Katz (1989) and Gallini and Wright (1990) provide more detailed analyses of how equity or royalty provisions in a sales contract can serve as a signal of the seller's information in cases where the input quality is fixed.
11. One might suspect that the fact that a firm tries to keep a worker would in itself serve as an indication of the worker's ability. But it may be that firms have sufficient reputations with their workforces that they can make credible promises of future promotions, etc., to their workers that are unobservable to outsiders. Or firms may be able to grant better working conditions that are difficult for outsiders to discern.

12. The owners themselves may not literally set this compensation scheme. Rather, they may delegate to high-level managers, who would then set the compensation of lower level managers.
13. For further analysis of agency with multiple tasks, see Holmstrom and Milgrom (1991).
14. Here, I am assuming that the owners of the acquired company do, in fact, know the quality of their firm. Where owners and managers are distinct groups, and managers possess the private information about quality, the equity arrangements discussed here would have to involve managerial participation.
15. Of course, this problem is mitigated to the extent that the shares of the acquiring firm are publicly traded and provide an unbiased predictor of their future value.
16. Indeed, the original acquisition agreement might have an explicit limitation on the acquired company's owners' ability to subsequently sell their shares.
17. Alternatively, his/her managerial compensation could be tied to firm performance. I will return to this point below.
18. This question was raised by Holmstrom and Hart (1987).
19. For a recent analysis of bankruptcy as a device with which to discipline managers, see Harris and Raviv (1990).
20. One might wonder why the firm cannot simply issue more stock and use the proceeds to undertake a large number of projects on its own. First, as Samuelson (1963) showed (cited in Diamond 1984), adding statistically independent projects in this manner may not reduce the decision maker's aversion to the risk of any one project. There is a difference between diversifying by taking on 1/*n*th of *n* projects and simply taking on *n* projects.
21. For an insightful analysis of the latter, see Diamond (1984).

References

Bernstein, Jeffrey I., and M. Ishaq Nadiri. (1988). "Interindustry R&D Spillovers, Rates of Return, and Production in High-Tech Industries," *American Economics Association Papers and Proceedings* 78, 429–434.

Bhattacharya, Sudipto, J. Glazer, and David Sappington. (1987). "Motivating Exchange of Knowledge in R&D Ventures: First-Best Implementation." Technical memorandum, Bell Communications Research.

Buckley, Peter J., and Mark Casson. (1988). "A Theory of Cooperation in International Business." In Farok J. Contractor and Peter Lorange (eds.), *Cooperative Strategies in International Business*. Lexington: Lexington Books, 31–53.

Contractor, Farok, J., and Peter Lorange. (1988). "Why Should Firms Cooperate? The Strategy and Economics Basis for Cooperative Ventures." In Farok J. Contractor and Peter Lorange (eds.), *Cooperative Strategies in International Business*. Lexington: Lexington Books, pp. 1–30.

Darrough, Masako N., and Neal M. Stoughton. (1989). "A Bargaining Approach to Profit Sharing in Joint Ventures," *Journal of Business* 62, 237–270.

d'Aspremont Claude, and Alexis Jacquemin. (1988). "Cooperative and Noncooperative R&D in Duopoly with Spillovers," *American Economic Review* 78, 1133–1137.

Diamond, Douglas W. (1984). "Financial Intermediation and Delegated Monitoring," *Review of Economic Studies*, 51, 393–414.

Dybvig, Philip H., and Jaime F. Zender. (1991). "Capital Structure and Dividend Irrelevance with Asymmetric Information," *The Review of Financial Studies* 4, 201–219.

Gallini, Nancy T., and Brian D. Wright. (1990). "Technology Transfer under Asymmetric Information," *RAND Journal of Economics* 21, 147–160.

Green, Jerry R., and Suzanne Scotchmer. (1992). "Antitrust Policy, the Breadth of Patent Protection and the Incentive to Develop New Products." Unpublished manuacript, University of California at Berkeley.

Greenwald, Bruce C. (1986). "Adverse Selection in the Labor Market," *Review of Economic Studies* 53, 325–347.

Grossman, Gene M., and Carl Shapiro. (1986). "Research Joint Ventures: An Antitrust Analysis, *Journal of Law, Economics and Organization* 2, 315–337.

Grossman, Sanford, and Oliver D. Hart. (1986). "The Costs and Benefits of Ownership: A Theory of Vertical and Lateral Integration," *Journal of Political Economy* 94, 691–719.

Harris, Milton, and Artur Raviv. (1990). "Capital Structure and the Informational Role of Debt," *The Journal of Finance* 45, 321–349.

Hart, Oliver. (1991). "Theories of Optimal Capital Structure: A Principal-Agent Perspective." Unpublished draft, MIT.

Hart, Oliver, and Bengt Holstrom. (1987). "The Theory of Contracts." In Truman Bewley (ed.), *Advances in Economic Theory, Fifth World Congress*. Cambridge: Cambridge University Press.

Hermalin, Benjamin E., and Michael L. Katz. (1993). "Diversification and Agency." Unpublished manuscript, University of California at Berkeley.

Holmstrom, Bengt. (1982). "Moral Hazard in Teams," *The Bell Journal of Economics* 13, 324–340.

Holmstrom, Bengt, and Paul Milgrom. (1991). "Multitask Principal-Agent Analyses: Incentive Contracts, Asset Ownership, and Job Design," *Journal of Law Economics, and Organization* 7, 24–52.

Jaffe, Adam B. (1986). "Technological Opportunity and Spillovers of R&D: Evidence from Firms' Patents, Profits, and Market Value," *American Economic Review* 76, 984–1001.

Katz, Michael L. (1986). "An Analysis of Cooperative Research and Development," *Rand Journal of Economics* 17, 527–543.

Katz, Michael L. (1989). "Vertical Contractual Relationship." In R. Schmalensee and R.D. Willig (eds.), *The Handbook of Industrial Organization*. Vol. 1. Amsterdam: North Holland Publishing, pp. 655–721.

Katz, Michael L., and Janusz A. Ordover. (1990). "Cooperation and Competition in R&D." In *Brookings Papers on Economic Activity: Microeconomics*, pp. 137–203.

Klein, Benjamin, and Keith B. Leffler. (1981). "The Role of Market Forces in Assuring Contractual Performance," *Journal of Political Economy* 89, 615–641.

Leland, Hayne, and David Pyle. (1977). "Informational Asymmetries, Financial Structure, and Financial Intermediation," *Journal of Finance* 32, 371–387.

Ordover, Janusz A., and Robert D. Willig. (1985). "Antitrust for High-Technology Industries: Assessing Research Joint Ventures and Mergers," *Journal of Law and Economics* 28, 311–333.

Perry, Martin. (1989). "Vertical Integration: Determinants and Effects." In R. Schmalensee and R.D. Willig (eds.), *The Handbook of Industrial Organization*, Vol. 1. Amsterdam: North Holland Publishing, pp. 183–255.

Reinganum, Jennifer F. (1981). "Dynamic Games of Innovation," *Journal of Economic Theory* 25, 21–41, (1985). "Corrigendum" 35, 196–197.

Reinganum, Jennifer F. (1989). "The Timing of Innovation Research, Development, and Diffusion." In Richard Schmalensee and Robert D. Willig (eds.), *The Handbook of Industrial Organization*, Vol. 1. Amsterdam: North Holland, pp. 849–908.

Ross, Stephen A. (1977). "The Determination of Financial Structure: The Incentive-Signalling Approach, *Bell Journal of Economics* 8, 23–40.

Samuelson, Paul A. (1963). "Risk and Uncertainty: A Fallacy of Large Numbers," *Scientia.*

Shapiro, Carl. (1983). "Premiums for High Quality Products as Returns to Reputations, *Quarterly Journal of Economics* 98, 615–641.

Spence, A. Michael. (1984). "Cost Reduction, Competition and Industry Performance," *Econometrica* 52, 101–121.

Williamson, Oliver E. (1983). "Credible Commitments: Using Hostages to Support Exchange," *American Economic Review* 73, 519–540.

Group Decision and Negotiation, 4: 401–409 (1995)

Noncooperative, Cooperative, and Delegative R&D

SUGATA MARJIT
Department of Economics, Monash University

HELING SHI
Department of Economics, Monash University

Abstract.

We discuss alternative organizational forms of research and development in a symmetric duopoly framework. Firms play a noncooperative game at the output stage but can collaborate at the R&D stage. In the absence of patent protection, technology licensing that prevents imitative R&D may emerge as an equilibrium outcome. In general, greater probabilities of "success" in R&D rule out noncooperative arrangement at the R&D stage. Delegative R&D, where firms move sequentially, tends to dominate the cooperative form of R&D.

Key Words: R&D, cooperative R&D, noncooperative R&D, licensing, delegative R&D

1. Introduction

In recent years a considerable amount of theoretical research has been done concerning the context of R&D behavior of oligopolistic firms. Most of the existing literature has focused on the analysis of noncooperative R&D strategies of the competing firms. Recently the phenomena of "cooperative R&D" and "R&D joint ventures" attracted the attention of economists. As d'Aspremont and Jacquemon (1988) note, some firms may cooperate in the R&D projects but compete in the product market. The incentives for cooperation in R&D and the welfare implications of such partial cooperation or full cooperation (when firms also collude in the product market) have been discussed in detail by Katz (1986), Ordover and Willig (1985), Gandal and Scotchmer (1989), Kamien, Muller, and Zang (1990), Ray Chaudhuri (1992), and others. Recently, Marjit (1991) has shown that when firms act in the absence of "spillovers," they will be interested in cooperating in R&D projects with "very high" or "very low" success probabilities, while they continue to choose noncooperative output levels in the product market.

At the same time, research has been done to analyze R&D preemptive technology licensing where the incumbent firm decides to share the market with an entrant just to subdue its incentive for further R&D. Gallini (1984)[1] has discussed a model where the incumbent does the research and the entrant only licenses it from the incumbent. Rockett (1990) discusses optimal licensing contracts when imitation is potentially possible and shows that

The authors would like to thank Amitava Bose, Debraj Ray, Suzanne Scotchmer, and Dennis Yao for thoughful comments. The presentation and the content of the article are vastly improved following the comments of two anonymous referees. The usual disclaimer applies.

the "quality" of technology can be endogenously determined by the principal. As a synthesis, all the above-mentioned articles discuss different organizational arrangements of R&D among competing firms. Typically, the firms can cooperate in R&D or can "delegate" the activity of R&D to one firm and subsequently share the knowledge. So the question is under what circumstance these firms will choose different alternative arrangements. The purpose of this article is to construct a model in which these alternatives can be compared and the equilibrium then identified. Some simple conjectures can be drawn regarding the situations which lead to the emergence of alternative organizational forms involving R&D activities. Our main conclusions is that a project with a moderate chance of "success" or "failure" will generally lead to noncooperative R&D; while a project with a high probability of "success" will generally lead to either cooperative or delegative R&D.

Institutional specifications play a very crucial role in shaping the organizational forms of R&D activities. When patent rights are easily enforceable, the winner in an R&D race does not need to worry about the subsequent imitation of the knowledge or the possible repetitive R&D activities by the competing firms; and therefore, either cooperative or noncooperative R&D will emerge, depending on the probability of success. However, it is a well recognized problem that patent laws are quite difficult to enforce, especially across national boundaries. As a result, GATT negotiators recently have been trying very hard to reach consensus on the international protection of intellectual property rights. In the latter half of the article, we discuss technology transfer (or licensing) as a possible means of thwarting imitative R&D activities. The theoretical structure discussed in the article fits in quite well with the observed strategies played by multinationals and local firms in a less developed country.

The article proceeds as follows: In the next section, we present a basic model with the description of market and the R&D activities of firms, along with the definitions of alternative forms of R&D arrangements. In the third section comparisons are made among different types of alternatives. The last section contains some concluding remarks.

2. The basic model

Consider an industry with two firms engaged in a Cournot–Nash game. They have equal constant marginal cost (c). We assume, for simplicity, that initially both of them earn negligible profits. Innovation takes the form of a reduction in marginal cost, and if it takes place at all, it is "drastic" in nature. Hence, if only one firm is a successful innovator of a new technology, it emerges as a monopolist. Innovative activity of R&D involves setting up an R&D lab with a fixed cost F, and, given that the lab is in operation, p is the "success" probability of innovation and $(1 - p)$ the "failure" rate. There is no correlation between p and F, except that one has to invest F prior to having a possibility of success. If both firms simultaneously emerge as successful, they play a symmetric Cournot–Nash game in the post-innovation situation. Throughout the article we assume that the firms cannot collude in the product market due to antitrust regulations. We also assume that there are no spillovers. Given this set up, let us first define three alternative arrangements:

Noncooperative R&D (NCR) is defined as a situation in which firms do independent R&D with independent draws and in which there is no communication at the R&D stage.

Cooperative R&D (CR) is defined as a situation in which firms cooperate in R&D. If it is a success, it is so for both of them. Similarly they equally share the possible failure. They jointly set up a lab by equally sharing F.

Delegative R&D (DR) is defined as a situation in which one firm moves first by setting up the lab and doing the R&D. In the next stage, it can sell the R&D output to another firm. The information is shared against a lump-sum fee determined by a simple bargaining rule. Firms compete subsequently in the product market.[2]

We further make a profitability assumption that even if both firms independently succeeded in R&D and they therefore engaged in a symmetric duopoly competition in the product market, it would still be profitable to do R&D.[3] If $\hat{\pi}$ is defined as each firm's profits in the above symmetric duopoly situation, this profitability assumption could be written as:

$$p\hat{\pi} > F. \tag{1}$$

Corresponding to the three R&D arrangements defined above, we first calculate the expected profits of firms under NCR, CR, and DR, respectively.

NCR:

Under the NCR, the expected profits for a firm are given by

$$p(1 - p)\pi_m + p^2\hat{\pi} - F, \tag{2}$$

where $p(1 - p)$ is the combined probability that one firms succeeds in R&D (with probability p) and another fails (with probability $(1 - p)$); π_m is defined as the monopoly profits in the post-innovation situation where one firm has been driven out of the market due to the "drastic" assumption on R&D. If both firms succeed in R&D with the probability of $\hat{\pi}$ will be the payoff in the symmetric duopoly situation. F is the fixed cost to set up an R&D lab.

CR:

Similarly, the expected profits for a firm under CR are

$$p\hat{\pi} - F/2. \tag{3}$$

If (1) holds, (2) and (3) must be positive, implying profitability under both of these arrangements.

DR:

To calculate the payoffs in the DR case, we first draw the extensive form of the game (see figure 1). Without loss of generality, let us assume that firm 1 sets up an R&D lab and incurs a fixed cost F in the first period. Then, the following situations can arise:

s: firm 1 succeeds in R&D;
f: firm 1 fails in R&D;
r: firm 1 reveals the information to the second firm against a fee P_s;
nr: firm 1 does not reveal the information;
D: firm 2 chooses to do R&D by itself;
ND: firm 2 chooses not to do R&D.

Let $\pi_i(\theta, \delta, \gamma)$ be the payoffs to the ith firm ($i = 1, 2$), when, in the first stage of the game, firm 1 succeeds in R&D ($\theta = s$) and chooses to adopt the strategy that either reveals the information to the second firm or does not reveal [$\delta(=r, nr)$]; while firm 2 then chooses either to independent R&D or not, [$\gamma(=D, ND)$]. Similarly $\pi_i(\theta, \gamma)$ is defined as the payoffs when firm 1 fails in R&D ($\theta = f$) in the first stage, and firm 2 chooses to do or not to do R&D in the second stage [$\gamma(=D, ND)$].

For example, $\pi_1(s, r, D)$ denotes the payoffs to the first firm when the first firm succeeds in the R&D, reveals the information to the second firm against a licensing fee P_s, and the second firm chooses to do independent R&D; while $\pi_2(s, r, D)$ denotes the payoffs to the second firm in the same situation. So, $\pi_1(s, r, D) = \hat{\pi} + P_s - F$, and $\pi_2(s, r, D) = \hat{\pi} - P_s - F$. Similarly, we can calculate the payoffs to each firm in various situations. The results are listed in figure 1 where the formulae in the top line are the payoffs to firm 1 and the bottom line to firm 2.

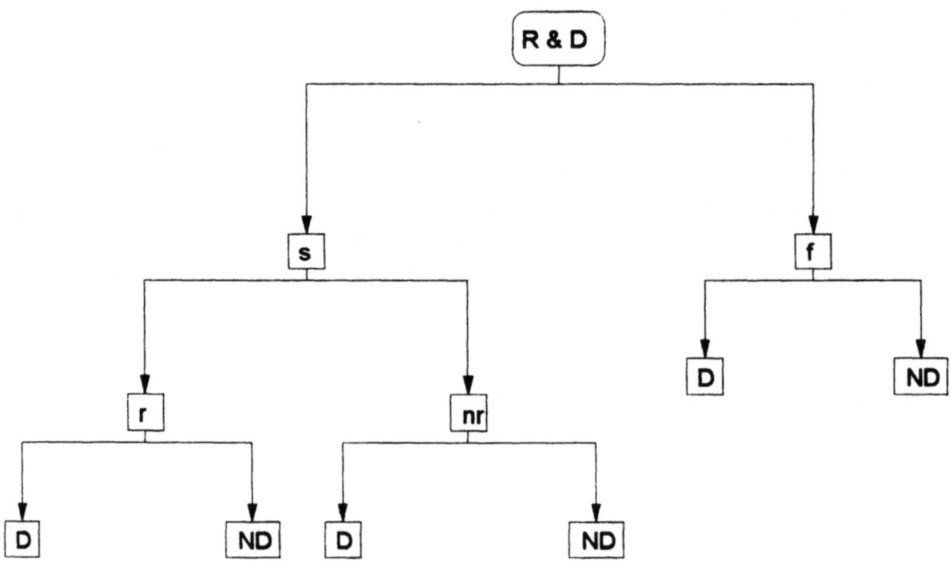

$$\begin{pmatrix} \hat{\pi} + P_s - F \\ \hat{\pi} - P_s - F \end{pmatrix} \begin{pmatrix} \hat{\pi} + P_s - F \\ \hat{\pi} - P_s \end{pmatrix} \begin{pmatrix} p\hat{\pi} + (1-p)\pi_m - F \\ p\hat{\pi} = F \end{pmatrix} \begin{pmatrix} \pi_m - F \\ 0 \end{pmatrix} \begin{pmatrix} -F \\ p\pi_m - F \end{pmatrix} \qquad \begin{pmatrix} -F \\ 0 \end{pmatrix}$$

Figure 1. Extensive form of delegative R&D game.

Let us start with s, i.e., firm 1 succeeds in R&D in the first stage. A simple calculation will result in two possible equilibria: (s, r, ND) and (s, nr, D). Checking the second stage, we have the following proposition:

Proposition 1: If $F > (1 - p)(\pi_m - 2\hat{\pi})$, then the unique subgame perfect equilibrium of the delegative research model is (s, r, ND). If $F < (1 - p)(\pi_m - 2\hat{\pi})$, then the unique subgame perfect equilibrium is (s, nr, D).

Proof. Since $p\hat{\pi} > F$, if the technology transfer does not take place, the second firm must go for independent R&D, leaving an expected payoff $\pi_1(s, nr, D)$ to the first mover. The first firm will prefer to transfer if,

$$\hat{\pi} + P_2 - F > p\hat{\pi} + (1 - p)\pi_m - F$$

or

$$P_s > (1 - p)(\pi_m - \hat{\pi}). \tag{4}$$

Similarly for the transferee,

$$\hat{\pi} - P_s > p\hat{\pi} - F$$

or

$$P_s < (1 - p)\hat{\pi} + F. \tag{5}$$

From (4) and (5), for technology transfer to be feasible,

$$F > (1 - p)(\pi_m - 2\hat{\pi}). \tag{6}$$

What this shows is that if firm 1 succeeds in R&D, it will share the knowledge with the second firm, and that the second firm will refrain from doing further R&D provided that condition in the proposition holds.

Going one step back, we now consider the possibility of failure for the first mover. In that case, the equilibrium payoff is $-F$. So the first mover will actually engage in R&D if

$$\hat{\pi} + P_s > F/p \tag{7}$$

If (7) holds, then the first mover will choose to invest in R&D, and at the subsequent stage the unique Nash equilibrium is (s, r, ND). From (1), inequality (7) follows directly. Hence, (s, r, ND) is the unique subgame perfect equilibrium of the game.

On the other hand, if $F < (1 - p)(\pi_m - 2\hat{\pi})$, there does not exist a transfer price P_s such that technology transfer will take place. So the subgame perfect equilibrium is (s, nr, D), and the payoffs are $p\hat{\pi} + (1 - p)\pi_m - F$ for the first firm, and $p\hat{\pi} - F$ for the second firm. □

Observe that for (s, r, ND) to be a subgame perfect equilibrium, p should be such that,

$$p\hat{\pi} > (1 - p)(\pi_m - 2\hat{\pi}) \qquad \text{(from (1) and proposition 1)}$$

or

$$p\hat{\pi} > \pi_m(1 - p) - 2(1 - p)\hat{\pi}$$

or

$$p > \frac{\pi_m - 2\hat{\pi}}{\pi_m - \hat{\pi}} \equiv \tilde{p}. \tag{8}$$

To determine the licensing fee for sharing the information in the post-R&D stage, the firms are assumed to follow a simple Nash-bargaining process.

Firms 1 and 2 bargain over a pie of size $2\hat{\pi} - F$ and face a disagreement point given by $(p\hat{\pi} + (1 - p)\pi_m - F, p\hat{\pi} - F)$. The bargaining solution is given by solving a maximization problem (9), which maximizes the product of differences in payoffs between two equilibria for the two firms, i.e.,

$$\operatorname*{Max}_{P_s}[\hat{\pi} - P_s - (p\hat{\pi} - F)][\hat{\pi} + P_s - F - (p\hat{\pi} - (1 - p)\pi_m - F)], \tag{9}$$

which gives us

$$\tilde{p}_s = [F + (1 - p)\pi_m]/2. \tag{10}$$

The ultimate individual payoffs in the R&D game are given by

$$\pi_1 = p(\pi + \tilde{p}_s - F) - (1 - p)(F) = p(\pi + \tilde{p}_s) - F \tag{11}$$

and

$$\pi_2 = p(\hat{\pi} - \tilde{p}_s) + (1 - p)(p\pi_m - F). \tag{12}$$

Note that

$$\pi_1 - \pi_2 = p(\hat{\pi} + \tilde{p}_s) - F - p(\hat{\pi} - \tilde{p}_s) - (1 - p)(p\pi_m - F)$$

$$= p(2\tilde{p}_s - (1 - p)\pi_m - F).$$

Substituting for $\tilde{p}_s$, we get

$$\pi_1 - \pi_2 = p(F + (1 - p)\pi_m - (1 - p)\pi_m - F) = 0.^{4} \tag{13}$$

Hence, ex ante both firms enjoy the same expected payoffs in the licensing arrangement.

3. Comparisons

3.1. NCR and DR

We know that if the technology agreement is feasible, i.e., DR is a possible outcome, then $\pi_1 = \pi_2$. Therefore, DR will be preferred to NCR, iff,

$$[p(\hat{\pi} + \tilde{p}_s) - F] - [p(1 - p)\pi_m + p^2\hat{\pi} - F] > 0$$

or

$$F > (1 - p)(\pi_m - 2\hat{\pi}). \tag{14}$$

If DR is at all feasible, then (14) will always be satisfied. This is evident from proposition 1. This leads us to the following proposition:

Proposition 2: If DR is at all feasible, it always dominates NCR.

Proof. Follows from Proposition 1 and condition (14). □

3.2. CR and DR

DR will be preferred to CR iff,

$$[p(\hat{\pi} + \tilde{p}_s) - F] - [p\hat{\pi} - 1/2F] > 0$$

or

$$(1 - p)(p\pi_m - F) > 0. \tag{15}$$

Proposition 3: If DR is at all feasible, it always dominates CR.

Proof. Note that (1) implies that (15) is positive. □

Proposition 4: For relatively high values of p, CR dominates NCR.

Proof. See Marjit (1991). □

In our construction, the delegated regime must dominate the cooperative arrangement. However, given our basic assumption, a cooperative regime is always feasible. But for a delegated regime to be feasible, we need condition (6) to be satisfied. By combining (1) and (6), we derived $\tilde{p}$ such that $\forall p > \tilde{p}$. One can get values of F satisfying both (1) and (6). In this sense, higher values of p would make the delegated regime more likely. Once the delegated regime is feasible, it dominates the cooperative form.

One should note that the cost-sharing cooperative arrangement seems to induce two effects: a decrease in costs from F to $F/2$ but also a decrease in the number of draws (from 2 to 1). The reason why licensing dominates cooperation seems to be that a sequential research program may limit costs of the draw by the first firm, if the draw by the first firm leads to the innovation, but also increase the chances of obtaining the innovation, since the second firm has a draw after the first firm's failure. Very recently, drawing on Marjit (1991), Combs, (1992, 1993) developed the case for an "alternative" cooperative arrangement where firms are allowed two draws, and where the existing results are modified. It is interesting to note that when firms are allowed two draws in CR, the payoff to each is just doubled up to $(2p\hat{\pi} - F)$, and DR does not dominate the cooperative arrangement any longer. Given the assumption on the particular type of cooperative arrangement, Proposition 3 holds.

4. Concluding remarks

We have discussed three alternative forms of R&D organization when firms behave noncooperatively on the product market. When patent rights are enforceable, the cooperative form dominates the noncooperative form of R&D for high values of p, the probability of success. When imitative R&D is allowed, sequential R&D and technology transfer tend to dominate the other forms. However, delegative R&D tends to emerge for greater values of p. Moderate or mild chances of success yield the noncooperative outcomes.

This article can be extended in various directions. First, we have not discussed the normative aspects of R&D organization, which are quite relevant for public policy. Social optimality of different R&D forms under alternative institutional structures should be an intriguing question. We have provided a simple workable model which would bear further analysis in that direction. Second, one can introduce "leap-frogging" behavior in the DR form where the follower can outsmart the leader and where there are potentially many subsequent stages rather than one. In that case, technology transfer might invade the leader's network of markets. Technology contract under potential threat of entry into "other" domains might lead to a whole set of results

Notes

1. Also notable are Gallini and Winter (1985), Katz and Shapiro (1985), Green and Scotchmer (1990), and Kabiraj and Marjit (1992, 1993). Gallini (1984) assumes that for the best technology, repetitive R&D is not profitable. Once one of the firms obtains the technology, the other gives up further research. But without patent protection, imitative R&D is possible and licensing can emerge just to eliminate the duplication effect of imitative R&D. Relative incentives for R&D in monopoly and duopoly situations have been discussed in Anton and Yao (1991).
2. This arrangement assumes that after a successful innovation by a firm, another firm can get the same technology and compete in the product market. It might come through independent R&D or through imitation, and there is no patent law to prevent the second firm from achieving this.
3. We consider only one-shot innovation, in the sense that if any one of the firms obtains the new technology, there is no scope for further innovation.
4. (13) is the outcome of the simple bargaining rule which we derived. π_1 would differ from π_2 if the sharing rules differed and, the two firms would then have different incentives for opting for the delegative regime. Since we are just focusing on the emergence of DR in lieu of CR or NCR, we abstract from the relative incentive problem.

References

Anton, J., and D. Yao. (1991). "Expropriation and Inventions—Appropriable Rents in the Absence of Property Rights." Mimeo, Wharton School.

Combs, K. (1992). "Cost Sharing vs. Multiple Research Project in Cooperative R&D," *Economics Letters* 39, 353–358.

Combs, K. (1993). "The Roles of Information Sharing in Cooperation Research and Development," *International Journal of Industrial Organization* 11, 535–551.

d'Aspremont, C., and A. Jacquemin. (1988). "Cooperative and Non-Cooperative R&D in Duopoly with Spillover," *American Economic Review* (December), 1133–1137.

Gallini, N. (1984). "Deterrence by Market Sharing," *American Economic Review* (December), 931-941.

Gallini, N., and R. Winter. (1985). "Licensing in the Theory of Innovation," *Rand Journal of Economics* 16, 237–252.

Gandal, N., and S. Scotchmer. (1989). "Coordinating Research through Research Joint-Ventures." Domestic Studies Program, Hoover Institution, Stanford University, CA.

Green, J., and S. Scotchmer. "Anti Trust Policy, the Breadth of Patent Protection and the Incentive to Develop New Products." Working paper, GSPP, University of California at Berkeley.

Grossman, G., and C. Shapiro. (1986). "Research Joint-Ventures—an Anti-Trust Analysis," *Journal of Law, Economics and Organization* 2, 315–337.

Kabiraj, T., and S. Marjit. (1992). "To Transfer or not to Transfer the Best Technology Under Potential Threat of Entry—The Case of Price Competition." In B. Dutta et al. (eds.), *Game Theory and Economic Application*. New York: Springer-Verlag.

Kabiraj, T., and S. Marjit. (1993). "International Technology Transfer Under Potential Threat of Entry—A Cournot–Nash Framework," *Journal of Development Economics* 42, 75–88.

Kamien, M., A.E. Muller, and I. Zang. (1990). "Research Joint-Venture and R&D Cartels." Mimeo, Kellogg Graduate School of Management, Northwestern Unversity.

Katz, M. (1986). "An Analysis of Cooperative Research and Development," *Rand Journal of Economics* 17, 528–533.

Katz, M., and C. Shapiro. (1985). "On the Licensing of Innovation," *Rand Journal of Economics* 16, 504–520.

Marjit, S. (1991). "Incentives for Cooperative and Non-Cooperative R&D in Duopoly," *Economics Letters* 37, 187–191.

Ordover, J.A., and R. Willig. (1985). "Anti-Trust for High Technology Industries—Answering Research Joint-Venture and Mergers," *Journal of Law and Economics* 28, 311–333.

Ray Chaudhuri, P. (1992). "Technological Asymmetry and Joint-Product Development." Mimeo, Indian Statistical Institute, Delhi.

Rockett, K. (1990). "The Quality of Licensed Technology," *International Journal of Industrial Organization* 8, 559–574.

Group Decision and Negotiation, 4: 411–428 (1995)

Networks of Innovators: Evidence from Canadian Patents

STÉPHANE GAUVIN
Département de Marketing, Université Laval, Ste-Foy, Québec, Canada, G1K 7P4
stephane.gauvin@fsa.uLaval.ca

Abstract.

Various forms of cooperative development have emerged in recent years, in response to increasing competitive pressures, development costs, and complexity. We use data on patents granted by the Canadian government between 1978 and 1989, in order to explore the formation of development coalitions, where two or more firms jointly develop and patent an innovation. Close to 2,600 firms have been involved in development coalitions. These coalitions can be mapped into more than 1,000 independent networks of innovators. The largest network interconnects 711 organizations.

The prevalence of development coalitions varies considerably across nations. Two-thirds of the Japanese firms holding more than five patents are involved in at least one development coalition. This figure is less than 20% for Canadian and American firms, and 35% for German firms. Coalitions tend to be domestic rather than international. They also tend to be intra-sectorial, except in Japan where they are more frequently inter-sectorial. Our analysis indicates that Japanese development networks are very loose, just as they are for their American and European counterparts.

Key Words: research and development, networks, alliances

1. Introduction

Faced with ever shorter product life cycles, an explosion of development costs, and, perhaps most importantly, increasingly complex technologies, many organizations turn to various forms of cooperative research and development. The *Industrial Research Institute* reports that a third of the firms surveyed expect an increase in cooperative R&D (Brodsky 1991); MERIT-CATI database suggests that the formation rate of research alliances has increased by more than 20% per year during the past decade (Hagedoorn 1990). The frequency of mentions of corporate alliances in trade journals increases even faster.[1]

For all the talk about research alliances, there is little empirical evidence to suggest that they are effective. The American experience with research consortia has received mixed reviews: firms are traditionally very secretive about their research projects, and learning to cooperate is not easy. Participants tend to keep their best researchers in-house; it is difficult to reach a consensus on the projects that should be supported; knowledge transfer takes too long, etc. (e.g., Mandell 1990; Evan and Olk 1990).

This research has been supported by a grant of the FCAR. The author would like to thank the participants of the First International Conference on Joint-Ventures and Strategic Alliances (University Park) and two anonymous reviewers for their helpful comments.

In a review of several national experiences with cooperative research, Alic (1990) concludes that cooperation is likely to remain marginal in applied R&D and that firms will continue to seek proprietary advantages in their core business through internal funding. Porter (1990) argues that government policy should give a limited role to cooperative research. He suggests that the evidence in favor of cooperative research is largely anecdotal—Japan is extremely successful in the global arena and relies extensively on research consortia. Porter notes, however, that other nations that do not encourage cooperative research are equally successful in complex technologies. He also claims that the importance of cooperative research has been misinterpreted: "[t]he most important role of Japanese cooperative research is to *signal* the importance of emerging technical areas and *stimulate proprietary firm research*, not to achieve efficiencies in R&D" (p. 636—emphasis in the original).

These critics are focused on large-scale cooperative agreements. Large-scale cooperation raises the problem of coordinating the activities of several economic agents that have only partially overlapping interests and where inefficiencies occur as the agents negotiate to resolve their disagreements. But cooperative research also exists on a smaller scale, between firms who share information or agree to jointly research a product or a process.

Von Hippel (1987) has documented how mini-mills engineers frequently exchange information. He found a distinct relationship between the amount of cooperation and the value of the information that is exchanged. When information has a modest value, firms trade it. They give information to rivals expecting that a similar favor will eventually be returned. When information has considerable value however, it is closely guarded. This behavior is consistent with a repeated Prisoner's Dilemma.

Suppose the following matrix game:

	Share	Protect
Share	3,3	1,X
Protect	X,1	2,2

As long as X is less than 3, firms will always share information. If X is greater than 3 and less than 5, they face a Prisoner's Dilemma. The individually optimal strategy for the one-shot game is to keep the information proprietary, even though the long-run optimal strategy for both participants would be to share information (Axelrod 1984). If X is greater than 5, the optimal long-run strategy is for both players to exploit each other alternately.

Von Hippel's analysis provides an interesting counterpoint to the arguments against cooperative research. According to his interpretation, cooperation is more likely to occur in the form of a large number of individually insignificant transactions rather than a small number of strategically vital operations. The emergence of this organizational form has been discussed by several authors. Dynamic networks (Miles and Snow 1986), network organizations (Galbraith and Kazanjian 1986), mutual organizations (Koenig and Thiétart 1990), and spot networks (Child 1987) are changing the way new products are being developed.

Two perspectives on organizational networking can be contrasted here. One view is that networks are formed as a web of fairly stable relationships designed by a firm to extend its market and/or technological reach. The design of an efficient network organization involves the identification of critical gaps in the focal firm's capabilities and of potential partners that will help in bridging these gaps, and the management of these key relationships (see Burt 1992).

The other perspective sees networks as the meshing of opportunistic firms that form short-lived partnerships to take advantage of coincident interests. Unlike network organizations, dynamic networks involve nonrecurrent transactions and require the ability to scan a large number of potential partners in order to find the one which is best suited for the specific task at hand. Network organizations are built on stable alliances, while dynamic networks thrive on short-lived coalitions.

Research alliances are connected by long-term exchanges of capital (e.g., cross-holdings), of personnel (e.g., interlocking corporate boards), or information (e.g., cross-licensing). This is often what we have in mind when we think of the Japanese approach to industrial policy: "[t]he New Competition is manifest in a variety of inter-firm complexes [such as the] giant Japanese organizational structures coordinating trading companies, banks and manufacturing enterprises" (Best 1990).

The raison d'être of such alliances is to reduce the level of rivalry between members of the group, and to gain market power as a group. The erosion of America's economic leadership over Japan has focused much attention on strategic alliances. Many felt that the strict American antitrust policy was hurting its competitiveness. As a result, several steps have been taken in the direction of a more liberal policy toward research alliances (see Moore 1988; Langenfeld and Scheffman 1989).

Development coalitions, perhaps a more potent form of cooperation, are based on the idea of dynamic networking. Here, firms interact dynamically with each other, as the need arises, in a series of short-term transactions. There is no alliance, but rather a series of coalitions between firms who have a common interest at one point in time. The key idea of dynamic networks is that firms do not attempt to integrate part of their activities, but instead accept to transact with others for the resources which they lack, when they need them.

While much has been said about Japanese alliances, we know relatively little on the extent of dynamic networking that occurs there. Several reasons may be suggested to explain this situation, one being that data on coalitions is difficult to gather. In this article, we use data on patents granted by Canada in order to explore this issue. We ask three basic questions. (1) How prevalent are development coalitions and how does their frequency vary across nations (U.S., Japan, Germany and Canada)? (2) What is the profile of coalitions' partners: are they from the same country, the same industrial sector? (3) If we consider the complete set of coalitions to build networks, are we likely to find several large industrial groups? Will these groups be organized around large organizations?

2. Data

Canada is the second largest issuer of patents, being second only to the United States (Etemad and Séguin-Dulude 1987). Approximately 16,000 patents are granted by the Canadian Patent Office each year. A comprehensive database (*PATDAT*) provides summary information on all patents granted since 1978. This database has two unique features. First, the Canadian system is the only one where the SICs of manufacture and use of patents are assigned on a case-by-case basis. Second, it is the only synthetic database to provide the names of all assignees of jointly owned patents.

The general limitations and advantages of patent data are well documented (Griliches 1990; Trajtenberg 1989). The most important limitations include uneven representation across sectors of activities and lack of information on the value of a given patent. Still, patent data have no real substitute in providing a fairly accurate account of the level of inventive activity.

A subset of the population of patents is jointly owned by more than one legal entity. Joint ownership (JO) of patents is admittedly a crude indicator of cooperative R&D. On the one hand, JO may underestimate the extent of cooperative R&D. When firms cooperate on a regular basis, they often prefer alternative mechanisms for securing a fair share of the revenues, such as R&D joint-ventures (e.g., IBM–Apple's Metaphor) or general licensing agreements (e.g., Bell Enterprise Canada–Northern Telecom). On the other hand, joint ownership does not necessarily imply joint development. A firm may retain residual rights on patents of a former subsidiary, or the patent office might assign joint ownership if it is unable to establish who was first to invent.

In order to assess the potential for bias we have interviewed representatives of several of the largest Canadian patent assignees. As one would expect, we have been able to identify many instances of cooperative research that have not resulted in joint ownership of patents,[2] but not a single case of joint ownership without joint development. It thus appears to be safe to assume that JO underestimates the number of joint development efforts, in particular those that are part of long-term relationships. In other words, the joint ownership of patents appears to be a reasonably good indicator of coalitions (i.e., opportunistic, short-lived instances of cooperative research) rather than of alliances (i.e., recurrent, long-term instances of cooperative research).

Despite these shortcomings, data on joint ownership of patents hold the potential to be among the better measures that can be used to assess the prevalence of cooperative R&D. Unlike survey data on informal alliances and private contractual agreements, the coverage is comprehensive and reliable, since both the patentees and the government have significant interests at stake. Patents also provide a reasonable standard for making international comparisons, since they are granted by one agency, using the same rules irrespective of the nationality of the inventor. Table 1 presents the elements of information used in this article.

Table 1. Definitions.

Name	Description
Country	Country of residence of the assignee. Four countries are used in this study: Canada, Germany, Japan, and the U.S.
Name	Legal name of the assignee
Number of assignees	Number of assignees who are granted a patent right for the same patent
SIC (assignee)	Computed for all assignees at the two-digit level. The SIC (assignee) is the most frequent SIC (patent) that was granted to this assignee
SIC (patent)	Industrial sector most likely to manufacture the product covered by the patent. Available at the four-digit level
Type	Three types of assignees: corporations, individuals, and government
Year	Calendar year during which the patent was granted
Joint Ownership (JO)	Patent assigned to more than one assignee

3. The prevalance of development coalitions

The evolution of the number of patents granted by Canada is presented in Table 2. The total number of patents granted has declined steadily in recent years, with close to 22,000 new patents per year in 1978, down 25% to 16,000 in 1989. The bulk of patents is granted to corporate assignees (85%). American assignees account for a little more than half of all patents granted during that period, Japan for about 10%, and Germany and Canada for 7% and 8% respectively. The share of all patents owned by American assignees has eroded (58% to 50%), while Japan's position has improved (7% to 13%).

The total number of JOs is small relative to the total number of patents, but fairly stable. During the past decade, approximately 600 joint patents were granted each year. This number represented about 2.7% of the total number of patents in 1978, and 4% in 1989. This upward trend is significant, and is the result of both an increase in the prevalence of corporate coalitions in the U.S., and of the increasing share of Japanese corporations.

The prevalence of development coalitions varies across types and countries of patentees. The rate of JO averages 1.5% for corporate assignees, but more than 17% for individuals. This is consistent with the idea that development coalitions generate economies of scale. Corporations are much more likely than are individuals to have reached the minimum efficient size for R&D. Thus corporations have less incentive to form a research coalition. However, economies of scale do not tell the whole story.

Table 3 presents data on corporate JO broken down by country of origin. American corporations are much less likely to engage in JO than their Canadian, German, or Japanese counterparts. The differences are important. JO represents approximately 0.9% of the American patents output, as compared to 11.7% of the Japanese. Less than 5% of all American corporations that were granted one patent or more have been involved in at least one JO, as compared to 40% of their Japanese counterparts. These figures climb to 13% and 64%, respectively, if we consider corporate assignees with more than five patents to their credit.

The difference in national propensities to form development coalitions is best illustrated by Tables 4 and 5. Table 4 presents the leading 20 patent assignees. These multinational corporations were all granted more than 1,000 patents, and without exception they were granted at least one JO patent. American corporations dominate this list, with 13 entries. Japan has only one firm figuring in the top-twenty (Sony).

Table 5 presents the list of the top-twenty corporate JO holdings. The contrast is revealing: there are now 10 Japanese but not a single American firm in the list.

The data on the prevalence of development coalitions is consistent with what we already knew of cooperative research. First, the incidence of cooperative development is much higher in Japan than it is in the U.S. Second, the absolute numbers are fairly low, but there is an increasing propensity in the U.S.

Even though these two facts—an upward trend in R&D coalitions and their prevalence in Japan, a very successful innovator—can be used to advocate that R&D coalitions can enhance innovator's productivity, there is no clear relationship between the prevalence of cooperative research and the performance of the agents that engage in it. For instance, the U.S. market share of patents continues to erode despite a doubling in the propensity to engage in JO; and even though the rate of JO appears to correlate with the rate of change in national productivity (Japan has a higher rate than Germany, which is itself higher than

Table 2. Patents granted by year, type, and country of assignee.

	Patents		Corporate		Government		Individuals		USA		Japan		Germany		Canada	
Year	Total	JO%[1]	Total	JO%	Total	JO%	Total	JO%	Total	JO%	Total	JO%	Total	JO%	Total	JO%
1978	21,792	2.7%	18,526	1.0%	664	3.3%	2,602	15.1%	12,586	1.9%	1,625	6.3%	1,474	2.8%	1,726	4.4%
1979	23,539	2.7%	19,951	1.0%	736	3.0%	2,852	14.8%	13,568	2.0%	1,673	4.9%	1,683	2.6%	1,701	4.5%
1980	23,895	2.7%	20,230	1.2%	764	3.6%	2,901	13.4%	13,548	1.8%	1,824	5.9%	1,682	4.5%	1,768	5.3%
1981	22,697	3.1%	19,231	1.3%	736	4.9%	2,730	15.7%	12,730	1.9%	1,778	7.0%	1,694	3.5%	1,607	5.7%
1982	23,147	3.6%	19,514	1.5%	783	4.8%	2,849	17.4%	12,761	2.0%	1,982	7.1%	1,663	4.4%	1,773	5.2%
1983	20,999	3.8%	17,664	1.6%	739	5.7%	2,595	18.5%	11,262	2.1%	1,887	6.8%	1,627	4.8%	1,637	5.8%
1984	20,545	4.0%	17,320	1.7%	689	5.5%	2,536	19.8%	11,034	2.1%	1,964	8.3%	1,598	4.3%	1,625	7.4%
1985	18,697	3.8%	15,956	1.7%	643	4.6%	2,099	19.3%	9,712	2.2%	2,021	8.0%	1,366	3.9%	1,550	5.1%
1986	17,250	3.8%	14,867	1.7%	516	7.2%	1,867	19.9%	9,123	2.2%	1,923	7.5%	1,095	3.0%	1,372	7.5%
1987	14,849	3.7%	12,660	1.8%	429	5.3%	1,760	17.2%	7,620	2.1%	1,587	6.8%	1,089	4.5%	1,207	6.3%
1988	16,846	3.8%	14,456	1.7%	464	7.8%	1,926	18.7%	8,715	2.4%	1,971	6.9%	1,224	2.9%	1,390	5.8%
1989	16,297	4.0%	14,023	2.1%	445	7.8%	1,829	18.1%	8,148	2.2%	2,081	7.5%	1,196	4.2%	1,284	7.4%
Total	240,553		204,398		7,608		28,548		130,808		22,315		17,390		18,639	

[1]Proportion of patents that are jointly owned.

Table 3. Corporate patents.

All Firms	U.S.	Japan	Germany	Canada
Firms	12,208	1,935	1,831	2,619
Patents	117,365	22,437	15,774	11,735
Average % of joint ownerships	0.9%	11.7%	4.4%	3.3%
% of firms with at least one joint patent	4.64%	40.1%	13.71%	5.99%
Firms with More than Five Patents	**U.S.**	**Japan**	**Germany**	**Canada**
Firms	1,953	420	289	242
Patents	100,008	19,822	13,222	8,172
Average % of joint ownerships	1.17%	17.15	6.56%	3.53%
% of firms with at least one joint patent	13%	65%	35%	18%

Table 4. Leading patent assignees.

Rank	Country	Name	Total	Joint
1	USA	General Electric Company	3,376	8
2	Netherlands	N.V. Philips Gloeilampenfabrieken	3,047	12
3	USA	International Business Machines Corporation	2,931	7
4	USA	Westinghouse Electric Corporation	2,147	7
5	Switzerland	Ciba-Geigy Ag	2,102	17
6	Germany	Hoechst Aktiengesellschaft	2,068	18
7	Japan	Sony Corporation	1,974	20
8	Germany	Bayer Aktiengesellschaft	1,942	40
9	USA	E.I. Du Pont De Nemours and Company	1,891	3
10	USA	Union Carbide Corporation	1,698	9
11	USA	Xerox Corporation	1,586	2
12	USA	Western Electric Company, Incorporated	1,393	1
13	USA	RCA Corporation	1,188	2
14	USA	Exxon Research and Engineering Company	1,186	11
15	Canada	Shell Canada Limited	1,142	7
16	USA	Dow Chemical Company (the)	1,121	4
17	USA	General Motors Corporation	1,121	3
18	Germany	Basf Aktiengesellschaft	1,082	3
19	USA	Eastman Kodak Company	1,072	3
20	USA	Mobil Oil Corporation	1,058	2
Total			33,125	179

the U.S.), Canada has a higher rate of development coalitions but loses ground relative to the U.S. in terms of productivity.

Part of the explanation for these inconsistencies may lie in the structure of cooperative research. The effectiveness of R&D coalitions may depend on the type of partners (domestic versus foreign, private versus public), on the number of firms involved in the coalition, and on the type of relationships between coalitions members (clique versus group with a clear leader, etc.). We examine these questions in the next two sections.

Table 5. Leading joint assignees.

Rank	Country	Name	Total	Joint
1	Japan	Hitachi Ltd.	911	122
2	Soviet Union	Soviet Union	119	117
3	Soviet Union	Soviet Union	903	115
4	Japan	Toyota Motor Co. Ltd.	189	53
5	Japan	Sumitomo Electric Industries Ltd.	308	51
6	Japan	Sumitomo Chemical Co. Ltd.	578	49
7	Japan	Mitsubishi Heavy Industries Ltd.	122	41
8	Germany	Bayer Aktiengesellschaft	1,942	40
9	Canada	Canada-Cities Service, Ltd.	39	39
10	Canada	Gulf Oil Canada Limited	58	38
11	Japan	Mitsubishi Chemical Industries Ltd.	152	35
12	Germany	Deutsche Gold- und Silber-scheideanstalt Vormals Roessle	153	34
13	Great Britain	Imperial Chemical Industries Limited	1,024	33
14	Canada	Imperial Oil Ltd.	124	33
15	Japan	Fujitsu Limited	447	31
16	Germany	Henkel KGAA	207	31
17	Germany	Bergwerksverband GMBH	66	31
18	Japan	Kawasaki Steel Corp.	166	29
19	Japan	Mitsui Toatsu Chemicals Inc.	211	28
20	Japan	Matsushita Electric Works Ltd.	89	28
Total			7,808	978

4. Profile of coalition partners

Data on JOs can be used to examine several dimensions of the profile of partners engaged in a cooperative research project: whether or not partners are likely to be of the same type, the same country, and the same industry. Table 6 presents the frequency of the various combinations of types of assignees.[3]

The profile of partnerships varies considerably across countries. Canada and the U.S. are characterized by a large proportion of their JOs involving two or more individuals relative to JOs involving two or more corporations (8 to 1 in Canada and 7 to 1 in the U.S.), while the opposite is true in Japan (1 to 6). Canada is the country where we find the highest proportion of governmental partnerships, followed by Japan, Germany, and finally the U.S., where they are virtually nonexistent.

Table 7 presents a breakdown of JOs into four categories according to the country of residence and the two-digit SIC of the assignees involved in a JO. The most important finding here is that unlike those of the other three nations, Japanese firms tend to be involved in partnerships with other Japanese firms that are specialized in different, and presumably complementary, industries. In other countries, firms tend to join forces with a domestic partner specialized in the same industry, presumably to reap economies of scale. This situation is particularly true of Canada where close to two-thirds of the JOs are of this type. This data is also useful for highlighting the fact that development coalitions are rarely used to span national boundaries. On average, 11% of the JOs are multinational; this figure dips to a mere 3% in Japan.

Table 6. Profile of domestic joint ownerships.

	U.S.	Japan	Germany	Canada
Assignees				
Corporations	367	779	251	156
Government	8	12	7	27
Individuals	2,534	354	396	1,697
JO				
Corporations	514	1,250	345	134
Government	6	72	13	69
Individuals	2,163	231	301	876
Instances				
Corporations	1,061	2,632	707	391
Government	12	154	27	230
Individuals	4,919	608	748	1,983
Partnerships				
C-C	310	1,063	253	105
C-G	3	0	0	80
I-I	2,082	173	271	848
C-G	4	154	23	54
C-I	153	153	28	32
G-I	0	1	1	9
C-G-I	0	0	0	0

Table 7. Prevalence of international and inter-sectorial joint ownerships.

	U.S.	Japan	Germany	Canada
Same country Same industry	255	584	229	119
Same country Different industry	202	902	164	28
Different country Same industry	94	44	51	24
Different country Different industry	51	17	23	18

The results reported in this section suggest that Japan differs from other nations not only in terms of the prevalence of corporate JOs, but also in terms of the type of partners that are involved in these coalitions. Japanese coalitions involve corporations belonging to different industries; while American coalitions mainly involve individuals, and when they involve corporations, they tend to belong to the same industry. American coalitions appear to be created in order to generate a critical mass of R&D and reap economies of scale; Japanese coalitions appear to be created in order to assemble complementary subunits and reap economies of scope.

The Japanese pattern is consistent with the existence of a dynamic network. However, it may also reflect the presence of *keiretsus*, those loose industrial groups that are coordinated by a strong central organization (Kaisha). The next section attempts to answer this question by looking at the networks' structures.

5. Networks of innovators

While JOs generally involve few partners, more than 500 firms have two partners or more, because they participated in several JOs. It is essentially through these polyadic coalitions that networks of innovators are created. As we will see in the next section, networks need not depend on a few focal firms with a large number of unrelated partners. They can also be the result of indirect relationships across firms with a limited number of direct partners.

The procedure used to construct networks is quite simple (see Freeman, White, and Romney 1989):

1. Create a matrix M of size N, where N is the number of firms.
2. The entries $m_{r,c}$ take a value of 1 if firm r is directly linked to firm c, and 0 otherwise. M is symmetric.
3. M is then block-clustered. Block-clustering is achieved by computing $M^k = M^{k-1} \times M^{k-1}$. All entries of M^k greater than 1 are set to 1. The procedure iterates until $M^k = M^{k-1}$. Rows and columns are then sorted in "blocks" of firms (i.e., networks).

In our case, there are no less than 1,047 independent networks of firms, but most networks (87%) involve one[4] or two corporations generally working on a single JO. Table 8 presents the distribution of networks broken down by the number of participating firms.

Table 8. Networks of corporate innovators: size and frequency.

Size of Network[1]	Frequency
1	464
2	447
3	83
4	33
5	11
6	1
7	5
13	2
711	1

These networks include all firms that are directly or indirectly related. The largest network involves 711 corporations. The next largest network involves only 13 firms.[5]

A clear implication of the existence of this global network is that networking of innovators is very loose. In order to directly connect all firms together, a network of 711 organizations would require more than a quarter of a million dyadic JOs $[(711^2 - 711)/2]$. What we have here instead, is a loose meshing of a large number of organizations indirectly connected by fewer than 2,000 direct links. Another implication is that although networking is largely done within a country, the network itself is international.

Figure 1 illustrates the "core" of the global network. The top 24 firms account for a total of more than 34,000 patents, including 363 JOs. They have direct relationships with an average of 7.3 firms, and indirect relationships in a network of 711 organizations which claims more than 53,000 patents.

As we can see from Figure 1, there are only eight direct links between these firms. Even though General Electric (leading patent holder) and Hitachi (leading JO holder) belong to the same network, the shortest path to Hitachi goes, from GE through Westinghouse, Allis–Chalmers, Kubota, Chugai Ro Kogyo, and Kawasaki Steel before reaching Hitachi.

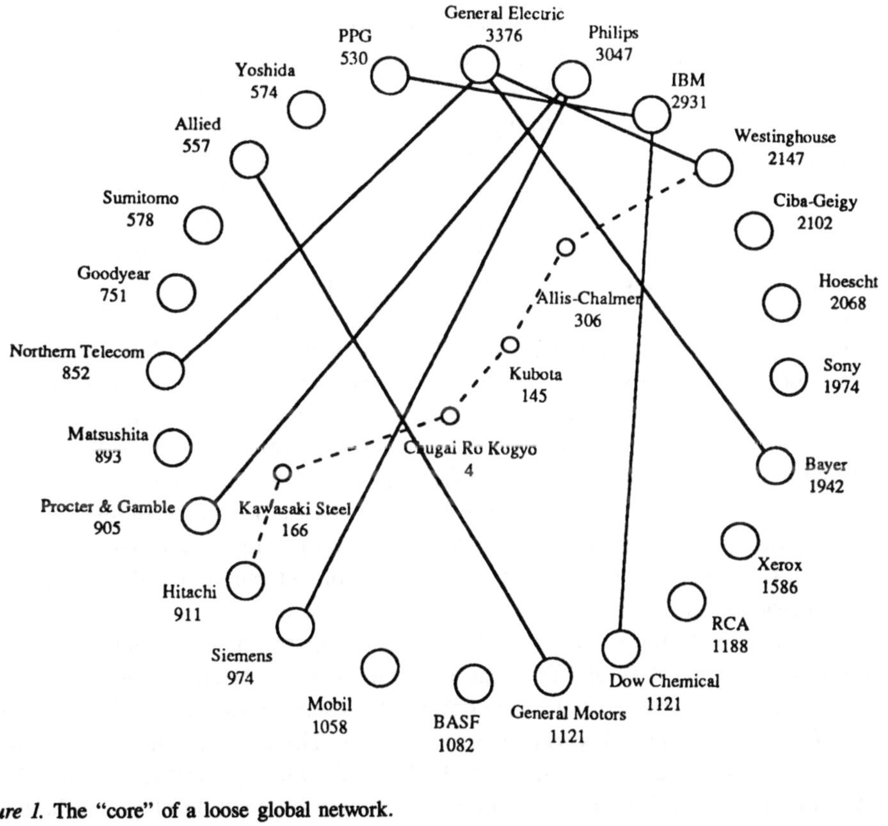

Figure 1. The "core" of a loose global network.

It is interesting to note that the propensity to network among "core" participants is a mirror image of what we have found so far. In general, Japanese firms are more likely to engage in coalitions than their American counterparts. If we focus on the "core" of the network of innovators, we would conclude otherwise. Of the 12 American firms, eight have participated in a JO with another core member. Three of the four corporate JOs in which General Electric was involved are with core members (Westinghouse, Bayer, and Northern Telecom). The one Canadian firm is also linked within the core. Only one of the four German corporations is linked (Bayer) in the core, but none of the five Japanese firms has a direct link with another core member.

In other words, large North American corporations are not only much less likely to engage in development coalitions than their foreign competitors, but, when they do, they tend to venture with equally massive partners. In contrast, Japanese and German corporations participate in the global network via an elaborate meshing of smaller organizations.

6. Positional analysis

Studying networks like these using conventional methods from the field of social network analysis (e.g., Freeman, White, and Romney 1989; Useem 1979) doesn't appear very promising. The vast majority of networks of innovators are trivially small, or too large and too loosely connected to provide for a meaningful analysis. An alternative is to study networking locally, at the firm level, considering each firm as the focal point of its own network.

Two generic types of networks are possible. At one extreme, a firm can be the hub of the network, connected to otherwise autonomous organizations. At the other extreme, all particpants in a network may be connected to each other, in what is usually called a clique. Mixtures of cliques and centralized networks will give more or less complex relational structures. Simple examples of networks are presented in Figure 2.

In the centralized network, the focal entity (A) developed a total of four patents. One is the result of an autonomous research project and the other three were developed through dyadic coalitions, with firms B, C, and D, respectively. The diagram can be mapped into a matrix form, with the entries denoting the frequency of transactions between the nodes of the diagram. In this example, four patents were developed by firm A itself (one alone and three with partners), one patent by firm A and B, one by A and C, and one by A and D. Zeros in the lower triangle mean that there was no instance of a collaboration involving two firms working in concert with the focal organization, while the zeros in the upper triangle mean that there was no instance of collaboration between firms B, C, or D other than those involving A.

In the clique network, the focal entity (A) developed one patent as a result of a polyadic coalition involving firms B, C, and D. In this example, only one patent has been developed, and all the firms are connected with each other. The lower triangle is filled with ones to reflect the fact that B, C, and D worked together with A. The upper triangle remains filled with zeros, because there is no instance of B, C, or D working together without A.

The third example is a little more complex, involving one patent developed in-house by the focal firm and five in-house by D; one coalition involved firms A, B, and D; one involved A, B, and C; one involved A and C; and finally one involved B and D. We do not

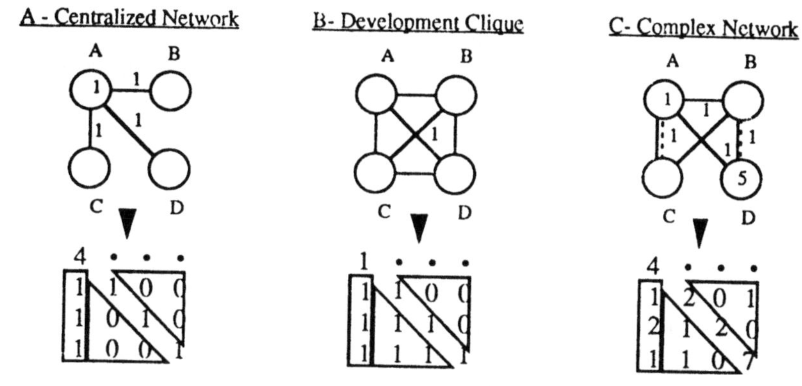

	A	B	C
Number of firms	4	4	4
Number of patents	4	1	10
Inner Coverage	0	1	.67
Outer Coverage	0	0	.33
Patent share	1	1	.4
Joint Herfindhal	.58	.25	.26
Global Herfindhal	.39	.25	.32

Figure 2. Positional indices.

have a perfect clique, since firms C and D never worked jointly with A. Note also the entry in the upper triangle, which reflects the coalition between B and D in which A was not involved.

We can now use these matrices to generate a parsimonious set of focal indicators. In addition to basic descriptors such as the total number of patents and firms involved in a network, the following indicators are computed:

Inner Coverage is the proportion of the lower triangle that is filled by nonzero values. *Inner Coverage* can take values between zero (centralized network) and one (clique). This index is computed at the first order level, i.e., using direct linkages between firms.

Outer Coverage is computed similarly, using the entries of the upper triangle. *Outer Coverage* is a measure of clique among the focal firm's partners. It is computed using the firms that belong to the first order network of the focal firm.

Share of Patents measures the ratio of the number of shares owned by the focal firm to the number of patents owned by firms that belong to its first-order network. This measure serves to capture the relative importance of a firm in its first-order network.

Joint Herfindah is the sum of the squares of the JO shares held by the participants to the first-order network. This measure provides an indication of the concentration of joint ownership of patents.

Global Herfindah is computed similarly for the shares of patents.

Table 9 shows how these focal indicators vary as a function of the country of residence of the focal firms, and firm size expressed in terms of the number of patents owned. The numbers of partners and patents have been computed for three orders of networking. Firms directly linked to each other form a first-order network. Second-order networks include firms with direct linkages plus firms that are directly linked to first-order partners (*JO 1*, *JO 2*, *JO 3*, and *Partners 1*, *Partners 2*, and *Partners 3*). The regression was run with firms having two or more direct corporate partners.

Regressions on the number of JOs and partners show once again the considerable differences in terms of corporate networking that exist between Japan, Germany, and the rest of the world. Results indicate that as we move outwards in a Japanese or German network, the number of partners involved increases dramatically. In contrast, North American networks tend to close on themselves. The average number of partners in a third-order Japanese network is close to 60; this figure is about 30 for Germany, 10 in the U.S., and seven in Canada. The average number of JOs in a third-order network is in excess of 120 for Japan, 60 for Germany, and 17 for the U.S. and Canada.

While there is no doubt that development coalitions are a much more salient feature of the Japanese and German industrial organizations, contrary to what many believe, the data suggest that the structure of their networks is quite similar to what we find in North America. If we partial out the impact of the number of patents and JOs on the focal firms' network structure, neither Japanese nor German networks are structured like cliques. The index of *Inner Coverage* is in fact significantly less than that of the nations that are included in the intercept. This index is also less than the intercept in the U.S., but not significantly. The difference between *Inner Coverage* in the U.S., Germany, and Japan is not statistically significant either. In contrast, Canadian firms are more likely to form cliques. This is apparent from significantly higher indices of *Inner* and *Outer Coverage*, and probably the result of cost reducing development coalitions, since Canada has a relatively small domestic market and correspondingly small firms.

Joint development is more concentrated in the U.S. than it is in Japan, not less as the concept of Kaishas would suggest; and the number of patents held by first-order networks is significantly higher in Japan and Germany, suggesting that networking is indeed an effective means of leveraging a firm's research budget.

7. Discussion

Our findings suggest that research coalitions play an important role in Japan. and, to a lesser extent, in Germany. The incidence of development coalitions is much higher than in North American: more than 40% of Japanese firms have participated in at least one development coalition, and these coalitions account for more than 10% of the total innovative output, measured in patents.

The structure of Japanese networks is not radically different from the structures of other countries. In particular, it exhibits about the same degree of centralization and is not more "cliquish" than what we find in the U.S., which suggests that Japanese networks cannot be dismissed as a legal artefact of the keiretsus-kaishas organization structure. Networking is a reality of the Japanese way of doing business.

One important difference deserves our attention: in general, coalitions involve partners of the same country and the same industry, while in Japan coalitions involve members of

Table 9. Country and portfolio effect on positional indices.

	Intercept	U.S.	Japan	Germany	Canada	Patents	JOs	R^2
Partners 1	3.713	−0.223	1.209**	0.991	0.919			0.03**
JO 1	5.787	−1.893	0.817	1.806	−0.208			0.01
Partners 2	6.250	−0.587	13.997**	6.676**	0.829			0.19**
JO 2	12.028	−3.345	27.502**	16.028**	4.420			0.12**
Partners 3	10.602	−1.217	47.472**	17.824**	−2.865			0.27**
JO 3	19.787	−2.393	102.736**	40.046**	−1.340			0.24**
Inner Coverage	0.808	−0.042	−0.088**	−0.096**	0.111**	−1.85 E−04**	−9.32 E−03**	0.35**
Outer Coverage	0.028	−0.018	0.005	0.008	0.065**	−7.25 E−06	−2.52 E−04	0.04**
Joint Herfindhal	0.345	0.022**	−0.012*	0.003	−0.071**	−2.35 E−05**	−6.50 E−04**	0.17**
Global Herfindhal	0.580	0.005	0.045	0.062	−0.146**	5.11 E−06	−4.42 E−03**	0.09**
Total Patents	85.586	93.916	180.332**	399.117**	−4.767	1.82 E+00**	1.30 E+01**	0.49**
Share of Patents	0.483	−0.017	−0.275**	−0.206**	0.066	1.27 E−04**	−3.37 E−04	0.18**

n = 585 in all cases
* = significant at .05 or better
** = significant at .01 or better

different industries. This piece of evidence suggests that Japanese coalitions aim at creating economies of scope rather than economies of scale. The success of the Japanese economy has been attributed to several factors, including nationwide coordination achieved by MITI's strong leadership. When we think of "this" Japan, we tend to think of large industrial groups, and many are tempted to see collusion rather than coordination: firms enjoy a captive domestic market, can share risks by sitting on a steering committee, and collude to fix prices in export markets. We cannot say much about collusion, but our data suggest that coordination is very much a reality in Japan: firms are more productive, because they tend to develop joint solutions to their problems; their involvement with suppliers and customers makes them more attentive to their needs, etc.

There is no clear evidence that networking contributes significantly to innovators' performance, however. The four countries used in this study are very successful by most standards, yet the prevalence of networking is remarkably different. On the other hand, it is possible to argue that the country with the largest share of patents (U.S.) is also the one with the fewest joint ownerships, a point in favor of a strong antitrust policy. One cannot be indifferent to recent trends, however, and to the fact that both Japan and Germany make greater use of networks than the U.S. does. Both countries have been very successful since World War II, and it is tempting to attribute part of this success to domestic coordination that would take both the form of long-term agreements and short-term interactions, a point in favor of a strong industrial policy.

To summarize, our basic findings are that: (1) Japanese and German corporations rely much more on coalitions than do their North American rivals; (2) Japanese corporations are involved in more vertical than horizontal partnerships; (3) despite these differences, the network structures are similar across these three economic blocks.

These results are consistent with anecdotal evidence, but provide little more than a better understanding of the similarities and differences in the practice of joint patent ownership in the economic triad. Several obvious limitations should be addressed in future research on this topic. First, the argument that joint ownership of patents can be used as a proxy for research coalitions deserves more scrutiny. As one anonymous reviewer observed, joint ownership may reflect national traditions with respect to the handling of subcontracted research, rather than true cooperation. Second, industry effects should be more carefully isolated—differences in the prevalence of joint ownership of patents could be attributed, in part, to differences in the national mix of industries.

But the most pressing questions bear on the impact that joint development has on performance, both at the national level and for the firms involved in these projects. For instance, the results reported in this article suggest a positive correlation between the speed of development and the frequency of joint ownerships of patents. But this interpretation is speculative, and the causation is not clear. Although formal models suggest that cooperative research may accelerate the pace of development (e.g., Kamien, Muller, and Zang 1992), the reverse—namely, that rapid development pace breeds joint development—is also plausible.

Notes

1. During the first ten months of 1991, 930 mentions of corporate alliances are found in ABI/Inform's citation index, up from 528 in 1990.

2. In particular, Bell Canada Enterprise and Northern Telecom have agreed to assign all patents to Northern Telecom. Hundreds of patents have been developed jointly during the period covered by this study, yet not one is reported as a jointly owned patent. On the basis of private conversations with R&D executives, I would estimate that between 1% and 5% of private R&D spendings end up in joint ownership of patents, while cooperative R&D represents between 10% and 20% of private R&D spendings.
3. The number of instances of joint ownership is a multiple of the number of JOs, because one patent involves more than one partner, For example, 567 U.S. corporate assignees have participated in at least one JO, and 514 JOs involved at least one American corporation with another American assignee. The number of instances of one American corporation involved in one JO is 1,061. These events include 310 JOs of two or more corporations, four JOs involving at least one corporation, and one government agency, etc.
4. Four-hundred and forty-seven "networks" involve one corporation and one or more noncorporate partner(s), generally individual co-owners of a patent.
5. The distribution on network sizes is striking, but we shouldn't conclude to a deliberate effort by firms to build a global network. In the absence of a normative theory on the distribution of network sizes, I ran several simulations to explore this question. Results suggest that random coalitions will generate network distributions similar to what I report in this article.

References

Alic, John A. (1990). "Cooperation in R&D," *Technovation* 10(5), 319–331.

Best, Michael. (1990). *The New Competition—Institutions of Industrial Restructuring*. Cambridge, MA: Harvard University Press.

Brodsky, Philip H. (1991). "Industrial Research Institute's Annual R&D Trends Survey," *Research-Technology Management* 34(1), 12–14.

Burt, Raymond. (1992). *Structural Holes*. Cambridge, MA: Harvard University Press.

Child, John. (1987). "Information Technology, Organization, and the Response to Strategic Challenges," *California Management Review* 30(1), 33–50.

Etemad, Hamid, and Louise Séguin Dulud. (1987). "Patenting Patterns in 25 Large Multinational Enterprises," *Technovation* 7, 1–15.

Evan, William M., and Paul Olk. (1990). "R&D Consortia: A New U.S. Organizational Form,'' *Sloan Management Review* 31(3), 37–47.

Freeman, Linton C., Douglas R. White, and A. Kimball Romney. (1989). *Research Methods in Social Network Analysis*. Fairfax VA: George Mason University Press.

Galbraith, Jay, and Robert Kazanjian. (1986). *Strategy Implementation: Structure, Systems and Process*. St. Paul: West Publishing.

Griliches, Zvi. (1990). "Patent Statistics as Economic Indicators: A Survey," *Journal of Economic Literature* 28(4), 1661–1707.

Hagedoorn, John. (1990). "Organizational Model of Inter-Firm Cooperation and Technology Transfer," *Technovation* 10(1), 17–29.

Kamien, Morton, Eitan Muller, and Israel Zand. (1992). "Research Joint Ventures and R&D Cartels," *American Economic Review* 82(5), 1293–1306.

Koenig, Christian, and Raymond Alain Thiétart. (1990). "The Mutual Organization: a New Form of Cooperation in a High-Technology Industry," in Ray Loveridge and Martyn Pitt (eds.), *The Strategic Management of Technological Innovation*. West Sussex, England: John Wiley & Sons.

Langenfeld, James, and David Scheffman. (1989). "Innovation and U.S. Competition Policy," *Antitrust Bulletin* 34(1), 1–63.

Mandell, Mel. (1990). "The Consortium: An Idea Whose Time Has Come (or Gone)?" *Across the Board* 27(6), 30–35.

Miles, Raymond, E., and Charles C. Snow. (1986). "Organizations: New Concepts for New Forms," *California Management Review* 28(3), 62–73.

Mitchell, Graham R. (1990). "Industrial Research Institute's Annual R&D Trends Survey," *Research-Technology Management* 33(1), 14–16.

Moore, John H. (1988). "Knowledge Transfers in the United States," *European Economic Review* 32(2), 591–603.
Olleros, Francisco-Javier, and Roderick Macdonald. (1988). "Strategic Alliances: Managing Complementarity to Capitalize on Emerging Technologies," *Technovation* 7, 155–176.
Porter, Michael. (1990). *The Competitive Advantage of Nations*. New York: The Free Press.
Rothwell, Roy. (1991). "External Networking and Innovation in Small and Medium Sized Manufacturing Firms in Europe," *Technovation* 11(2), 93–110.
Russo, Margherita. (1985). "Technical Change and the Industrial District: The Role of Interfirm Relations in the Growth and Transformation of Ceramic Tile in Italy," *Research Policy* 14, 329–342.
Trajtenberg, Manual. (1989). "The Welfare Analysis of Product Innovations, with an Application to Computed Tomography Scanners," *Journal of Political Economy* 97(2), 444–479.
Useem, Michael. (1979). "The Social Organization of the American Businesses Elite," *American Sociological Review* 44(4), 553–572.
von Hippel, Eric. (1987). "Cooperation between Rivals: Informal Know-How Trading," *Research Policy* 16, 291–302.

Group Decision and Negotiation, 4: 429–452 (1995)

Patterns of Strategic Alliances between Rival Firms

BERNARD GARRETTE
HEC, School of Management, 78351 Jouy-en-Josas, France

PIERRE DUSSAUGE
HEC, School of Management, 78351 Jouy-en-Josas, France

Abstract.

This article describes the results of a research project which examined 171 alliances set up by competing firms in an international context. It presents an empirically-based taxonomy of such alliances constructed on the basis of a set of variables chosen for their demonstrated or assumed influence on the evolution and outcomes of strategic partnerships. Three contrasted types of allliances are identified: quasi-concentration alliances, market penetration alliances and shared supply alliances. They differ according to two fundamental dimensions: their symmetrical or dissymmetrical nature and the way in which they alter competition. Legal structure, often emphasized in previous research on the subject, does not emerge as a strongly discriminating factor. Hypotheses on the likely evolution and outcomes of each type of alliance are derived from the taxonomy.

Key Words: alliance, cooperation, interfirm collaboration, competition, globalization, taxonomy, configurations

1. Introduction

Interfirm collaboration is becoming an increasingly common phenomenon (Harrigan 1985). In this context, collaboration between rival firms raises specific issues, because it blurrs the distinction between competition and cooperation (Porter and Fuller 1986; Doz, Hamel, and Prahalad 1989). This article focuses on strategic alliances set up by competing firms. Such alliances are defined as collaborative projects implemented by firms operating in the same industry, which nevertheless retain their strategic autonomy. This definition therefore excludes mergers and acquisitions that lead to the loss of autonomy by at least one partner. It also excludes vertical partnerships set up by suppliers and buyers.

Research on interfirm collaboration has examined the questions of the stability of such partnerships (Franko 1971; Beamish 1985; Kogut 1988b), of their effectiveness as compared to other organizational forms (Hennart 1988; Teece 1986; Anderson and Gatignon 1986; Kogut and Singh 1988), of the relative benefits derived by each partner firm (Doz 1988; Doz, Hamel, and Prahalad 1989; Hamel 1991), as well as of the anticompetitive aspects of interfirm cooperation (Pate 1969; Pfeffer and Nowak 1976; Duncan 1982). All of these questions deal with the issue of the evolution of alliances over time, and of the

We are grateful to Barbara Gray, Stuart Hart, Aneel Karnani, Will Mitchell, Michel Tenenhaus, and to two anonymous reviewers for their very valuable and helpful comments on earlier drafts of this article. Our research project was funded by "Fondation HEC," whose support we gratefully acknowledge.

various consequences which they produce. Empirical research on the subject has not yet reached the point where clear answers to these questions have been formulated (Kogut 1988a). On the other hand, interfirm cooperation has been shown to be a phenomenon which is more heterogeneous than is usually thought to be the case (Hergert and Morris 1987). Even when focusing on collaboration between rival firms, the diversity of observed cases is considerable (Ghemawat, Porter, and Rawlinson 1986). This diversity, which is reflected in the wide range of strategic and organizational factors that have been used to categorize alliances, is probably what makes it difficult to anticipate the evolutions and outcomes of alliances: indeed, it appears very unrealistic to hypothesize that these evolutions follow a single pattern. Therefore, a necessary preliminary stage in modeling the evolutions and outcomes of interfirm collaboration is to build a taxonomy of strategic alliances. Such an approach draws on Miller's conceptualization of strategy and structure configurations (Miller 1986). Indeed, Miller argued that research on the influence of strategic and organizational factors upon firm performance should be based on the previous identification of coherent configurations of strategy and structure, or "gestalts." In the same way, as particular configurations of strategy and structure produce contrasted developments and lead to differing levels of firm performance (Rumelt 1974), it can be assumed that partnerships corresponding to different strategic and organizational patterns should be managed differently and lead to contrasting outcomes.

In this context, the objective of our research is to build an empirically based taxonomy of strategic alliances between rival firms, on the basis of which contrasting evolutions and outcomes can be anticipated (Galbraith and Schendel 1983). While previous taxonomies of strategic alliances are either theoretical (Astley and Fombrun 1983; Gray and Yan 1992) or based on small samples (Killing 1988), the taxonomy which we are producing is based on a statistical analysis of the attributes of a large sample of such alliances. The attributes considered were chosen on the basis of their hypothesized influence on the evolutions of alliances over time, and they are essentially strategic and organizational factors. This will therefore make it possible for us to formulate in the discussion section of this article a set of hypotheses on the likely evolutions and outcomes of alliances pertaining to each identified pattern of collaboration.

2. The main attributes of alliances suggested in prior research

To identify the attributes of alliances that should be considered in the building of the taxonomy, we have examined what factors were shown in previous research to influence the evolution of alliances. Previous empirical research has analyzed strategic alliances according to a number of descriptive dimensions, such as the scope of the alliance (Ghemawat, Porter, and Rawlinson 1986; Mariti and Smiley 1983; Harrigan 1985), the legal form adopted (Pisano, Russo, and Teece 1988), the distribution of equity ownership (Kogut 1988a), partner asymmetries (Harrigan 1988b), the countries of origin of partner firms (Hergert and Morris 1987), and the industries concerned (Harrigan 1988a; Hergert and Morris 1987). Several of these studies have established or speculated on the existence of relations between certain of these attributes and different aspects in the evolution of partnerships over time, such as joint venture survival (Kogut 1988b; Harrigan 1988b) and manager satisfaction (Killing 1982; Harrigan 1988b).

Clinical studies on interfirm collaboration suggest additional factors which are directly related to strategic management issues—namely, similar or different contributions made by the partner firms, skill appropriability (Doz, Hamel, and Prahalad 1989), task complexity, organization of tasks (Killing 1988), and management structures (Killing 1983; Kogut 1988b). These factors are rarely operationalized in statistical studies. However, their importance is critical, since they affect the essential question of skill transfer and appropriation between allied firms (Teece 1977, 1986; Hamel 1991).

Other significant attributes of strategic alliances can be derived from more theoretical approaches. Transaction cost theory suggests a distinction between "scale" and "link" joint ventures (Williamson 1975, 1985). On this basis, alliances in which all partner firms contribute similar assets in order to benefit from size and scale effects have been distinguished from alliances in which partner firms contribute assets of different natures (Hennart 1988). This distinction considerably alters the relationship between the partner firms and can thus be hypothesized as having a strong influence on the evolution of alliances over time.

Conceptual approaches on competition and cooperation stress the importance of examining the more or less collusive, or competitive, nature of strategic alliances (Porter and Fuller 1986; Contractor and Lorange 1988; Buckley and Casson 1988; Bresser 1988; Jorde and Teece 1989). While some alliances preclude all direct competition between the allied firms, others alter the forms of competition to a lesser extent.

Some of these factors suggested in the literature have been operationalized in statistical studies. However, other factors, whose importance has been stressed, have not been operationalized to date. We have designed original variables intended to operationalize such factors and take them into account in a statistical analysis.

In addition, what has been examined in most previous research is the isolated influence of one or the other of the above-mentioned factors. On this basis, our expected contribution is to demonstrate that the various factors that have been shown to affect the dynamics of interfirm collaboration cohere to form distinct patterns of alliances. It could then be hypothesized that contrasted evolutions can be associated to these various alliance patterns.

3. Variable definition and justification

All the variables used in this study are categorical. A first set of variables (variables 1 to 3) was used to control the representativeness of the sample. The taxonomy of alliances is built on the basis of the second set of variables (variables 4 to 14).

Illustrative variables:

- Country of origin of the firms: *variable 1*
- Year that the alliance was formed: *variable 2*
- Industry: *variable 3*

These first three variables were included in the study to control the distribution of the sample by geographical zone, year, and industry. The sample was designed to be consistent in terms of these three dimensions with previous studies which extensively recorded alliance formation announcements (Hegert and Morris 1987; Ghemawat, Porter, and Rawlinson

1986). Thus, these variables were used in an illustrative way, i.e., they were not taken into account in the building of the taxonomy. Indeed, these attributes of alliances can be hypothesized as having only an indirect impact on the evolution of alliances. For example, it is often asserted that alliances with Japanese partners produce very unbalanced benefits (Mankin and Reich 1986; Doz, Hamel, and Prahalad 1989). However, this is not because of the attribute of nationality, but because of other underlying features, which happen to be correlated with nationality. Including these variables in the study in an illustrative way makes it possible to observe whether they are statistically linked with other features or with the patterns of alliances.

Active variables:

- Number of partner firms: *variable 4*

Transaction cost literature (Williamson 1975), as well as empirical studies on the defense and aerospace industry (Hartley 1983; Kolodziej 1987), suggest that the complexity and cost of managing networks and partnerships increases with the number of players involved. Therefore, it can be hypothesized that joint-venture stability decreases as the number of partners increases. On this basis, we have chosen to distinguish bilateral partnerships from multilateral alliances.

- Structure set up: *variable 5*

Clinical as well as theoretical studies (Killing 1982, 1988; Gray and Yan 1992) have shown that the distribution of ownership and control in joint ventures has an influence on the evolution of alliances. From a broader perspective, transaction cost theory would suggest that more structured partnerships lead to more stable alliances. Therefore, variable 5 distinguishes three increasing levels of alliance structuration. First, alliances that have not led to the formation of a legal entity remain very close to market relations. Second, balanced equity joint ventures, in which each ally owns the same share of the JV's equity, are hybrid forms situated in an intermediate position between market and hierarchy. Indeed, as none of the partners is in a dominant position, all decisions must be negotiated. Finally, dominated equity joint ventures, in which one partner owns a larger share of the JV's equity than any other, are close to hierarchy, as one partner is in a position to impose a particular decision in case of conflict.

- Equity participations: *variable 6*

Equity participations of one partner in the other's equity signal an increased degree of internalization and institutionalization of the relationship. It has been suggested that such participations also increase the stability of alliances (Lorange and Roos 1992).

- Relative competitive positions: *variable 7*

The influence of the symmetry or asymmetry in size between allies upon the dynamics of alliances has been stressed in empirical studies (Harrigan 1985, 1988b). These studies suggest that alliances between similar firms tend to be more successful than asymmetric partnerships. In addition, it has been argued that weaker partners tend to increase their dependence rather than reinforce their position when they enter into alliances with stronger partners (Doz, Hamel, and Prahalad 1989). The operationalization of this factor is difficult because of data collection and reliability problems, especially in an international context. We considered a partnership to be unbalanced when, at the time the alliance is created, the sales of one of the partner firms in the business in which the alliance is formed are at least twice as large as the sales of any other partner firm in that same business. A similar indicator was used by Franko (1971) for international joint ventures set up by U.S. firms and by Ravenscraft and Scherer (1987) for takeovers.

- Entry into the business: *variable 8*

Alliances have been shown to be a way for new competitors to enter a business (Mitchell and Singh 1992). It has been argued that, in such cases, entering firms use the alliance to acquire capabilities which they lack and which are essential to compete successfully in the targeted business (Teece 1986; Pisano, Shan, and Teece 1988). We have thus distinguished alliances in which one partner firm enters the business by joining the alliance from others.

- Entry into new geographic markets: *variable 9*

Alliances have also been shown to be a means for competitors present in other markets to enter new geographic zones (Porter and Fuller 1986; Kogut and Singh 1988). When this is the case, the entering partner is likely to progressively gain autonomy in the targeted geographic market (Harrigan 1985; Mankin and Reich 1986). We have thus identified when the alliance is aimed at exporting an existing product, developed by one partner, to the domestic market of the other partner.

- Configuration of the alliance: *variable 10*

The nature of the assets contributed to an alliance by the partner firms have been argued in theoretical developments to have a significant impact on the dynamics of alliances (Hennart 1988; Porter and Fuller 1986; Teecc 1986). This question is directly linked with the more or less anticompetitive impact of alliances (Schmalensee 1992; Jorde and Teece 1992). The configuration variable captures both the nature of the assets contributed by each partner firm and the way in which rivalry between the allies is modified by the alliance. This variable is designed to characterize (1) the respective contributions of each partner firm to the alliance in terms of assets and (2) the output of the alliance:

1. We classified assets into three types: research facilities, production plants, and distribution networks. When the assets contributed to the partnership by the allies are different in nature (for example, a production facility on one side and a distribution network on the other), we have considered the configuration of the alliance to be "complementary." When the assets contributed by the partner firms are similar in nature (for example, production facilities on both sides), we have distinguished configurations according to the output of alliances.

2. In this second case, when the alliance results in the same common product marketed by all allies, we have considered the alliance to have a "scale" configuration. When the assets contributed by the partner firms are similar in nature and the result of the alliance is incorporated in separate products, specific to each ally, we have considered the alliance to have a "pool" configuration. Thus the three possible configurations can be represented in the following way.

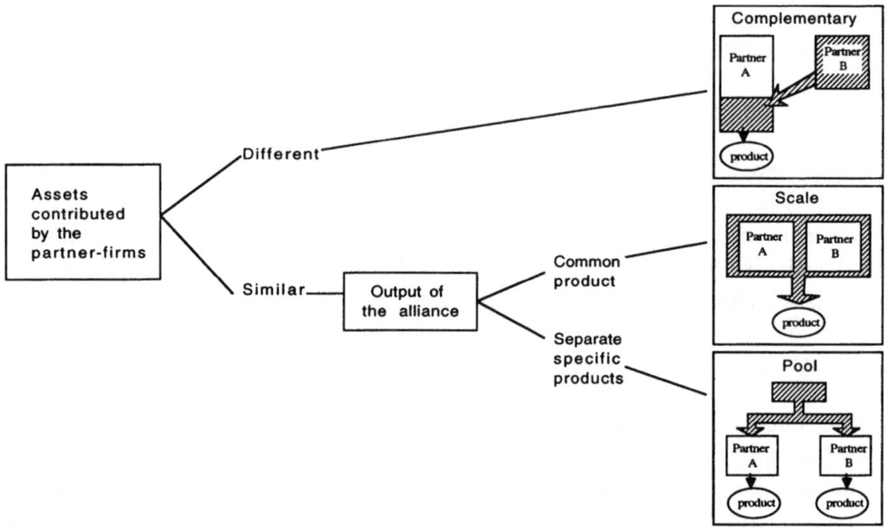

Figure 1. Configurations of strategic alliances.

- The functions covered by the alliance: *variable 11*

Empirical studies almost systematically trace the scope of alliances and examine the functions which they cover, on the basis of the value chain concept (Porter 1985; Porter and Fuller 1986). In addition, theoretical work supports the idea that the competitive impact of alliances varies greatly according to their scope and the functions which they cover (d'Aspremont and Jacquemin 1988; Vickers 1985; Jacquemin and Slade 1989).

- Organization of tasks: *variables 12 to 14*

Technology transfer and skill appropriation have been shown to be a strong incentive in the formation of alliances between competitors (Doz, Hamel, and Prahalad 1989; Hamel 1991). When such transfers take place, they may entail a significant change in the relative competitive positions of the partner firms. The organization of tasks is directly linked with the issue of protecting, capturing, or transferring capabilities (Killing 1988; Doz 1988; Teece 1986; Hamel 1991). The distribution of tasks among the partner firms limits the transfer of capabilities and can result from, or lead to, a specialization of each firm within the alliance. Carrying out tasks jointly favors the transfer of capabilities between allies, or the building of common capabilities. When tasks are duplicated, this can be interpreted as a means of counterbalancing a specialization process induced by the alliance. We considered that a task is carried out jointly (variable 12) when it takes place in a common facility, using jointly owned assets (i.e., a jointly owned research facility, plant, or distribution network). We considered a task to be distributed (variable 13) when it is allocated to one partner and to no other. The corresponding job is then carried out separately in that partner's own facilities. Finally, tasks are duplicated (variable 14) when they are carried out simultaneously and separately by several partner firms within the scope of the alliance.

The set of variables is listed in Table 1.

Table 1. The distribution of the sample on all variables.

I. Illustrative variables	
(1) Countries of origin of the firms involved in the alliance	
Intra-U.S.A.	6
Japan–U.S.A.	17
U.S.A.–Europe	38
Intra-Japan	2
Japan–Europe	25
Intra-Europe	83
(2) Year in which the alliance was formed	
60: 1960 to 1969	17
70: 1970 to 1979	19
80: 1980 to 1990	135
(3) Industry in which the alliance was formed	
Aerospace	35
Automobile	45
Telecommunications	33
Computers	20
Other industries	38
II. Active variables	
(4) Number of partner firms involved in the alliance	
Bilateral	135
Multilateral	36
(5) Structure set up for the management of the alliance	
No legal entity	72
JV =: balanced equity JV	48
JV ≠: unbalanced equity JV	51
(6) Equity participations of the various partner firms in one another's equity	
Equity participations	37
No participations	134
(7) Relative competitive positions of the partner firms	
Unbalanced partnership	126
Balanced partnership	45

Table 1. Continued.

(8) Entry into the business	
New entrant	30
No entrant	141
(9) Entry into new geographic markets	
Geographic entry	72
No geographic entry	99
(10) Configuration of the alliance	
Scale	52
Pool	47
Complementary	72
(11) Functions covered by the alliance	
R&D	28
Dev/Mfg	14
Mktg	33
Mfg + Mktg	24
R&D + Mfg + Mktg	72
(12) Tasks carried out jointly	
No tasks carried out jointly	75
R&D carried out jointly	13
Dev/Mfg carried out jointly	27
Mktg carried out jointly	27
Mfg + Mktg carried out jointly	10
Tasks carried out jointly in all functions	19
(13) Tasks distributed among the partner firms	
No distribution of tasks	52
Distributed R&D	30
Distributed Dev/Mfg	20
Distributed Mktg	37
Distributed Mfg + Mktg	4
Distributed tasks in all functions	28
(14) Duplicated tasks	
No duplication	133
Duplicated Mfg	26
Duplicated Mktg	12

4. The studied sample

We created an original database for this study. Each observation included in the sample is a strategic alliance between competing firms, or at least potential competitors, in manufacturing industries. The features of alliances which the set of variables was designed to capture were observed at the time each alliance began implementing the operations which it was formed to carry out. If any of these features were subsequently altered, this was not considered in our data. The sample contains 171 alliances uniting firms originating from developed countries. It is stratified by industries and reproduces the distribution observed by Hergert and Morris (1987). The study includes alliances formed between 1960 and 1990.

In a first stage, the information used in the study was gathered from secondary sources. Due to the very detailed nature of the data required, these sources were mainly specialized industry-specific publications. The data on each case was validated, or complemented, by interviews with industry analysts and company executives when the descriptions available in the above-mentioned secondary sources were either incomplete or ambiguous.

The distribution of the sample on all the considered variables is given in Table 1.

5. Statistical methods

The data were processed according to two methods: multiple correspondence analysis and agglomerative hierarchical clustering (Lebart, Morineau, and Warwick 1984).[1]

These statistical methods were chosen in order to produce:

1. a synthesis of all the variables used in the study into a few major dimensions according to which the studied sample can be described in a satisfactory way. Each such major dimension corresponds to a combination of variables; along these dimensions, groups of categorical values (i.e., attributes of alliances), often associated in the observed cases, emerge.
2. a taxonomy of the observed alliances. Such a taxonomy identifies contrasting groups of alliances: two cases included in the same class share numerous common features, while cases pertaining to different classes have very few common features. By combining these two stages of the analysis, it is possible to interpret the taxonomy of strategic alliances on the basis of the major dimensions which discriminate between alliance patterns.

5.1. Multiple correspondence analysis

Multiple correspondence analysis (Lebart, Morineau, and Warwick 1984; Tenenhaus and Young 1985; Weller and Romney 1990) is similar to principal component analysis, but is aimed at dealing with categorical variables. Multiple correspondence analysis converts the set of categorical variables into a set of dummy variables and uses the chi-square distance given in the following formula:

$$d^2(i, i') = \sum_j \sum_l \frac{1}{n_{jl}} (x_{ijl} - x_{i'jl})^2.$$

In this formula, x_{ijl} takes on the value 1 when in observation i, variable j takes on the categorical value l; x_{ijl} takes on value O in the opposite case. n_{jl} is the frequency of the categorical value l of variable j.

The principal components to be considered are those which are associated with eigenvalues whose percentage of the total of eigenvalues is greater than the inverse of the number of variables. Such principal components summarize more information than any one variable individually. On this basis, both the observed cases and the attributes of alliances can be positioned according to their coordinates on the selected principal components. In this representation, each case is plotted at the center of gravity of the categorical values that apply to it.

5.2. Agglomerative hierarchical clustering

The taxonomy of alliances is obtained by a clustering method which is based on the Ward criterion. This method measures the distance between two groups (G_1 and G_2) of observations with the following formula:

$$d^2(G_1, G_2) = \frac{n_1 n_2}{n(n_1 + n_2)} d^2(g_1, g_2).$$

In this formula, n is the total number of observations; n_1 and n_2 are the number of observations in G_1 and G_2, respectively; g_1 and g_2 are the center of gravity of G_1 and G_2, respectively; and d is the chi-square distance.

First, the two closest observations are grouped, then this procedure is repeated until a single cluster (containing the whole sample) is obtained. The number of classes to be considered is identified by finding the point where the Ward criterion drops the most significantly in the classification tree, when moving back down from a single class to n classes. The resulting taxonomy is analyzed by examining the cross-tabulation of the taxonomy and the categorical variables.

Finally, a general synthesis of the results can be obtained by plotting the alliances belonging to each class according to the dimensions which emerged from the multiple correspondence analysis.

6. Findings

6.1. Interpreting the results of the multiple correspondence analysis

As there are 11 active variables, the axes which are associated with eigenvalues whose percentage of the total is greater than 1/11 (9.1%) are to be considered. Three such axes emerge from the multiple correspondence analysis (see Table 2). These three axes summarize 37.5% of the information contained in the data (14.6% for the first axis, 12.4% for the second and 10.5% for the third).

Table 3a presents the coordinates of the categorical values of the active variables on the three axes, the contributions of these values to the formation of each axis, and the squared cosine of each value with each axis. In this table (which is to be read like a principal components analysis), the "contribution" measures the influence of each categorical value on the formation of the axes, and the "squared cosine" measures the quality of the projection of each categorical value on the axes.

Table 2. Eigenvalues associated with the principal components produced by the multiple correspondence analysis.

Ranking	Eigenvalue	Percentage of the Total of Eigenvalues	
1	0.3320	14.61%	
2	0.2817	12.40%	
3	0.2382	10.48%	9.10%
4	0.1628	7.16%	
5	0.1433	6.31%	
6	0.1310	5.76%	
7	0.1294	5.69%	
8	0.1111	4.89%	
9	0.0999	4.40%	
10	0.0878	3.87%	
	2.2727	100%	

In order to interpret the meaning of each of the three axes, one should consider those categorical values that most contribute to the formation of each considered axis and have strong coordinates and squared cosine. Table 3a shows that, for each categorical value on each axis, these three measures are linked, thus demonstrating that the data are represented in a satisfactory way in the resulting system of axes.

The *configurations*, the *functions covered*, the *distributed tasks* and the *tasks carried out jointly* appear as the variables that most discriminate between the cases. Indeed, their contributions to the formation of the three axes are much stronger than those of other variables.

Axis 1 discriminates between:

(i), on the negative side:

- the complementary configuration
- geographic entry
- agreements limited to marketing or covering manufacturing and marketing
- the distribution of marketing tasks

and (ii), on the positive side:

- the scale or the pool configuration
- no geographic entry
- agreements covering the entire value chain or limited to R&D
- the distribution of R&D tasks

Though their contributions to the formation of axis 1 are weaker, the "balanced partnership" and "multilateral agreement" categories have strongly positive coordinates on axis 1. In addition, though they were not taken into account in the formation of the axes, the intra-Europe and intra-U.S.A. categories have strongly positive coordinates on axis 1, while the

Table 3a. Formation of the three principal components on the basis of the active variables.

Variables and Categorical Values	Coordinates			Contributions %			Squared Cosine		
	Axis 1	Axis 2	Axis 3	Axis 1	Axis 2	Axis 3	Axis 1	Axis 2	Axis 3
Number of partners									
Bilateral	−0.22	−0.08	−0.01	1.0	0.2	0.0	0.17	0.03	0.00
Multilateral	0.81	0.31	0.03	3.8	0.7	0.0	0.17	0.03	0.00
Variable total				4.8	0.8	0.0			
Structure									
No legal entity	−0.19	0.24	−0.97	0.4	0.8	15.2	0.03	0.04	0.69
JV =	0.19	−0.03	0.6	0.3	0.0	3.9	0.01	0.00	0.14
JV ≠	0.09	−0.31	0.81	0.1	0.9	7.4	0.00	0.04	0.28
Variable total				0.8	1.7	26.5			
Equity participations									
Equity participations	−0.31	−0.47	−0.14	0.6	1.6	0.2	0.03	0.06	0.01
No participation	0.09	0.13	0.04	0.2	0.4	0.0	0.03	0.06	0.01
Variable total				0.7	2.0	0.2			
Relative competitive position									
Balanced partnership	0.72	0.42	−0.18	3.8	1.5	0.3	0.19	0.06	0.01
Unbalanced partnership	−0.26	−0.15	0.06	1.3	0.5	0.1	0.19	0.06	0.01
Variable total				5.1	2.0	0.4			
Business entry									
New entrant	−0.33	−0.25	0.12	0.5	0.3	0.1	0.02	0.01	0.00
No entrant	0.07	0.05	−0.02	0.1	0.1	0.0	0.02	0.01	0.00
Variable total				0.6	0.4	0.1			
Geographic entry									
Geographic entry	−1.02	0.00	0.10	12.0	0.0	0.2	0.76	0.00	0.01
No geographic entry	0.74	0.00	−0.07	8.7	0.0	0.1	0.76	0.00	0.01
Variable total				20.8	0.0	0.3			
Configuration									
Scale	0.84	−1.07	−0.02	5.8	11.2	0.0	0.30	0.50	0.00
Pool	0.69	1.32	0.10	3.6	15.4	0.1	0.18	0.66	0.00
Complementary	−1.05	−0.09	−0.05	12.8	0.1	0.0	0.81	0.01	0.00
Variable total				22.1	26.7	0.1			
Functions									
R&D	0.91	1.60	−0.68	3.7	13.5	2.9	0.16	0.50	0.09
Dev/Mfg	0.40	1.10	1.24	0.4	3.2	4.8	0.01	0.11	0.14
Mktg	−1.31	−0.01	−0.61	9.1	0.0	2.7	0.41	0.00	0.09
Mfg + Mktg	−1.04	0.18	0.88	4.1	0.2	4.2	0.18	0.01	0.13
R&D + Mfg + Mktg	0.51	−0.89	0.01	3.0	10.8	0.0	0.19	0.58	0.00
Variable total				20.3	27.7	14.7			
Tasks carried out jointly									
No tasks carried...	−0.21	0.13	−0.98	0.5	0.2	16.2	0.03	0.01	0.76
R&D carried...	0.70	0.90	0.09	1.0	2.0	0.0	0.04	0.07	0.00
Dev/Mfg carried...	−0.34	0.60	1.27	0.5	1.8	9.7	0.02	0.07	0.30
Mktg carried...	0.42	−0.94	0.30	0.8	4.5	0.6	0.03	0.17	0.02
Mfg + Mktg carried...	−0.36	0.20	1.19	0.2	0.1	3.1	0.01	0.00	0.09
Tasks in all functions...	0.42	−0.76	0.96	0.5	2.1	3.9	0.02	0.07	0.12
Variable total				3.5	10.7	33.6			
Distributed tasks									
No distribution	0.06	0.19	0.98	0.0	0.4	11.2	0.00	0.02	0.42
Distributed R&D	0.72	1.25	−0.46	2.5	8.8	1.4	0.11	0.33	0.04
Distributed Dev/Mfg	0.66	−1.02	0.28	1.4	3.9	0.3	0.06	0.14	0.01
Distributed Mktg	−1.34	0.02	−0.41	10.6	0.0	1.4	0.49	0.00	0.05
Distributed Mfg + Mktg	−1.33	0.42	−0.57	1.1	0.1	0.3	0.04	0.00	0.01
Distributed tasks in all functions	0.59	−1.06	−0.90	1.6	5.9	5.1	0.07	0.22	0.16
Variable total				17.2	19.1	19.7			
Duplicated tasks									
No duplication	−0.08	0.26	0.12	0.1	1.6	0.4	0.02	0.23	0.05
Duplicated Mfg	0.78	−1.2	−0.78	2.6	7.1	3.6	0.11	0.26	0.11
Duplicated Mktg	−0.83	−0.22	0.34	1.3	0.1	0.3	0.05	0.00	0.01
Variable total				4.0	8.8	4.3			
Total				100	100	100			

Table 3b. Coordinates of the illustrative variables on the three principal components.

Variables and Categorical Values	Coordinates		
	Axis 1	Axis 2	Axis 3
Countries of origin			
Intra-U.S.A.	0.88	1.10	0.01
Japan–U.S.A.	−1.43	0.06	−0.31
U.S.A.–Europe	−0.11	−0.12	0.22
Intra-Japan	0.55	1.38	0.79
Japan–Europe	−0.85	−0.01	0.35
Intra-Europe	0.52	−0.06	−0.16
Year			
60	0.88	−0.71	−0.28
70	0.11	−0.03	0.02
80	−0.13	0.09	0.03
Industry			
Aerospace	0.87	−0.94	−0.36
Automobile	−0.44	0.50	−0.13
Telecommunications	−0.13	0.14	−0.17
Computers	0.04	0.71	0.10
Other industries	−0.19	−0.21	0.59

U.S.–Japan and Japan–Europe categories have strongly negative coordinates on the same axis (see Table 3b).

In view of these results, this first axis can be interpreted as discriminating between symmetrical alliances and asymmetrical alliances. We will refer to it as the *symmetry dimension* of alliances. Indeed, both the "scale" and the "pool" configurations are symmetrical in nature, because they unite firms which contribute similar assets. Equal competitive positions as well as the "non-geographic" purpose of the agreement are also indicators of symmetry. On the contrary, partner firms contributing complementary assets in unbalanced partnerships and tending to have geographic entry strategies form more asymmetrical alliances.

Axis 2 discriminates between:

(i), on the negative side:

- alliances covering the entire value chain
- the scale configuration
- the distribution of tasks in all functions (R&D, manufacturing and marketing)
- marketing tasks carried out jointly
- duplication of some manufacturing tasks

and (ii), on the positive side:

- alliances limited to R&D or to R&D and manufacturing
- the pool configuration

- the distribution of R&D tasks
- R&D or manufacturing tasks carried out jointly

The "aerospace industry" value of the illustrative *industry* variable has a strongly negative coordinate on axis 2. The "intra-U.S.A." and "intra-Japan" categories have strongly positive coordinates on this axis, as does the "computer industry" category (see Table 3b).

This second axis can be interpreted as discriminating between anticompetitive agreements and precompetitive agreements. We will refer to it as the *competitive dimension* of alliances. It measures the degree to which competition is altered by alliances. Toward the negative side of axis 2, alliances tend to be anticompetitive. Indeed, when alliances cover the entire value chain, coordination between the partner firms must be very tight. In addition, when alliances have a "scale" configuration, they result in the production of a product common to all allies. Competition between the allied firms is therefore cancelled on this common product and can only subsist in areas not covered by the alliance. The fact that marketing tasks tend to be carried out jointly is a confirmation that direct market competition is no longer an issue. Toward the positive side of axis 2, alliances tend to be precompetitive. By sharing the burden when R&D tasks are distributed, or by benefitting from economies of scale through joint manufacturing, all allies increase their efficiency. However, as the scope of these alliances is limited and does not cover marketing functions, the impact on competition is less significant. In addition, in a "pool" configuration, each partner firm manufactures and markets its own products, even though these products incorporate common elements. Thus, open competition can continue to exist between the allied firms.

Axis 3 discriminations between:

(i), on the negative side:

- no tasks carried out jointly
- no legal entity
- the distribution of tasks in all functions (R&D, manufacturing and marketing)

and (ii), on the positive side:

- tasks pertaining to one or several functions carried out jointly
- joint venture
- no tasks distributed among the partner firms
- partnerships limited to manufacturing or development and manufacturing

The third axis can be interpreted as opposing simple contractual agreements to structured partnerships. We will refer to it as the *structural dimension* of alliances. Indeed, alliances positioned at the extremes of axis 3 are organized in totally different forms. Simple contractual agreements, in which tasks are organized on the basis of a division of labor between the partner firms, do not require the creation of a separate legal entity. In structured partnerships, on the contrary, certain tasks are carried out by an equity joint venture specifically created to that effect.

By combining the three principal components which emerge from the multiple correspondence analysis, an analytical model of strategic alliances can be constructed (see Figure 2).

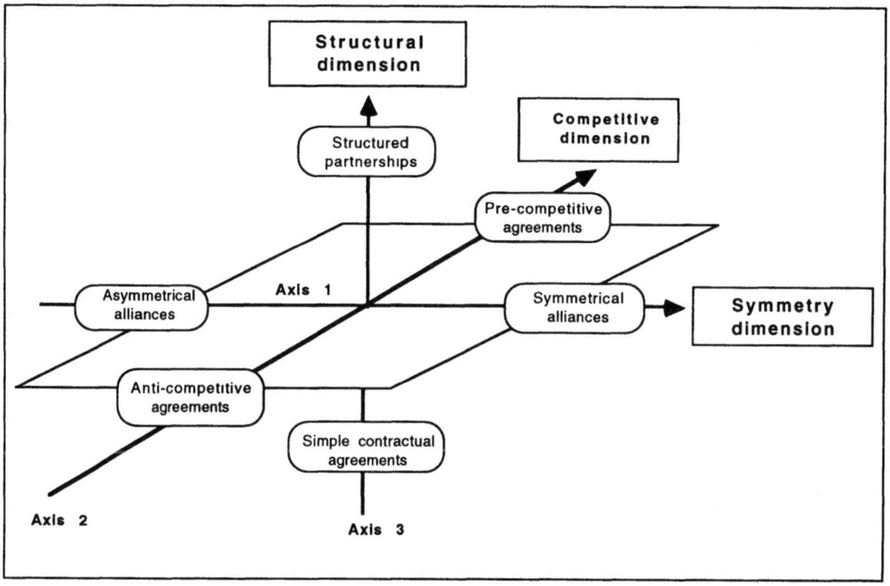

Figure 2. An analytical model of strategic alliances.

6.2. The taxonomy of strategic alliances

Contrasted patterns of strategic alliances can emerge from the data only if the partnerships in the sample are not distributed evenly in the space defined by the previously identified axes. To determine this, we undertook a clustering of the sample. The criterion described in the previous section supports the partition of the sample in three classes (see Table 4).

Each of the three classes of alliances can be described on the basis of the categorical values most frequently represented in it. Table 5 lists the categories which characterize the three classes of alliances, and Table 6 presents the chi-square tests of independence between the three-class taxonomy and each variable.

Table 4. Ward criterion in the clustering of the sample.

Number of Classes	Ward Index	Δ
1	0.23976	—
2	0.23148	0.00828
3	0.16114	0.07034
4	0.13821	0.02293
5	0.13574	0.00247
6	0.12602	0.00972
7	0.10814	0.01788
8	0.10431	0.00383
9	0.08431	0.02000
10	0.07254	0.01177

Table 5. The attributes of the three patterns of strategic alliances.

Class 1: Quasi-Concentration Alliances (60 cases)	Class 2: Market Penetration Alliances (75 cases)	Class 3: Shared Supply Alliances (36 cases)
Scale	Geographic entry	Pool
R&D + Mfg + Mktg	Complementary	R&D
No geographic entry	Distributed Mktg	Distributed R&D
Aerospace	Mktg	No geographic entry
Duplicated Mfg	Mfg + Mktg	No duplication
Distributed tasks in all functions	U.S.A.–Japan	Balanced partnership
Distributed Dev/Mfg	Japan–Europe	R&D carried out jointly
Intra-Europe	Unbalanced partnership	Multilateral
Tasks carried out jointly in all functions	Bilateral	Intra-U.S.A.
Mktg carried out jointly	Automobile	Computers
60s		Dev/Mfg
		Intra-Europe

In each class, the categories are listed according to their decreasing frequency in the corresponding class and to the decreasing frequency of the class in the category.

Table 6. Chi-square tests of independence between the taxonomy and each variable.

Variable	Chi-Square Variable/Taxonomy	Degrees of Freedom	Probability Level
Functions	252.97	8	0.0000
Configurations	254.97	4	0.0000
Geographic entry	136.66	2	0.0000
Distributed tasks	159.74	10	0.0000
Industry	71.19	8	0.0000
Countries of origin	74.63	10	0.0000
Tasks carried out jointly	65.56	10	0.0000
Duplicated tasks	49.86	4	0.0000
Relative competitive positions	21.05	2	0.0000
Number of partner firms	19.73	2	0.0001
Year	16.98	4	0.0020
Structure	10.27	4	0.0361
Equity participations	3.06	2	0.2167
Business entry	1.81	2	0.4053

Class-1 alliances are of the scale configuration and cover the entire value chain. They are not aimed at facilitating the entry of an existing product into a new market and are formed primarily in the aerospace industry. Most cases in this class are coproduction projects, such as the Airbus aircraft, which are organized on the basis of a distribution of most tasks between the partner firms. In the case of Airbus, for example, one partner is responsible for designing and manufacturing the wings, while other partner firms make the fuselage, the cockpit, or other elements of the aircraft. In such alliances, marketing tasks are sometimes carried out jointly; for instance, the Airbus aircraft are not marketed directly by the consortium partners, but by a specifically created joint sales organization. Finally, unlike in other types of alliances, some manufacturing tasks are sometimes found to be duplicated in class-1 alliances. In the Concorde supersonic airliner project, each partner firm set up an assembly line to be able to roll out completed aircraft. Thus, even though only 14 Concordes were ever manufactured, half were assembled in the UK, while the other seven were assembled in France. Class 1 also includes alliances in which the partner firms have merged their operations in a certain business; in such cases, all tasks are carried out jointly by a common subsidiary. In our sample, most alliances formed in the 1960s are included in this class and correspond to European aerospace coproduction projects. Class-1 alliances are predominantly intra-European. As class-1 alliances associate firms that contribute similar assets to develop, manufacture, and market a common product, we will refer to them as *quasi-concentration alliances*. The competitive impact of such alliances is similar in nature to industry concentration, even though such a concentration does not formally take place. In addition, the fact that similar manufacturing tasks are often duplicated reveals that the rationalization of operations is only partial.

Class-2 alliances are generally aimed at marketing an existing product, previously developed by one partner, in new geographic markets in which the other partner firm has a priviledged access. Class-2 alliances are of the complementary configuration. They tend to be purely commercial agreements or can entail some manufacturing. Such alliances are usually bilateral and unite firms with very different competitive positions. They are frequent in the automobile industry and often involve Japanese partners. The well-known Nummi joint venture between General Motors and Toyota, as well as agreements between Chrysler and Mitsubishi or Ford and Mazda, fall into this category. On the basis of their common features, we will refer to class-2 partnerships as *market penetration alliances*.

Class-3 alliances are of the pool configuration. They are often R&D agreements in which the tasks are, in most cases, distributed among the partner firms and sometimes carried out jointly. This class also includes agreements for the development and manufacture of common components. Class-3 alliances are often balanced multilateral partnerships. Their purpose is not geographic expansion, and they avoid duplicating tasks. They are frequent in the computer industry (joint research consortia and joint manufacture of electronic components) and are often intra-American or intra-European. Peugeot, Renault, and Volvo, three major European automobile manufacturers, created an alliance of this type to develop and manufacture a V6 engine that they each use for their respective models of cars. We will refer to these class-3 alliances as *shared supply alliances*.

Though the *industry* variable is only illustrative and the three classes are not industry-specific, alliances in particular industries tend to be more frequent in certain classes than in others. Most alliances in the aerospace industry are of the quasi-concentration type, while most alliances in computers, telecommunication equipment, and automobiles are of either the market penetration or shared supply types. In the aerospace industry, alliances between European firms, which are predominant in our sample, can be interpreted as fulfilling the same role as mergers and acquisitions when such moves are impossible for political reasons. The fact that most European governments refuse to give up control of local aerospace manufacturers explains the development of many European international quasi-concentration alliances in this industry. These European alliances in aerospace can be contrasted to agreements signed by U.S. firms with foreign partners (e.g., Boeing with JCAC, a Japanese consortium, or McDonnell–Douglas with a Chinese company). Indeed, such agreements appear to be closer to our market penetration type than to quasi-concentration (Tucker 1991; Moxon, Roehl, and Truitt 1988). However, in these agreements, the position of the U.S. partner firm is so dominant, and the share of the foreign partner so small, that they appear as subcontracting agreements rather than actual strategic alliances. They were therefore not included in our database.

The geographic origins of the partner firms, which is also only an illustrative variable, appears to be related to the three classes of alliances. Unlike others, alliances involving a Japanese partner tend to be of the market penetration type. Conversely, most market penetration alliances unite partners from different continents and tend to include a Japanese partner. Alliances uniting firms that originate in the same continent are generally of the quasi-concentration or shared supply type. Alliances between European firms are distributed among these two types, while most alliances between U.S. firms are of the shared supply type. This difference may be interpreted as reflecting the more tolerant attitude of European authorities—at the EC level, and, even more so, at the level of the different national governments—toward potentially collusive behaviors. In contrast, in the U.S., antitrust concerns seem to strongly inhibit the formation of quasi-concentration alliances. Additional analysis of the data shows that, when intra-European alliances are of the quasi-concentration type, they tend to unite firms originating in different European countries. In contrast, domestic intra-European alliances (like domestic alliances in the U.S.) are predominantly of the shared supply type. Even when uniting firms from different countries, intra-European alliances are very rarely of the market penetration type. An interpretation of these observations is that market penetration alliances are a response to globalization, while quasi-concentration alliances are a response to the fragmented nature of the European market, which should be considered neither like a unified domestic market nor like the juxtaposition of several separate domestic markets. This might call into question the usually accepted dichotomy between global and multi-domestic markets.

6.3. A synthetic interpretation of the patterns of alliances

A projection of the individual cases in the sample on the three axes identified in the multiple correspondence analysis (see Figure 1) reveals that the three classes of alliances are clearly separated on the plane defined by axis 1 and axis 2 (see Figure 3). By contrast, axis 3 does not discriminate significantly between the three classes.

By relating the three-class taxonomy with the interpretation of the three principal dimensions depicted in Figure 1, we can synthesize the features of the three identified patterns of strategic alliances in the following way:

(i) *quasi-concentration alliances* (class 1) can be interpreted as being symmetrical (axis 1) and anticompetitive (axis 2).
(ii) *market penetration alliances* (class 2) can be interpreted as being asymmetrical (axis 1).
(iii) *shared supply alliances* (class 3) can be interpreted as being symmetrical (axis 1) and precompetitive (axis 2).

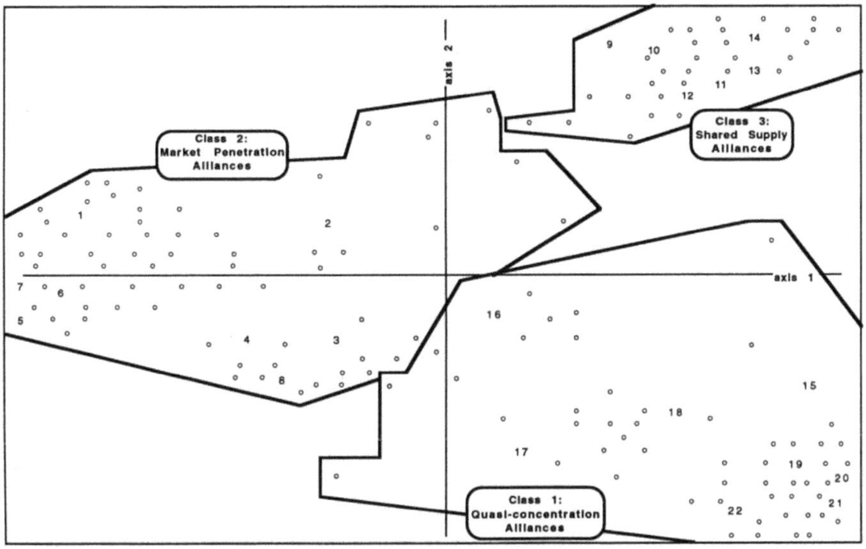

Number on the Figure	Name of Case	Partner Firms	Type of Project or Business	Industry
Market penetration alliances				
1	Nummi	GM, Toyota	Car production	Automotive
2	APT	ATT, Philips	Switching equipment	Telecommunications
3	Honda-Rover	Honda, Rover	Car production	Automotive
4	Diamond Star	Chrysler, Mitsubishi	Car production	Automotive
5	ATT-Olivetti	ATT, Olivetti	PABX	Telecommunications
6	GM-Suzuki	GM, Suzuki	Car distribution	Automotive
7	Ford-Mazda	Ford, Mazda	Car distribution	Automotive
8	Laboratoires Takeda	Roussel, Takeda	Cephalosporines	Pharmaceuticals
Shared supply alliances				
9	X31	Rockwell, Deutsche Aerospace	Experimental Aircraft	Aerospace
10	Française de Mécanique	Peugeot, Renault	Engines	Automotive
11	IBM-Siemens	IBM, Siemens	Integrated circuits	Computers
12	Sematech	15 partners all from the U.S.A.	R&D consortium	Semiconductors
13	JESSI	Siemens, Philips, SGS-Thomson	R&D consortium	Semiconductors
14	PRV	Peugeot, Renault, Volvo	V6 engines	Automotive
Quasi-concentration alliances				
15	Olivetti Bull	Olivetti, Bull	ATMs	Computers
16	Sevel	Peugeot, Fiat	Light trucks	Automotive
17	Ericsson-GE	Ericsson, GE	Mobile communication	Telecommunications
18	GPT	GEC, Plessey	Switching equipment	Telecommunications
19	Concorde	Aerospatiale, British Aerospace	Supersonic transport	Aerospace
20	Airbus	Aerospatiale, DASA, BAe, Casa	Airliner	Aerospace
21	Ariane	Aerospatiale, Matra, BAe, DASA, etc.	Space launcher	Aerospace
22	BK 117	DASA, Kawasaki	Helicopter	Aerospace

Figure 3. Projection of the sample and visualization of the taxonomy (axis 1–axis 2).

The structural dimension of alliances (axis 3) does not come into play in the characterization of the three patterns. Structural differences are internal to each of the three patterns, and thus appear as second-level discriminating factors. Therefore, a range of structural arrangements can be found within each pattern. This result was already apparent in Table 6: the *structure* variable is one of the few variables taken into account which cannot be considered as directly linked to the construction of the three-class taxonomy.

7. Hypotheses on the dynamics of strategic alliances

The variables taken into account in this study were chosen because of their demonstrated or assumed influence on the dynamics of strategic alliances. It is therefore possible to generate a set of hypotheses on the likely evolution of alliances according to the pattern to which they belong.

Market penetration alliances, unlike the two other types, are fundamentally characterized by the asymmetry existing between the partners. As the partner firms contribute different assets to the alliance, there is a clear division of labor between them, induced by their preexisting specialization. We can hypothesize that, for one partner to gain autonomy in the considered activity, it may try to acquire the assets and capabilities contributed by the other partner. A further hypothesis is that, in addition to their intrinsic appropriability, the extent to which assets and capabilities can be transferred is determined by organizational factors: (i) where tasks are carried out jointly, an easier transfer can take place, (ii) the distribution of tasks, on the contrary, will make the transfer more difficult, (iii) in addition, the creation of an equity joint venture will make it possible to transfer the ownership of assets. The dynamics of market penetration alliances are likely to be conditioned by the attitude of the partner firms with respect to their mutual dependence. In this context, issues of capability appropriation are critical and can give rise to opportunistic behaviors. It can be assumed that it is mainly in market penetration alliances that one partner can be strengthened and the other weakened by involvement in the partnership. Clinical studies that emphasize the danger of skill appropriation through alliances, notably when collaborating with Japanese partners, are likely to have mainly examined cases of market penetration alliances. The fact that in our sample U.S.A.–Japan and Europe–Japan alliances, as well as unbalanced partnerships, are overrepresented in the market penetration type, seems to confirm this interpretation.

Shared supply alliances associate very similar partner firms which contribute similar assets and skills to the alliance. There is no preexisting specialization between the allied firms. As the alliance is limited to a particular input, it does not affect direct market competition between the partners. Potential conflicts between the partner firms are centered on the management of the common operation and on the conditions in which they can each have access to the common input. A hypothesis on the dynamics of shared supply alliances is that they add the difficulties of jointly managing common operations to the problems traditionally encountered in vertical integration (loss of efficiency and of flexibility). All major decisions to improve or adapt the joint venture's activity will require extensive negotiations between the partners. Likely evolutions of shared integration alliances are: reinforced control of the joint venture by the parent companies, accelerated loss of efficiency when an agreement is difficult to reach, and takeover by one partner when external markets for the considered product make such an outcome possible.

Quasi-concentration alliances associate similar partner firms which develop, manufacture, and market a common product. As in shared supply alliances, there is no preexisting specialization between the allies. Competition between the allies is no longer possible in the area covered by the alliance. Therefore, marketing tasks are either carried out jointly or distributed on the basis of a geographic allocation to the various partner firms. The dominant form of organization being the distribution of tasks (i.e., each partner firm develops and manufactures different parts of the final product), it is likely that the alliance will induce an increasing specialization of the allied firms. The corresponding loss of capabilities implies that each partner firm is likely to see its ability to compete autonomously in the future considerably reduced. It can be assumed that firms engaged in quasi-concentration alliances will often try to avoid this induced specialization. In this context, it is not surprising to observe the existence of duplicated tasks in such alliances. Preliminary observations of major European aerospace coproduction projects (Dussauge and Garrette 1993) reveal that, by participating in several such projects, and by assuming responsibility for different parts in each project, a given firm can retain its overall capabilities. A hypothesis on the dynamics of quasi-concentration alliances is that, when the induced specialization takes place, the industry undergoes a process similar in nature to concentration even though the apparent number of competing firms remains the same. When the competitors in the industry can avoid specializing, they will do so by managing several alliances simultaneously, in order to cover the entire activity and retain the complete scope of capabilities.

8. Concluding remarks and limitations

In summary, the statistical analysis which we have conducted contributes to the understanding of interfirm cooperation by identifying three distinct patterns of strategic alliances defined by a coherent set of features. These patterns incorporate and synthesize most of the variables usually used to construct more partial typologies based on one or two variables. They also take into account variables which were designed specifically for this study, in order to operationalize factors deemed important by prior researchers, but which had not been previously examined in empirical research using large samples.

The general taxonomy of strategic alliances between rival firms provides a framework with which to analyze the issues faced by the partner firms in the context of a particular partnership. Indeed, the results of our research show that alliances between rival firms should not be analyzed with a unifying model. It is likely that contributions made previously on the subject apply to one or the other of the patterns that we have identified rather than to all alliances indiscriminately. On the other hand, the identification of three distinct patterns makes it possible to generalize findings obtained from the observation of particular cases to the population of alliances corresponding to the relevant pattern. For example, a lot of conclusions drawn from the observation of alliances set up with Japanese partner firms, i.e., asymmetry in the benefits gained by each ally (Doz, Hamel, and Prahalad 1989; Hamel 1991) could probably be extended to most market penetration alliances—alliances with Japanese partners being over-represented in this pattern—but should not be generalized to all partnerships between competitors. In the same way, the evaluation of the extent to which alliances alter competition should not be carried out indiscriminately. Indeed, the anticompetitive impact of alliances varies considerably according to the pattern to which they correspond.

A next step in this stream of research should be to validate the hypothetized linkages between the identified patterns of alliances and contrasted evolutions and outcomes of strategic partnerships. Indeed, at this stage, our results only make it possible to infer a set of hypotheses on the likely evolutions of each type of alliance, on the basis of the features determining these types. Testing these hypotheses would require longitudinal data that is yet to be gathered. In addition, our results should not be generalized without some care, since our sample probably overrepresents European alliances and underrepresents intra-Japanese partnerships. This is due to the very detailed nature of the information used, which often required close contact with the firms involved, thus making it easier for us to obtain data on cases to which we had easier access.

Note

1. The data were processed with the SPAD-N software (developed and marketed by C.I.S.I.A., Centre International de Statistique et d'Informatique Appliquées, Paris).

References

Anderson, E., and H. Gatignon. (1986). "Modes of Foreign Entry: A Transaction Cost Analysis and Propositions," *Journal of International Business Studies* (Fall), 1–26.

Astley, W.G., and C.F. Fombrun. (1983). "Collective Strategy: Social Ecology of Organizational Environments," *Academy of Management Review* 8(4), 576–587.

Beamish, P.M. (1985). "The Characteristics of Joint Ventures in Developed and Developing Countries," *Columbia Journal of World Business* 20(2), 13–19.

Bresser, R.K.F. (1988). "Matching Collective and Competitive Strategies," *Strategic Management Journal* 9(4), 375–385.

Buckley, P.J., and M. Casson. (1988). "A Theory of Cooperation in International Business." In F. J. Contractor and P. Lorange (eds.), *Cooperative Strategies in International Business*. Lexington, MA: Lexington Books, pp. 31–54.

Contractor, F.J., and P. Lorange. (1988). "Why Should Firms Cooperate? The Strategy and Economics Basis for Cooperative Ventures." In F.J. Contractor and P. Lorange (eds.), *Cooperative Strategies in International Business*. Lexington, MA: Lexington Books, pp. 3–30.

Contractor, F.J., and P. Lorange, eds. (1988). *Cooperative Strategies in International Business*. Lexington, MA: Lexington Books.

D'Aspremont, C., and A. Jacquemin. (1988). "Cooperative and Non Cooperative R&D in Duopoly," *American Economic Review* (December).

Doz, Y.L. (1988). "Technology Partnerships between Larger and Smaller Firms: Some Critical Issues." In F.J. Contractor and P. Lorange (eds.), *Cooperative Strategies in International Business*. Lexington, MA: Lexington Books, pp. 317–338.

Doz, Y.L., G. Hamel, and C.K. Prahalad. (1989). "Collaborate with Your Competitors—and Win," *Harvard Business Review* 67(1), 133–139.

Duncan, L. (1982). "Impacts of New Entry and Horizontal Joint Ventures on Industrial Rates of Return," *Review of Economics and Statistics* 64, 120–125.

Dussauge, P., and B. Garrette. (1993). "Industrial Alliances in Aerospace and Defence: An Empirical Study of Strategic and Organizational Patterns," *Defence Economics* 4(1), 45–62.

Franko, L.G. (1971). *Joint Venture Survival in Multinational Corporations*. New York: Praeger.

Galbraith, C., and D. Schendel. (1983). "An Empirical Analysis of Strategy Types," *Strategic Management Journal* 4(2), 153–173.

Ghemawat, P., M.E. Porter, and R.A. Rawlinson. (1986). "Patterns of International Coalition Activity." In M.E. Porter (ed.), *Competitive Advantage*. New York: Free Press, pp. 346–366.

Gray, B., and A. Yan. (1992). "A Negotiations Model of Joint Venture Formation, Structure and Performance: Implications for Global Management." In S.B. Prasad (ed.), *Advances in International Comparative Management*, Vol. 7, pp. 41–75.

Hamel, G. (1991). "Competition for Competence and Inter-Partner Learning Within International Strategic Alliances," *Strategic Management Journal* 12 (Special Issue, Summer), 83–103.

Harrigan, K.R. (1985). *Strategies for Joint Ventures*. Lexington, MA: Lexington Books.

Harrigan, K.R. (1988a). "Joint Ventures and Competitive Strategy," *Strategic Management Journal* 9(2), 141–158.

Harrigan, K.R. (1988b). "Strategic Alliances and Partner Asymmetries." In F.J. Contractor and P. Lorange (eds.), *Cooperative Strategies in International Business*. Lexington, MA: Lexington Books, pp. 205–226.

Hartley, K. (1983). *NATO Arms Co-operation: A Study in Economics and Politics*. London: George Allen & Unwin.

Hennart, J.F. (1988). "A Transaction Cost Theory of Equity Joint Ventures," *Strategic Management Journal* 9(4), 361–374.

Hergert, M. and D. Morris. (1987). "Trends in International Collaborative Agreements," *Columbia Journal of World Business* 22(2), 15–21.

Hladik, K.J. (1985). *International Joint Ventures: an Economic Analysis of U.S. Foreign Business Partnerships*. Lexington, MA: Lexington Books.

Jacquemin, A., and M.E. Slade. (1989). "Cartels, Collusion, and Horizontal Merger." In R. Schmalensee and R.D. Willig (eds.), *Handbook of Industrial Organization*, Vol. 1. Amsterdam: North Holland.

Jorde, T.M., and D.J. Teece. (1989). "Competition and Cooperation: Striking the Right Balance," *California Management Review* 31(3), 25–37.

Jorde, T.M., and D.J. Teece, eds. (1992a). *Anti-Trust, Innovation and Competitiveness*, Oxford: Oxford University Press.

Jorde, T.M., and D.J. Teece. (1992b). "Innovation, Cooperation, and Anti-Trust." In T.M. Jorde and D.J. Teece (eds.), *Anti-Trust, Innovation and Competitiveness*, Oxford: Oxford University Press, pp. 47–81.

Killing, J.P. (1982). "How to Make a Global Joint Venture Work," *Harvard Business Review* 60 (May–June), 120–127.

Killing, J.P. (1983). *Strategies for Joint Venture Success*. New York: Praeger.

Killing, J.P. (1988). "Understanding Alliances: The Role of Task and Organizational Complexity." In F.J. Contractor and P. Lorange (eds.), *Cooperative Strategies in International Business*. Lexington, MA: Lexington Books, pp. 55–68.

Kogut, B. (1988a). "Joint Ventures: Theoretical and Empirical Perspectives," *Strategic Management Journal* 9(4), 319–332.

Kogut, B. (1988b). "A Study of the Life Cycle of Joint Ventures." In F.J. Contractor and P. Lorange (eds.), *Cooperative Strategies in International Business*. Lexington, MA: Lexington Books, pp. 169–186.

Kogut, B., and H. Singh. (1988). "Entering the United States by Joint Venture: Competitive Rivalry and Industry Structure." In F.J. Contractor and P. Lorange (eds.), *Cooperative Strategies in International Business*. Lexington, MA: Lexington Books, pp. 241–251.

Kolodziej, E.A. (1987). *Making and Marketing Arms*. Princeton: Princeton University Press.

Lebart, L., A. Morineau, and K.M. Warwick. (1984). *Multivariate Descriptive Statistical Analysis*. Chichester: Wiley.

Lorange, P., and J. Roos. (1992). *Strategic Alliances: Formation, Evolution and Implementation*. London: Basil Blackwell.

Mankin, E., and R. Reich. (1986). "Joint Ventures with Japan Give Away our Future," *Harvard Business Review* 2, 78–86.

Mariti, P., and R.H. Smiley. (1983). "Cooperative Agreements and the Organization of Industry," *Journal of Industrial Economics* 31(4), 437–451.

Miller, D. (1986). "Configurations of Strategy and Structure: Towards a Synthesis," *Strategic Management Journal* 7(3), 233–249.

Mitchell, W., and K. Singh. (1992). "Incumbents' Use of Pre-Entry Alliances before Expansion into New Technical Subfields of an Industry," *Journal of Economic Behavior and Organization* 18, 347–372.

Moxon, R.W., R.W. Roehl, and J.F. Truitt. (1988). "International Co-operative Ventures in the Commercial Aircraft Industry: Gains, Sure, but What's my Share?" In F.J. Contractor and P. Lorange (eds.), *Cooperative Strategies in International Business*. Lexington, MA: Lexington Books, pp. 255–277.

Mowery, D.C., ed. (1988). *International Collaborative Ventures in U.S. Manufacturing*. Cambridge, MA: Ballinger.

Pate, J.L. (1969). "Joint Venture Activity, 1960–1968," *Economic Review* (Federal Reserve Bank of Cleveland), 16–23.

Pfeffer, J. and P. Nowak. (1976). "Joint Ventures and Interorganizational Interdependence," *Administrative Science Quarterly* 21, 398–418.

Pisano, G., M.V. Russo, and D.J. Teece. (1988). "Joint Ventures and Collaborative Arrangements in the Telecommunications Equipment Industry." In D.C. Mowery (ed.), *International Collaborative Ventures in U.S. Manufacturing*. Cambridge, MA: Ballinger, pp. 23–70.

Porter, M.E. (1985). *Competitive Advantage*. New York: Free Press.

Porter, M.E., ed. (1986). *Competition in Global Industries*. Cambridge, MA: Harvard University Press.

Porter, M.E., and M.B. Fuller. (1986). "Coalitions and Global Strategy." In M.E. Porter (ed.), *Competition in Global Industries*. Cambridge, MA: Harvard University Press, pp. 315–344.

Ravenscraft, D.J., and F.M. Scherer. (1987). "Life After Takeover," *Journal of Industrial Economics* 36(2), 147–156.

Rumelt, R.P. (1974). *Strategy, Structure and Economic Performance*. Cambridge, MA: Division of Research, Graduate School of Business Administration, Harvard University.

Schmalensee, R. (1992). "Agreements Between Competitors." In T.M. Jorde and D.J. Teece (eds.), *Anti-Trust Innovation and Competitiveness*. Oxford: Oxford University Press, pp. 98–118.

Stopford, J., and L. Wells. (1972). *Managing the Multinational Enterprise*. New York: Basic Books.

Teece, D.J. (1977). "Technology Transfer by Multinational Firms," *Economic Journal* 87, 242–261.

Teece, D.J., (1986). "Profiting from Technological Innovation: Implications for Integration, Collaboration, Licencing, and Public Policy," *Research Policy* 15(6), 285–305.

Tenenhaus, M., and F.W. Young. (1985). "An Analysis and Synthesis of Multiple Correspondence Analysis, Optimal Scaling, Dual Scaling, Homogeneity Analysis, and Other Methods for Quantifying Categorical Multivariate Data," *Psychometrika* 50(1), 91–120.

Tucker, J. (1991). "Partners and Rivals: A Model of International Collaboration in Advanced Technology," *International Organization* 45(1), 83–120.

Vickers, J. (1985). "Pre-Emptive Patenting, Joint-Venture, and the Persistence of Oligopoly," *International Journal of Industrial Organization* 3, 261–273.

Weller, S.C., and A.K. Romney. (1990). *Metric Scaling, Correspondence Analysis*. Newbury Park, CA: Sage Publications.

Williamson, O.E. (1975). *Markets and Hierarchies*. New York: Free Press.

Williamson, O.E. (1985). *The Economic Institutions of Capitalism*. New York: Free Press.

Group Decision and Negotiation, 4: 453–467 (1995)

Agency Costs and the Structure and Performance of International Joint Ventures

J. MICHAEL GERINGER
Global Strategy and Law Area, School of Business Administration, California Polytechnic State University, San Luis Obispo, CA 93407

C. PATRICK WOODCOCK
Faculty of Administration, University of Ottawa, Ottawa, Ontario K1N6N5 Canada

Abstract.

This article develops a principal-agent contractual model for the issue of the structure and performance of international joint ventures. From this model, hypotheses are generated relating the number of partners in a joint venture and the cross-cultural divergence of the partners with joint venture performance. These hypotheses are empirically assessed using a population of over 3,500 developed-country joint ventures.

Key Words: joint ventures, strategic alliances, agency theory, international business

During the past two decades, the use of joint ventures has become increasingly popular as a means of competing internationally (Hergert and Morris 1988; Harrigan 1988). Both managers and academics agree that these ventures have become an important international competitive weapon given the environmental uncertainty facing many firms and industries (McCormick and Stone, 1990; Harrigan 1990). Yet, despite their increasing popularity, joint ventures have often been viewed as an inferior competitive alternative due particularly to the additional complexity associated with the shared-ownership and decision-making nature of these ventures. This concern is further supported by evidence of the failure of many joint ventures to achieve their strategic objectives (Harrigan 1986, 1988).

One of the most prominent theoretical arguments for explaining joint venture performance problems is the complex issue of how they are structured, especially in terms of their ownership and management control. This issue has been studied extensively from both a theoretical and an empirical perspective, and a variety of issues associated with ownership and management control have been cited as reasons for joint venture performance problems, including partner-firm size divergence, mutual trust and commitment, degree of ownership control, and partner selection technique (Beamish 1984; Beamish and Banks 1987; Blodgett 1987; Buckley and Casson 1988; Geringer and Hebert 1989; Geringer and Woodcock 1989; Killing 1983; Schaan 1983). All of these studies have explicitly or implicitly taken either an organizational control, organizational resource, or transaction cost perspective in their analyses.

The authors would like to acknowledge the useful comments of Colette Frayne on earlier drafts of this manuscript.

This article takes an alternative conceptual approach, namely, agency theory, to examine IJV structure and performance. Agency theory was selected as the theoretical paradigm in which to frame the argument, because it combines a contractual approach with a socio-psychological perspective. These broad conceptual characteristics have been cited as being important to the success or failure of international joint ventures (Beamish 1984; Blodgett 1987; Geringer and Hebert 1989). Although agency theory has not previously been applied to either joint venture analysis or cross-cultural comparative studies, it would appear to be particularly useful because of the focused and parsimonious manner in which this theory organizes itself around the control, or owner-manager, relationship.

This study focuses on two issues which are central to an agency theory perspective and which have received relatively cursory attention in the joint venture literature. The study examines whether either the total number of partners participating in a joint venture, or the cross-cultural divergence among these partners, may influence the subsequent performance of international joint ventures. Although prior research has suggested that the number of partners may influence the level of decision-making complexity and consequently the performance of joint ventures (Daniels, Ogram and Radebaugh 1983; Geringer 1988; Harrigan 1986; Killing 1983), there have been no empirical tests of this asserted relationship in the literature on joint ventures. Similarly, a variety of normative (Deal and Kennedy 1982; Ouchi 1981; Schein 1985; Schneider 1988) and empirical (England 1975; Hofstede 1980) studies have contended that substantial differences in work-related attitudes and values exist between various cultures. Differences in values attributable to divergence among the partner organizations' cultures can be particularly troublesome in joint ventures, due to the shared nature of both their ownership and their decision making (Beamish 1984; Cieslik 1983; Friedmann and Beguin 1971; Pucik 1988; Sullivan and Peterson 1982). Yet, despite the potential value for advancing joint venture theory and practice, there have been essentially no prior efforts to empirically test the relationship between cross-cultural divergence among partners and the performance of international joint ventures.

This article briefly reviews agency and cross-cultural management theory. Then a principal-agent contractual model is developed specifically for the issue of the efficient structure of joint ventures. Finally, the model is applied to the international joint venture situation, several hypotheses are generated, and exploratory empirical tests of these hypotheses are completed.

1. Theoretical framework

This study defines joint ventures in a manner consistent with previous studies in the joint venture literature. In this regard, joint ventures are defined as ventures involving two or more legally distinct organizations (the parents or principals) which share in the ownership and decision-making activities of the jointly owned entity (Geringer and Hebert 1989). An international joint venture is defined as a joint venture having parents with different nationalities, or a parent of different nationality from the joint venture (Geringer and Frayne 1990).

1.1. Agency theory

Agency theory postulates that the attributes and perspectives of two parties regarding a potential relationship influence the type of relationship which these two parties may develop with one another. Formally, it is described as the principal-agent relationship, in which one party (the principal) delegates work to the other (the agent), who performs that work. The relationship is described metaphorically as a "contract" providing economic utility between the two parties. This principal-agent relationship has been used to describe many types of relationships, but a common application has been the study of owner-manager relationships in a company. As such, it provides an excellent theoretical foundation upon which to study the complex issues associated with the efficient structuring of joint venture relationships.

The fundamental argument in agency theory is that the principal-agent contract should reflect efficient organization of information and risk-bearing costs (Jensen and Meckling 1976). The focus of the theory is on the principal-agent contract, and what factors influence its efficiency and effectiveness from both parties' perspectives. The contract is theoretically described as a contingent entity which is influenced by the principal's and agent's self-interest, bounded rationality, and risk aversion. These actor-specific factors can produce a variety of effects, including goal conflicts and information asymmetry between the principal and agent, which, in turn, will influence the choice and efficiency of the principal-agent contract selected (Eisenhardt 1989).

Two types of contractual arrangements exist. They are delineated as behaviorally based and outcome-based contracts. A behaviorally based contract is a contract in which the principal monitors the behavior of the agent. It is best suited to a situation in which the principal can monitor the agent relatively efficiently, outcomes are difficult to measure, goal conflict is minimal, and risk aversion is not important to the principal. An outcome-based contract is a contract in which the principal monitors an agreed-upon outcome of the agent's efforts. An outcome-based contract is best suited to the situation where information monitoring is inefficient, the outcome is clearly measurable by the principal, goal conflict is high, and risk aversion by the principal motivates him or her to pass risk on to the agent. Table 1 more fully delineates the various contingent influences of the contract type and its inherent

Table 1. Contingent influences on princpal-agent contracts.

Contingent Contractual Factors	Behavioral-Based Contract[a,b]	Outcome-Based Contract[a,b]
1. Good information systems	+	−
2. Outcome uncertainty	+	−
3. Risk aversion of the agent	+	−
4. Risk aversion of the principal	−	+
5. Outcome measurability	−	+
6. Goal conflict	−	+
7. Task programmability	+	−
8. Length of relationship	+	−

Notes:
[a] + positively influences the selection of this type of contract
[b] − negatively influences the selection of this type of contract

efficiency. In regard to efficiency, the two types of contracts are not independent of one another. If a contingent factor provides positive efficiencies for one type of contract, it will decrease the efficiency of the other contract type if selected in the same context.

The situational and actor-specific influences thus tend to induce one type of contract to be more efficient than another type. This basic framework has been utilized in an attempt to describe many principal-agent relationships in regard to the actions of either actor, and the resulting efficiency of the total organization (Eisenhardt 1989; Levinthal 1988).

1.2. Cross-cultural theory

A growing body of cross-cultural literature documents a wide variety of work in this field. Unfortunately, much of this literature is focused on single-culture descriptive work, or comparative work on macro-level organizational, structural, or financial issues (Adler and Graham 1989). Some cross-cultural comparative work has focused on sociopsychological characteristics. These studies have been based on within-culture sampling techniques and have generally been exploratory and lacking in theoretical arguments. Finally, work on cross-cultural interaction theory and on causal modeling relating culture to outcomes represents a relatively new and unresearched area in the management field (Adler and Doktor 1986; Bhagat and McQuaid 1982; Roberts 1970).

Research on cross-cultural, sociopsychological comparative management issues is probably best represented by the work of Hofstede (1980). This research explored the attitudinal and value differences of managers in one organization across a wide variety of countries. Hofstede controlled for organizational type, and, unlike previous work, provided a minimal theoretical and descriptive reasoning for variable selection. Hofstede concluded that culture does influence work-related attitudes and values. Unfortunately, Hofstede's noncausal study could not provide statistical evidence of such a dependence. This empirical problem has continued to weaken the conclusions of research of this type. A variety of arguments has occurred over the validity of the variables selected for use in Hofstede's and other similar research efforts (Yeh 1989). Yet, all of the major cross-cultural comparative, work-related attitudinal studies have supported a divergence between certain cultural groups (Ronen and Shenkar 1985; Townsend, Scott, and Markham 1990). Additional work in the sociopsychological field has tended to support these findings (Adler and Doktor 1986).

Cross-cultural interaction provides a more rigorous test of the cross-cultural divergence concept. This approach, rather than relying on separate observation of the cultures, studies the interactions between two cultures to conclude that meaningful managerial behavior differences exist. There are generally two propositions in this line of research. The first is that cultural attitudinal differences will result in behavioral changes when individuals move from a homogeneous to a heterogeneous cultural interaction. The second is that the individual can adapt to a new cultural situation rather quickly and interact in a manner which is consistent with that culture (Bouchner and Ohsako 1977; Bouchner and Perks 1971; Rubin and Brown 1975). The majority of sociopsychological research has found evidence of both effects, but clearly a cultural difference causes changes in interaction behavior. Adler and Graham (1989) completed an empirical study to see whether managerial interaction was contingent upon the culture mix. Their results indicated that in seven out of 24 cases significant behavioral differences were evident. They concluded that culture was an important variable when considering cross-cultural interactions.

Thus, one should expect that joint ventures involving heterogeneous cultural principals would tend to encounter increased diversity in terms of interaction behaviors. Agency theory is based on contractual interaction postulates and, therefore, it may allow one to predict the performance of international joint ventures to some degree.

1.3. Joint venture agency model

The joint venture, principal-agent model developed herein utilizes this agency theory model of efficiency and applies it to multi-partner international joint ventures. The primary difference between the principal-agent model described above and a joint venture model is that in a joint venture there are two or more principals, each of which shares in both the venture's ownership and decision making. Historically, agency theory has considered the relevant principal's perspective as being singular in nature. In cases where there were multiple principals, the average principal's perspective has been used (Levinthal 1988). The averaging concept has allowed organizational economists to compare contract efficiencies of firms having owner-operated ownership structures to widely held stock-ownership structures. The argument for averaging is that stockholders tend to have similar perspectives because of their gross inability to monitor agent behavior, along with their desire to minimize overall risk. In this context, the averaging approach may be appropriate. In joint ventures, however, the principals may favor either type of contract, depending upon the context and attributes of each principal. Thus, the model must take into account the potential divergence in self-interest, bounded rationality, and risk aversion attributes of the principals.

The model is illustrated in Figure 1. The delta indicates the potential divergence in principal attributes which would influence the efficiency of one type of contract over the other. For example, in a joint venture which has two principals, if delta is significant and effective in producing divergent positions with respect to a contingent contractual influence,

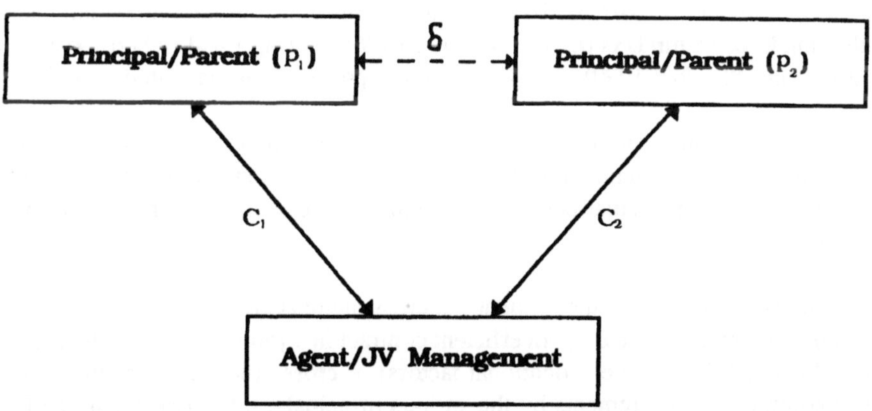

Figure 1.

one principal may find that a behaviorally based contract (C_1) is more efficient, while the other principal may find that an outcome-based contract (C_2) is more efficient. The final contract which is negotiated therefore may not be efficient for one or more of the principals, any more than for the joint venture. The other potential is that the joint venture agent has to live up to two pseudo-contracts, one with each principal. Again, the attributes of the agent specify that he or she will be most efficient at accommodating one type of contract over the other. The agent will be inefficient at simultaneously maintaining two or more contracts of divergent types.

2. Hypotheses regarding agency theory as applied to joint ventures

A variety of potential hypotheses may be generated from the joint venture agency model developed above. This article introduces several which are particularly relevant to multi-partner (i.e., two to four principals) international joint ventures.

The first hypothesis questions the efficiency of joint venture contractual relationships as the number of principals increases. For example, it can be expected that joint ventures having just two principals would be intrinsically more efficient than those having four principals. On a pure probability basis, the potential for divergent contractual perspectives increases as additional principals are added to a joint venture. Considerable research has broadly considered the issue of how to efficiently structure these ventures, but, to date, empirical research has not specifically examined the issue of the effect of the number of principals on organizational efficiency. However, research on organizational groups has demonstrated that increasing group size has a negative effect on group cohesiveness and produces increased conflict because of a divergence in goal, cognitive, and behavioral attributes (Cartwright and Zander 1968). In addition, on a conceptual level, prior research has argued that the number of partners participating in a joint venture may have important implications for the dynamics within these organizations (Daniels, Ogram, and Radebaugh 1983; Geringer 1988; Harrigan 1986). In this regard, risks of conflicts, coordination and communication problems, and overall decision-making complexity have been argued to escalate as the number of partner firms increases, thus constituting a potentially serious destabilization force within IJVs (Bivens and Lovell 1966; Geringer and Hebert 1989; Killing 1983; Zeira and Shenkar 1990). Thus, the first hypothesis can be stated as follows:

Hypothesis 1. In a joint venture, as the number of principals increases, there is greater probability for poor organizational performance because of the increased chance for divergent principal-agent contractual perspectives, and thus for contract inefficiencies by one or more of the parties.

The second issue explored is the influence of cross-national situational and cross-cultural values on the potential for yielding an efficient contract in a joint venture. Different cross-national situational factors (i.e., locational factors) or cross-cultural values may produce divergent contractual requirements by the various principals, thus creating an inefficient principals-agent contract. Brown, Rugman, and Verbeke (1989) developed a framework that distinguished between economic and cultural modes of failure in international joint ventures. They considered cultural incompatability to be an important cause of joint venture failure. In this regard, a variety of studies have indicated that different values exist among different cultures (Deal and Kennedy 1982; England 1975; Hofstede 1980; Laurent 1983; Ouchi 1981; Schein 1985; Schneider 1988). A divergence in the principals' values would tend to increase the probability of incurring contractual inefficiency by one or more of the principals. Furthermore, a longer term contractual relationship tends to favor a behaviorally based contract (Lambert 1983), while geographic separation tends to favor an outcome-based contract because of the difficulty of monitoring the agent's behavior. Thus, it is hypothesized that:

Hypothesis 2. In a joint venture, as the cross-cultural content of the principals increases, there is greater probability for poor organizational performance because of the increased chance for divergent principal-agent contractual perspectives, and thus contract inefficiencies by one or more of the parties.

A stronger test of the cross-cultural value hypothesis would involve specific values which are related to the contingent contractual factors delineated in Table 1. Studies detailing specific value-based behavioral or cognitive cross-cultural characteristics are rather limited. Probably the most widely accepted dimensionalization of cross-cultural values is the work by Hofstede (1980). For example, one of the values identified by Hofstede, namely, *individualism*, is related to goal congruence. Individualism is defined as the degree to which individuals identify with themselves as individuals versus as members of a group. This value would indicate a positive attitude toward goal congruence, and would indicate a preference for an outcome-based contract if the principal had an individualistic attitude. Thus, incongruity by joint venture principals on this value may lead to contractual inefficiencies, as stated in the following hypothesis:

Hypothesis 3. In a joint venture, as divergence in the principals' values toward individualism increases, there is greater probability for organizational inefficiency because of the increased chance of divergent principal-agent contract perspectives, and thus contract inefficiencies by one or more of the parties.

Another value identified by Hofstede was the value of *uncertainty avoidance*. This value is related to the contingent contractual influence of risk aversion. Uncertainty avoidance is defined as the extent to which people feel threatened by ambiguous situations, and the extent to which they try to avoid these situations. This value could indicate an attitude toward risk aversion, and would indicate a preference for an outcome-based contract if the principal had a risk-averse attitude. Incongruity by joint venture principals on this value may lead to contractual inefficiencies, as stated in the following hypothesis:

Hypothesis 4. In a joint venture, as divergence in the principals' values toward uncertainty avoidance increases, there is greater probability for organizational inefficiency because of the increased chance of divergent principal-agent contract perspectives, and thus contract inefficiencies by one or more of the parties.

A final cross-cultural value identified by Hofstede and which appears to be related to one of the contingent contractual influences is the cross-cultural *power distance value*. Power distance is defined as the extent to which less powerful members accept the unequal distribution of power in their organization. This value reflects a tolerance for task programmability, indicating a preference for a behaviorally based contract if the principal has a high power distance attitude. Incongruity by joint venture principals on this value may lead to contractual inefficiencies, as stated in the following hypothesis:

Hypothesis 5. In a joint venture, as divergence in the principals' values toward power distance increases, there is greater probability for organizational inefficiency because of the increased chance of divergent principal-agent contract perspectives, and thus contract inefficiencies by one or more of the parties.

3. Research Methodology

3.1. Selection of sample

This study utilized a proprietary database listing the entire population of two-, three-, and four-parent, Canada-based joint ventures which existed in 1981. After adjusting for missing cases, the database contained 3,556 Canadian joint ventures. Of this total, 70% were two-parent joint ventures, 22% were three-parent joint ventures, 8% were four-parent joint ventures, and 22% of the joint ventures had at least one non-Canadian parent, and thus represented international joint ventures.

3.2. Analytical techniques employed

The analytical techniques used were generalized logit and log-linear logit modeling. Generalized logit modeling was utilized when a categorical dependent variable was being modeled in the relationship. Log-linear logit modeling is useful when all of the variables are categorical. It tends to be somewhat more robust than generalized logit analysis because of its contingency table analysis technique, but it may not make full use of all of the information in non-categorical data because of its analysis technique (Aldrich and Nelson 1984; Knoke and Burke 1980).

3.3. Joint venture efficiency measure

Prior research has assessed joint venture efficiency, or performance, using a variety of both subjective and objective measures. Unfortunately, both approaches have received criticism. Although some authors have argued for the use of objective financial measures of performance, these measures are often unavailable for joint venture-level performance, or they have been tampered with or contain inherent bias because of a desire to maximize cash flow to the principals (Beamish 1984; Schaan 1983). Subjective measures have been employed in an attempt to qualitatively measure the extent of goal attainment of the joint venture relative to the parents' expectations. Subjective performance measures have proved difficult to obtain for any large database, however, and their reliability has been questioned because of the measures' qualitative nature. An alternative measure which has been used in several prior studies is *venture survival*. This measure has been empirically shown to be highly correlated with both objective and subjective measures of joint venture performance, including overall and profit performance versus initial venture objectives, as well as parents' overall assessments of satisfaction with the venture's performance (Geringer and Hebert 1991). Data on venture survival were also available for firms in this study's database. Therefore, survival was used as the proxy for joint venture efficiency. The survival period was from 1981 to 1988, the two dates available from the database.

3.4. Number of principals measure

The number of principals was defined as the number of equity partners involved in the joint venture relationship. This number ranged from two to four in this database.

3.5. Percentage cross-cultural content measure

This variable was operationalized as the percentage of the principal relationships which were of the same nationality. For example, if all principals were of the same nationality, then this variable was 100% while if they were all different this variable was 0%.

3.6. Measures of cross-cultural values influencing agency contract efficiency

The cross-cultural values were based upon the national value figures delineated by Hofstede (1980). The total value divergence within each joint venture was based upon the summation of the absolute value of the differences between (among) all of the principals involved in the joint venture. These figures were then recoded into dichotomous categorical variables because of the predominance of contingency cells which had counts of less than five. The point separating cultural-value congruence with cultural-value incongruence was ten. This point was selected atheoretically based upon the need to maximize the dimensions which would have cell counts of greater than five.

3.7. Geographic diversification measure

Finally, the analyses always controlled for geographic diversification. The reason for implementing this control variable was because of its potential autocorrelation with cultural diversity. Furthermore, recent empirical research on international geographic diversification has indicated that this variable tends to be significantly related with organizational efficiency (Daniels and Bracker 1989; Geringer, Beamish and daCosta 1989).

Geographic diversification was controlled for by defining it as a dichotomous variable in which geographic diversification was considered to have taken place if none of the joint venture principals were Canadian, and geographic diversification was considered not to have occurred if at least one principal was Canadian.

4. Analysis and results

The initial test for Hypotheses 1 and 2 utilized logit analysis techniques on all 3,556 joint venture cases. The dependent variable was organizational efficiency or survival. The independent variables were the percentage of principal relationships which were cross-cultural in nature, and the number of principals in the joint venture. In addition, the model controlled for geographic diversification through the use of a dummy variable. The results of this model are delineated in Table 2. Using generalized logit modeling techniques, the parameter estimates were in the direction predicted as well as being statistically significant ($p \leq 0.05$). However, the residuals of the generalized model indicated a potential violation of assumptions. Unfortunately, there has been little research on violations of assumptions for this type of analytical model (Aldrich and Nelson 1984). Thus, to verify results, log-linear logit analysis was implemented. The results from this model are also detailed in Table 2. The estimate for the number-of-partners variable became nonsignificant for this latter analysis.

To further verify the significance of this parameter, a subset of the database was tested to ensure that autocorrelation problems with the percent cross-cultural principal content were not causing instability problems. The selected subsample controlled for percent cross-cultural content and geographic diversification by using only those joint ventures having all Canadian principals. These results also indicated that the number of partners estimate was nonsignificant. It was thus concluded that Hypothesis 1, stating that the number-of-partners parameter estimate would be significantly related with joint venture performance, was not supported. Hypothesis 2, that increased cross-cultural content would be related to decreased venture performance, was supported in both analyses, as shown in Table 2.

The analysis of Hypotheses 3, 4, and 5 required that the model control for both the number of joint venture principals and geographic diversification. Geographic diversification was controlled for by considering only joint ventures which had not undergone geographic diversification. A problem of low numbers made analysis of the subsample having geographic diversification too unstable. The number of principals was therefore controlled for by dividing

Table 2. Results for the total estimated joint venture agency model.

Defined Variable	Logit Parameter Estimate	Significance of Generalized Logit	Significance of Log-Linear Logit
Number of principals	−0.12284	$p = 0.025$	$p = 0.280$
Percent cross-cultural content	−0.07617	$p = 0.002$	$p = 0.006$
Total model	—	$p = 0.001$	—

Table 3. Results of cultural variability on joint venture survival.

Hypothesis Tested	Two Principal Joint Ventures	Three Principal Joint Ventures	Four Principal Joint Ventures
Hypothesis #3 (individualism)	+*	+*	+
Hypothesis #4 (uncertainty avoidance)	+**	+**	+[a]
Hypothesis #5 (power distance)	−*[a]	+	+[a]

Notes:
\+ indicates that the direction of the relationship supports hypothesis
− indicates that the direction of the relationship does not support hypothesis
[a]in these statistical tests, at least one cell had a count of less than 5
$^{**}p \leq 0.01$
$^{*}p \leq 0.05$

the sample into further subsamples based upon this variable. This was done to eliminate autocorrelation problems with the cross-cultural values' variables. The analysis used log-linear logit analysis. The results are detailed in Table 3. As shown, the majority of the estimates were in the hypothesized direction, and 44% of the relationships were both in the hypothesized direction and statistically significant at the 0.05 level.

On an individual basis, the hypotheses received different degrees of support. Hypothesis 3 predicted that divergence between principals in the individualism cross-cultural value would negatively influence organizational effectiveness. This hypothesis was significant for the two- and three-principal joint ventures, as shown in Table 3. The four-principal joint venture test was not significant. However, the four-principal subsample test was conducted on a small sample size. Therefore, significance in the prediction was more difficult to obtain because of the potential for small numbers instability in the contingency table analysis. The direction of the parameter estimate was in the correct direction in all cases for Hypothesis 3. Thus, it can be stated that Hypothesis 3 was partially supported.

Hypothesis 4 predicted that divergence between principals in the risk-aversion, cross-cultural value would negatively influence organizational efficiency. This hypothesis was supported by statistically significant results for the two- and three-principal joint ventures, but not for the four-principal joint ventures. As indicated in a note to Table 3, the four-principal joint venture analysis had at least one cell with less than the minimum cell count of five required for this statistical technique, a problem which could occasion instability in results. The parameter estimates were in the predicted direction in all cases for this hypothesis test. Thus, Hypothesis 4 was partially supported in a manner similar to that of Hypothesis 3.

Hypothesis 5 predicted that the divergence between principals in the power-distance cross-cultural value would negatively influence organizational efficiency. In the analysis for this hypothesis, only two of the parameter estimates were in the predicted direction, and neither of these estimates was statistically significant. Furthermore, the two-principal joint venture estimate was significant but not in the predicted direction, although it also had a small numbers problem. Thus, it was concluded that Hypothesis 5 was not supported.

5. Discussion and implications

This article attempted to develop an agency-theory-based model specific to the joint venture form of organization. The model attempted to account for the divergent attributes and values of principals in the joint venture, and the influence these may have on the principal-agent contract and on the subsequent performance of the joint venture. Five hypotheses were then developed to test the model for multi-partner, international joint ventures. The resulting empirical analysis revealed mixed support for this joint venture, agency-theory model.

This article makes several contributions to existing theory, particularly as it relates to joint ventures. First, this article extends existing conceptual frameworks by applying agency theory to multi-principal contexts, including the specific case of joint ventures. In addition, this article has attempted to develop an explicitly theory-based orientation toward culture and its relationship to the structure and performance of joint ventures. This is in contrast to much of the prior literature examining culture and joint ventures, literature which often has not been grounded within a strong theoretical framework. Also, in contrast to several prior studies, of both joint ventures and organizational phenomena in general, the agency-theory-based conceptual model developed in this article had the potential to be empirically tested. Having generally drawn the focal variables from prior conceptual and empirical studies, facilitated their operationalization. The use of a large-scale, population-based sample of developed-country joint ventures for empirical analysis represents another unique attribute of this study.

In contrast to assertions of prior joint venture studies, the hypothesis suggesting that the number of principals in a joint venture would produce contractual inefficiencies, and thus result in lower venture performance, was not supported. Although organizational process variables such as principal selection may also have been useful in assessing this relationship (Geringer 1988, 1991), they were not included in the model's initial conceptualization and were also unavailable for use in its empirical assessment. In addition, a joint venture contract could be multitiered on a princpal-agent, pseudo-contract basis. For example, one principal might have an owner-manager role, while the others would be passive investors. The first principal might desire a behavior-based contract, while the others might desire an outcome-based contract with the first principal. Such a multidimensional contract is possible; the resulting efficiencies, theoretical development, and empirical analysis would necessarily have to consider such a contract's multidimensionality.

The culture-related hypotheses received mixed support. However, results for Hypothesis 2 suggested that there was sufficient evidence to indicate that agency theory may provide some explanatory power for assessing cross-national, joint venture performance. In this regard, the partial support for Hypotheses 3 and 4 and the lack of support for Hypothesis 5 may indicate that some cross-cultural factors are more important than others in influencing the efficiency of the principal-agent contract. Clearly, the cross-cultural effects are complex and multidimensional. These effects may be interdependent and spuriously defined in their present form. Thus, further conceptual refinement may be warranted in order to develop a broader and more robust theoretical basis for testing potential cross-cultural effects.

Although unique in many respects regarding its conceptualization and operationalization, our model represents only an initial effort at constructing an agency-theory-based model of joint ventures and may thus be susceptible to several limitations. First, there is a need for conducting further empirical tests of this model in order to assess and refine the nature and direction of relationships among the research variables. This task may prove daunting, however, due to the inherent difficulty of accessing a database of sufficient size and scope, which contains data of the requisite breadth and depth, and which will permit analysis which may be generalizable within and across populations of joint ventures. The scarcity of such databases and the limited access to those which do exist continue to constrain efforts to advance theory and practice regarding the effective formation and management of international joint ventures.

In addition, it may be valuable to undertake efforts aimed at further extending the conceptual model itself. For example, the first hypothesis suggested that the number of principals in a joint venture would influence the likelihood of contractual inefficiencies. Organizational-process variables such as principal selection represent important potential influences on venture efficiency (Geringer 1988), yet they were not included in the current model. Finally, other theoretical lines of reasoning, such as organization-control, transaction-cost, strategic-contingency, and organizational-process theories, could indicate additional conceptual relationships which would enhance the explanatory powers surrounding this complex issue of organizational control in multi-partner, international joint ventures. Efforts to test relationships such as those proposed in this article, conducted either in conjunction with or parallel to an agency-theory-based analysis, could yield substantial additional insights into the joint venture phenomenon.

References

Adler, N.J., and R. Doktor (with S.G. Redding). (1986). "From the Atlantic to the Pacific Century: Cross-Cultural Management Reviewed," *Journal of Management* 12(2), 295–318.

Adler, N.J., and J.L. Graham. (1989). "Cross-Cultural Interactions: The International Comparison Fallacy?" *Journal of International Business Studies* 20(3), 515–537.

Aldrich, J.H., and F.D. Nelson. (1984). *Linear Probability, Logit, and Probit Models*. Beverly Hills, CA: Sage Publications.

Beamish, P.W. (1984). "Joint Venture Performance in Developing Countries." Unpublished doctoral dissertation, University of Western Ontario, London, Ontario.

Beamish, P.W., and J.C. Banks. (1987). "Equity Joint Venture and the Theory of Multinational Enterprise," *Journal of International Business Studies* 19(2), 1–16.

Bhagat, R.S., and S.J. McQuaid. (1982). "Role of Subjective Culture in Organization: A Review and Direction for Future Research," *Journal of Applied Psychology Monogram* 67(5), 635–685.

Bivens, K.K., and E.B. Lovell. (1966). *Joint Ventures with Foreign Partners: International Survey of Business Opinion and Experience*. New York: National Industry Conference Board.

Blodgett, L.L. (1987). "A Resource-Based Study of Bargaining Power in U.S. Foreign Equity Joint Ventures." Unpublished doctoral dissertation, University of Michigan, Ann Arbor.

Bouchner, S., and T. Ohsako. (1977). "Ethnic role in Salience in Racially Homogenous and Heterogenous Societies," *Journal of Cross-Cultural Psychology* 8, 477–492.

Bouchner, S., and R.W. Perks. (1971). "National Role Evocation as a Function of Cross-Cultural Interaction," *Journal of Cross-Cultural Psychology* 2, 157–164.

Brown, L.T., A.M. Rugman, and A. Verbeke. (1989). "Japanese Joint Ventures with Western Multinationals: Synthesising the Economic and Cultural Explanations of Failure," *Asia Pacific Journal of Management* 6(2), 225–242.

Buckley, P.J., and M. Casson. (1988). "A Theory of Cooperation in International Business." In F. Contractor and P. Lorange (eds.), *Cooperative Strategies in International Business*. Lexington, MA: Lexington Books, pp. 31–53.

Cartwright, C., and A. Zander. (1968). *Group Dynamics: Research and Theory.* New York: Harper & Row.
Cieslik, J. (1983). "Western Firms Participating in the East-West Industrial Co-operation: The Case of Poland," *Management International Review* 23(1), 69–75.
Daniels, J.D., and J. Bracker. (1989). "Profit Performance: Do Foreign Operations Make a Difference?" *Management International Review* 29(1), 46–56.
Daniels, J.D., E.W. Ogram, and L.H. Radebaugh. (1983). *International Business: Environments and Operations*, 3rd ed. Reading, MA: Addison-Wesley.
Deal, T., and A. Kennedy. (1982). *Corporate Cultures: The Rites and Rituals of Corporate Life.* Reading, MA: Addison-Wesley.
Eisenhardt, K.M. (1989). "Agency Theory: An Assessment and Review," *Academy of Management Review* 14(1), 57–74.
England, G.W. (1975). *The Manager and His Values: An International Perspective from the United States, Japan, Korea, India, and Australia.* Cambridge, MA: Ballinger.
Friedmann, W.G., and J.-P. Beguin. (1971). *Joint International Business Ventures in Developing Countries.* New York: Columbia University Press.
Geringer, J.M. (1988). *Joint Venture Partner Selection: Strategies for Developed Countries.* Westport, CN: Quorum Books.
Geringer, J.M. (1991). "Strategic Determinants of Partner Selection Criteria in International Joint Ventures," *Journal of International Business Studies* 22(1), 41–62.
Geringer, J.M., P.W. Beamish, and R.C. daCosta. (1989). "Diversification Strategy and Internationalization: Implications for MNE Performance," *Strategic Management Journal* 10(2), 109–119.
Geringer, J.M., and C.A. Frayne. (1990). "Human Resource Management and International Joint Venture Control: A Parent Company Perspective," *Management International Review* 30 (Special Issue), 103–120.
Geringer, J.M., and L. Hebert. (1989). "Control and Performance of International Joint Ventures," *Journal of International Business Studies* 20(2), 235–254.
Geringer, J.M., and L. Hebert. (1991). "Measuring Performance of International Joint Ventures," *Journal of International Business Studies* 22(2).
Geringer, J.M., and C.P. Woodcock. (1989). "Ownership and Control of Canadian Joint Ventures," *Business Quarterly* 54(1), 97–105.
Harrigan, K.R. (1990). "Bases of Interorganizational Co-operation: Propensity, Power, Persistence," *Journal of Management Studies* 27(4), 417–434.
Harrigan, K.R. (1988). "Joint Ventures and Competitive Strategy," *Strategic Management Journal* 9(2), 141–158.
Harrigan, K.R. (1986). *Managing for Joint Venture Success.* Lexington, MA: Lexington Books.
Hergert, M., and D. Morris. (1988). "Trends in Collaborative Agreements." In Farok Contractor and Peter Lorange (eds.), *Cooperative Strategies in International Business.* Lexington, MA: Lexington Books, pp. 99–109.
Hofstede, G. (1980). *Culture's Consequences: Inter-National Differences in Work Related Values.* Beverly Hills, CA: Sage.
Jensen, M., and W. Meckling. (1976). "Theory of the Firm: Managerial Behavior, Agency Costs, and Ownership Structure," *Journal of Financial Economics* 3, 305–360.
Killing, J.P. (1983). *Strategies for Joint Venture Success.* New York: Praeger.
Knoke, D., and P.J. Burke. (1980). *Log-Linear Models.* Beverly Hills, CA: Sage Publications.
Lambert, R. (1983). "Long-Term Contracts and Moral Hazard," *Bell Journal of Economics* 14, 441–452.
Laurent, A. (1983). "The Cultural Diversity of Western Conceptions of Management," *International Studies of Management and Organizations* 13(1–2), 75–96.
Levinthal, D. (1988). "A Survey of Agency Models of Organizations," *Journal of Economic Behavior and Organization* 9, 153–185.
McCormick, J., and N. Stone. (1990). "From National Champion to Global Competitor: An Interview with Thomson's Alain Gomez," *Harvard Business Review* 68(3), 126–135.
Ouchi, W.G. (1981). *Theory Z: How American Business Can Meet the Japanese Challenge.* Reading, MA: Addison-Wesley.
Pucik, V. (1988). "Strategic Alliances with the Japanese: Implications for Human Resources Management." In F. Contractor and P. Lorange (eds.), *Cooperative Strategies in International Business.* Lexington, MA: Lexington Books, pp. 487–498.

Roberts, K.H. (1970). "On Looking at an Elephant: An Evaluation of Cross-Cultural Research Related to Organizations," *Psychological Bulletin* 74(5), 327–350.

Ronen, S., and O. Shenkar. (1985). "Clustering Countries on Attitudinal Dimensions: A Review and Synthesis," *Academy of Management Review* 10(3), 435–454.

Rubin, J.Z., and B.R. Brown. (1975). *The Social Psychology of Bargaining and Negotiation*. New York: Academic Press.

Schaan, J.-L. (1983). "Parent Control and Joint Venture Success: The Case of Mexico." Unpublished doctoral dissertation, University of Western Ontario, London, Ontario.

Schein, E. (1985). *Organizational Culture and Leadership*. San Francisco: Jossey-Bass.

Schneider, S.C. (1988). "National versus Corporate Culture: Implications for Human Resource Management," *Human Resource Management* 27(2), 231–246.

Sullivan, J., and R.B. Peterson. (1982). "Factors Associated with Trust in Japanese-American Joint Ventures," *Management International Review* 22(2), 30–40.

Townsend, A.M., K.D. Scott, and S.E. Markham. (1990). "An Examination of Country and Culture-Based Differences in Compensation Practices," *Journal of International Business Studies* 21(4), 667–678.

Yeh, R.-S. (1989). "On Hofstede's Treatment of Chinese and Japanese Values," *Asia Pacific Journal of Management* 6(1), 149–160.

Zeira, Y., and O. Shenkar. (1990). "Interactive and Specific Parent Characteristics: Implications for Management and Human Resources in International Joint Ventures," *Management International Review* 30 (Special Issue), 7–22.

Bargaining Power, Management Control, and Performance in U.S.–China Joint Ventures: A Comparative Case Study

AIMIN YAN
Organizational Behavior Department, School of Management, Boston University, 621 Commonwealth Avenue, Boston, MA 02215

BARBARA GRAY
Department of Management and Organization, The Smeal College of Business Administration, The Pennsylvania State University, 408 Beam Business Administration Building, University Park, PA 16802

Abstract.

This article reports a comparative case study of four international joint ventures created between the United States and the People's Republic of China. The findings of this study suggest that the relative bargaining power of potential joint-venture partners significantly contributes to the structural configuration of the joint venture with respect to parent control, and that the structure of management control exercised by the parents affects venture performance. Several informal control mechanisms interacting with formal control structure and influencing performance are identified. The article also investigates the dynamic evolution of joint ventures over time as a result of changes in the environment, adjustments in the parents' strategies, mutual learning between the partners, and the maturity of the joint venture. Finally, an integrative model is presented and several propositions for future research are offered.

Key Words: international joint ventures, bargaining power, control, performance

International joint ventures are a rapidly growing organizational form that has received increasing interest from researchers in a variety of academic disciplines. Despite this attention, our understanding of joint ventures is still limited in scope and in depth. High failure/instability rates among joint ventures have been reported by previous studies (Franko 1971; Harrigan 1986; Levine and Byrne 1986; Kogut 1989), and the factors predictive of successful venture performance remain unclear (Geringer and Hebert 1991; Parkhe 1993a). In addition, the empirical work that has been done to test existing conceptual models has either produced contradictory results or been difficult to compare because of differences in how variables were operationalized across studies.

This article adopts an inter-partner negotiations perspective on joint-venture formation. It envisions joint ventures as mixed motive games between partners who cooperate and compete simultaneously (Lax and Sebenius 1986; Hamel, Doz, and Prahalad 1989). The negotiations perspective hypothesizes that the relative bargaining power between the joint-venture partners impacts the pattern of management control that is adopted by the venture.

The authors would like to thank Martin Kilduff, Jim Thomas, Michael Hitt, and two anonymous reviewers of the *Academy of Management Journal* for their insightful comments on the earlier versions of this article, part of which was presented at the 1992 Academy of Management Meeting, Las Vegas, Nevada.

In addition, parent control is hypothesized to be a critical factor that determines performance. While the first relationship has been empirically investigated by previous researchers (Fagre and Wells 1972; Killing 1983; Lecraw 1984; Blodgett 1991), the studies are difficult to compare, because they have measured both variables differently. Research findings on the relationship between control and performance offer conflicting results (see Geringer and Hebert 1989, for a review). Lecraw (1984) notes that the relationship between parent control and performance represents a continuing controversy in the international joint-venture literature.

Additional problems with prior research also make further study warranted. For example, (1) conflicting results have been obtained for joint ventures in developing as compared to developed countries (Beamish 1984, 1985, 1988); (2) longitudinal studies are underrepresented in research to date and, as a result, there is little known about how joint ventures evolve over time; (3) most joint venture research in developing countries adopts the perspective of the multinational partner and excludes the views of the developing-country partner; (4) finally, only two studies have examined the relationships between bargaining power and control and control and performance simultaneously (Lecraw 1984; Killing 1983).

This article utilizes a comparative case study approach to reexamine the relationships among bargaining power, control, and performance. We have sought to overcome the above-mentioned limitations in several ways. First, we look at the relationships among all three variables in the same study. By adopting in-depth, comparative case studies, we try to sort out the confusion and inconsistencies with respect to these relationships in the existing literature. By providing detailed explanations that survey methods miss, case studies offer the prospect of new insights into the connections among these variables (Glaser and Strauss 1967; Eisenhardt 1989; Yin 1989). Second, we sought to improve on existing models by accounting for the dynamic aspects of joint ventures, a topic largely ignored in research to date (Parkhe 1993a). By tracing the evolution of joint ventures, we identify changes in the venture over time. In this respect, comparative case studies are useful, because they are particularly appropriate for studying organizational changes (Van de Ven and Poole 1990). Third, our data reflect the interpretations of both parents. Fourth, research on international joint ventures that examines bargaining power, control, and performance relationships has primarily focused on ventures created among developed-country partners. In our study, we aimed at a deeper understanding of joint ventures in a developing country, namely, China, thus, enriching the literature with the Chinese experience.

Recent research has focused on the rapid proliferation of international joint ventures in the transformational (from centrally controlled to market-oriented) economies, such as that of the People's Republic of China (Child 1991; Pomfret 1991; Pearson 1991; Davidson 1987; Daniels, Krug, and Nigh 1985; Beamish 1993). Very little research on the relationships among bargaining power, control, and performance has been reported on joint ventures in China. What research exists either focuses on the macro-environments for direct foreign investment in China (e.g., Tung 1982; Mathur and Chen 1987; Campbell 1988; Ho 1990; Shan 1991) or is descriptive in nature (e.g., Hendryx 1986; O'Reilly 1988, Campbell 1988; Mann 1989; Schnepp, Von Glinow, and Bhambri 1990; Eiteman 1990). In-depth empirical research on the management and organizational issues in international joint ventures in China has been limited, though more work has been done recently (e.g., Lo 1989; Teagarden and Von Glinow 1990; Child 1991; Pearson 1991; Newman 1992;

Beamish 1993). Still, the applicability of research findings generated in the West to the Chinese setting remains an open question (Child 1991).

The economic reforms in China have stimulated a growth of joint ventures in the past decade. More than 20,000 international partnerships with a total investment of more than $26 billion were signed in the 1980s (The U.S.-China Business Council 1990). This rapid growth of Chinese joint ventures presents an interesting and challenging opportunity to study international alliances in a new institutional context (Child 1991).

In the next section, we introduce the preliminary framework derived from the existing literature. Following Yin (1989), who argues that case studies should start with theoretical propositions,[1] this research began with a theoretical framework linking bargaining power, management control, and performance. We then used analytic induction (Znaniecki 1934; Cressey 1953; Glaser and Strauss 1967) to analyze four U.S.-Chinese joint ventures. Section 2 describes our research method. Section 3 reports our findings and offers a revised model that captures the dynamic relationships among the key variables. These relationships are incorporated in several propositions for further investigation. Finally, in section 4, we discuss the findings and suggest directions for future research.

1. Theoretical background

As noted earlier, we adopt a negotiations perspective to explain the distribution of control among the partners in a joint venture. The negotiations perspective suggests that the relative bargaining power of the partners is a critical variable in determining patterns of control in joint ventures (Lecraw 1984; Harrigan and Newman 1990; Blodgett 1991). Below we develop the meaning of each of these constructs and provide support for the relationships among them.

1.1. Bargaining power

Bargaining power refers to the capability of the bargainers to favorably change the bargaining set (Lax and Sebenius 1986), to win accommodations from the other (Dwyer and Walker 1981; Tung 1988), and to influence the outcome of a negotiation (Schelling 1956). Two sources of bargaining power are identified in the bargaining and resource dependence literatures, respectively.

Bargaining theory proposes that the stakes of the bargainers in the negotiation and the availability of alternatives influence their bargaining power (Bacharach and Lawler 1984). Stakes refer to the level of dependence of each bargainer on the negotiating relationship and on the important outcomes of the negotiation. Stakes are negatively related to bargaining power. Alternatives available to a negotiator specify the extent to which the bargainers have a choice of different arrangements for achieving the same goals. Thus, availability of alternatives is positively related to bargaining power. The partner who has more alternatives is more powerful, because it can threaten to walk away from the current bargaining and exercise its best alternative to a negotiated agreement (BATNA) (Fisher and Ury 1981). Since stakes and availability of alternatives are associated with the context in which the negotiation occurs, we refer to them as sources of context-based bargaining power.

Another theoretical vein, resource dependence theory (Pfeffer and Salancick 1978) suggests that the possession or control of critical resources constitutes power in interorganizational relations. If a firm contributes more critical resources to an interorganizational arrangement than its partner does, it will be more powerful than the partner in managing the partnership between them. Put simply, the relative bargaining power of potential joint-venture partners is determined by who brings what and how much to the party (Harrigan 1986). A partner gains bargaining power if the joint venture depends heavily on resources contributed by this partner that are "costly or impossible for other partners to replace" (Root 1988, p. 76) and critical to the venture's success (Harrigan and Newman 1990).

1.2. Management control

Management control refers to the process by which an organization influences its subunits and members to behave in ways that lead to the attainment of organizational objectives (Arrow 1964; Ouchi 1977; Flamholtz, Das, and Tsui 1985). Conceptualization of control in joint ventures is more problematic, however, because two or more parents may exert influence on the venture's activities. In this study, we focus on the structure of management control exercised by the sponsoring organizations in influencing the joint venture's strategic decisions and regulating the venture's important activities.

Geringer and Hebert (1989) characterize parent control in international joint ventures as a multidimensional construct comprised of three parts: scope, extent, and mechanisms of control. The scope of control specifies the areas of the joint venture's operation in which control is exercised. The extent of control is the degree to which the parents exercise control. The mechanisms of control refer to the means by which control is exercised. Since previous studies each focus on different dimensions of control (e.g., Killing 1983, Lecraw 1984, on extent; Geringer 1986, on scope; Schaan 1983, 1988, on scope and mechanisms), their results are virtually noncomparable. In this study, we adopt a multidimensional approach to management control so as to enhance comprehensiveness and comparability with other studies.

1.3. Relationships between bargaining power and management control

Prior research has attempted to articulate the relationship between the partners' bargaining power and the level of control which they exercise in the joint venture. Lecraw (1984) found that three aspects of bargaining power (the technical leadership, advertising intensity, and export capability of the multinational partner) significantly contributed to the partners' control over their joint ventures. In a study of 35 international joint ventures between developed countries, Killing (1983) reported that the partners' respective contributions shaped the control structure of the joint venture. For example, if one partner contributes technology, while the other has expertise in marketing, shared control will be the most feasible arrangement. Other studies (Fagre and Wells 1972; Blodgett 1991) also reported a positive relationship between bargaining power and control, but in these studies control was measured by ownership split between the partners.

1.4. Performance

Configuration of performance has been a controversial topic in the organizational literature (for a review, see Goodman and Pennings 1980; Lewin and Minton 1986). The controversy derives from the fact that multiple perspectives exist under which performance can be evaluated and that there are few indicators of performance that have been widely accpted. Performance evaluation becomes even more problematic in joint ventures, because more than one entity is involved in the partnership, and each is likely to adopt idosyncratic criteria. The literature on joint-venture performance reveals three areas in which major inconsistencies occur: (1) whose perspectives (one parent's, both parents', or the joint-venture management's) are used for performance measurement, (2) variation in the types of performance measures used (ranging from subjective judgments to financial indicators), and (3) variation in the appropriateness of different performance measures as the venture matures (for a review, see Yan and Gray 1995). These inconsistencies make cross-study comparisons and generalizations about joint-venture performance particularly problematic.

Consistent with Schaan (1983, 1988) and Yan and Gray (1995), in this study, we adopt a multidimensional approach to joint-venture performance and incorporate the perspectives of multiple players in the venture in the performance assessment. Specifically, we use each partner's assessment of the extent to which it has achieved its strategic objectives as a measure of performance.

1.5. Relationship between management control and performance

Studies of the parent control-performance relationship have produced ambiguous results (Geringer and Hebert 1989). In a study of international joint ventures between developed-country partners, Killing (1983) found that dominant parent joint ventures outperform shared-management ones and that the relationship between control and performance is U-shaped. Drawing from a sample of international joint ventures in a developing country, Beamish (1984, 1985) reported that dominant control by foreign firms was negatively related to performance. But when local partners dominated the venture, no such relationship was found. Therefore, Beamish suggests that the type of economy in which the joint venture operates may moderate the control-performance relationship. However, Lecraw's (1984) study shows that the status of the economic development of the joint venture's host country may not be as critical as Beamish suggested. Using a sample of joint ventures in five Asian, developing countries, Lecraw (1984) found a positive, roughly linear association between control and performance, a finding consistent with Killing's (1983). Other researchers note that the control-performance relationship is indirect, thus subject to contingent factors (for a review, see Geringer and Hebert 1989). We argue that additional research is needed to sort out the conditions under which a positive relationship would exist between control and performance and that the type of economy in which joint ventures operate still deserves to be one of the important contingent factors.

1.6. Structural reconfiguration in international joint ventures

Researchers have characterized joint ventures as transitional forms of organization (Vernon 1977; Davidson 1982; Harrigan 1986; Porter 1990). Though not all international joint ventures are necessarily transitional or unstable, they are far more dynamic than single, standalone organizations (Franko 1971). Structural changes or reconfigurations in joint ventures are likely over time for several reasons. First, international partnerships may be an expedient alternative to wholly owned affiliates for multinational corporations entering foreign markets, when conditions prohibit whole foreign ownership (Fayerweather 1982; Davidson 1982). Whenever such constraints are removed, joint ventures shift toward wholly owned affiliates (Contractor 1990). Second, a joint venture can be faded out because its importance to one or both parents' overall strategies depreciates (Bartlett and Ghoshal 1986; Harrigan and Newman 1990). A third predictable transition in joint ventures is the "obsolescing bargain," a term initiated by Vernon (1977, p. 151) to refer to substantial learning by one partner over time which devalues the expertise or knowledge contributed by the other, thereby deconstructing the initial pattern of the bargaining relationship between them (Hamel 1991). The obsolescing bargain also occurs when the partners gain bargaining power over time as a result of environmental changes (Harrigan and Newman 1990). Dymsza (1988) notes that, in joint ventures between developed- and developing-country partners, the former's contribution is likely to become less important over time, thus, it should turn major managerial responsibilities over to the latter partner. Similarly, Hamilton and Singh (1991) and Gray and Yan (1992) note that joint ventures need to reconfigure over time in response to changes in the partners' relative bargaining power so as to ensure stability and overall performance.

However, the dynamic aspect of joint ventures has been understudied and has received "the least amount of systematic attention in the existing literature." This represents "a critical omission in the development of a more complete theory of international joint ventures" (Parkhe 1993a, p. 234). Previous research on changes in joint ventures has focused on different dimensions and remained fragmented in orientation. Particularly, empirically grounded findings on the dynamic characteristics of international partnerships have been very sketchy. In this regard, this case study attempts to provide inductively generated accounts for how joint ventures evolve over time, what factors trigger their structural reconfigurations, and how the parents deal with changes in their joint ventures.

1.7. Summary

The above review suggests that while many pieces of work on bargaining power, management control, and performance exist in the literature, previous studies suffer from inconsistent conceptualizations and noncomparable empirical results. In Figure 1, we offer a model that synthesizes past research on bargaining power, management control, and performance in international joint ventures. Although the main theoretical thesis of the model may apply to all joint ventures, the nature and strength of the relationship depicted in the model may vary from international to domestic joint ventures and from ventures in developed countries to those in developing countries. This research investigated the model by focusing

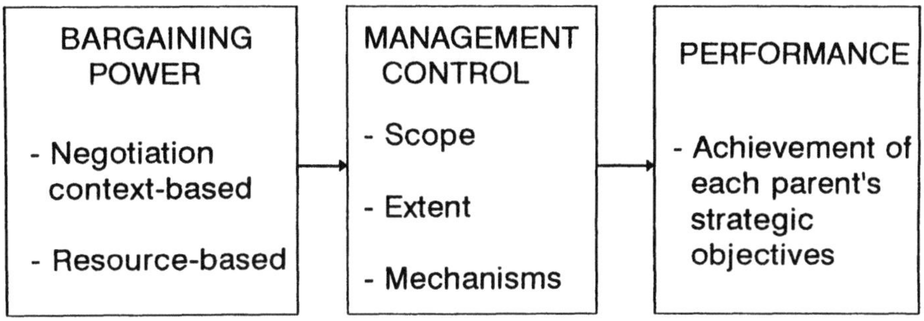

Figure 1. A theoretical model of bargaining power, management control, and performance.

on international joint ventures in a developing country. Following Yin (1989), we use the model in Figure 1 as a benchmark in analyzing our data. Using analytic induction, we conducted constant comparison of our data against the model, in order to see if the proposed relationships were present in our data and/or whether the case suggested modifications to the preliminary model (Znaniecki 1934; Robinson 1951; Cressey 1953; Glaser and Strauss 1967).

2. Method

2.1. Case selection

Recently, calls for rigorous case studies of international joint ventures have been made (Parkhe and Shin 1991; Parkhe 1993a). In this study, we case analyze four joint ventures between the United States and the People's Republic of China. Table 1 summarizes the major characteristics of these partnerships. The companies and individuals in each case are disguised in order to ensure confidentiality. (Detailed descriptions for each joint venture are available from the authors.)

We considered several factors in selecting the cases. First, we limited our study to manufacturing ventures so as to minimize extraneous variation (Eisenhardt 1989) that might be derived from industrial differences between service and manufacturing sectors (Chowdhury 1988). Second, the sample was widely representative of U.S.–China joint ventures operating in various industrial sectors. Manufacturing ventures represent 69% of U.S.–China joint ventures (The U.S.–China Business Council 1990), and the four ventures included in this study represent three industrial sectors in which about 50% of all U.S.–China manufacturing joint ventures were found. A third factor considered for case selection was that the joint ventures had to be in operation for a period of time, so that their performance data were available. A final and practical factor was access to informants. By design, we needed at least two parties from each partnership to agree to participate. The joint ventures eventually included in this study are among the first organizations for which agreement for interviews was obtained from the multiple parties involved.

Table 1. A summary of the major characteristics of the joint ventures.

Joint Venture	OfficeAid	IndusCon	DailyProduct	BioTech Ltd.
Product	Electronic office equipment	Industrial process control	Personal hygiene products	Pharmaceuticals
Length of negotiation (years)	4	3	2	3
Formation	1987	1982	1981	1982
Total investment ($ Million)	30	10	2.85	10
Equity share (% US/PRC)	51/49	49/51	50/50	50/50
Duration (years)	30	20	20	15
Product market	Mainly local; small percent for export	Local, import substitution	50% for export	Mainly local; small percent for export
Parents' objectives	U.S.: 1. Profit 2. Market share 3. Low-cost sourcing PRC: 1. Technology and management 2. Export for ForEx.	U.S.: 1. Business growth 2. Market penetration 3. Profit PRC: 1. Import substitution 2. Manufacturing technology 3. Upgrade suppliers' technology	U.S.: 1. Learn how to do business in China 2. Establish credibility 3. Profit 4. Business expansion PRC: 1. Profit 2. Export for ForEx. 3. Technology 4. Growth	U.S.: 1. Market 2. Profit PRC: 1. Technology 2. Learn mgmt. expertise 3. Businss expansion

2.2. *Data collection*

We collected data for this study from two sources: interviews and archives. Following a predesigned interview protocol, in-depth interviews were conducted with executives of both the U.S. and Chinese partners and the managers of the joint venture. Most of our informants (see Table 2) personally participated in the initial negotiations and/or were involved in the venture's management in its early stages. Each interview lasted an average of three hours; some informants were interviewed more than once. Interviews were tape recorded unless informants objected. In order to ensure the accuracy of the interview data, member checks (Lincoln and Guba 1985) were conducted, in which the original informants verified our tape transcripts or interview notes. All the interviews were conducted within a period of eight months, between May 1991 and January 1992. In addition to interviews, approximately 20 pages of archival data were collected for each partnership, including the highlights

Table 2. Sources of the interview data.

Joint Venture	Interviewees
OfficeAid	Manager for business strategy of the U.S. parent, member of the joint venture's board of directors, former head negotiator of the U.S. team, and the first general manager of the joint venture
	Chairman of the board and general manager of the Chinese parent firm
	Deputy general manager of the joint venture, member of the joint venture's board of directors, former executive general manager and head negotiator of the Chinese partner
	Two department managers of the joint venture, one for marketing, who was on the Chinese negotiation team, and the other for quality control
IndusCon	Directing manager for international joint ventures of the U.S. parent, member of the joint venture's board of directors, and former deputy general manager of the joint venture
	Deputy general manager of the joint venture, member of the joint venture's board of directors, former member of the Chinese negotiation team
	Manager of marketing of the joint venture
DailyProduct	Regional general manager for China operation of the U.S. parent, vice chairman of the joint venture's board of directors, one of the two members of the former U.S. negotiation team, former second general manager of the joint venture
BioTech Ltd.	Director of finance for the Asia-Pacific region of the U.S. parent, and active participant in the joint venture negotiations
	Vice president of the joint venture, former member of the Chinese negotation team
	Director for general administration of the joint venture

of the joint-venture contracts, the joint venture's and the parents' organizational charts, corporate brochures and annual reports, published case descriptions, and newspaper/magazine reports about these partnerships.

2.3. Data coding

Data from different sources were coded using typical content analysis procedures (Lincoln and Guba 1985; Diesing 1972; Strauss 1987; Taylor and Bogdan 1984). First, all data were coded into a number of categories according to the proposed theoretical model (Yin 1989). These categories are: (1) negotiation context factors, (2) strategic objectives of the partners for participating in the venture, (3) initial contributions of each partner to the joint venture, (4) the venture's management structure when it was formed, (5) changes that occurred during the joint venture's operation in each of the above areas, and (6) the extent to which each partner achieved its strategic objectives. Table 3 provides examples of data coding.

Second, subcategories were created using classifications adopted in previous research when appropriate (e.g., partner contributions in product design, special equipment, and production know-how were grouped into "technology"). Third, within each subcategory,

Table 3. Example of data coding.

Coding Category	Example
Negotiation context	"The Chinese were negotiating with a Japanese company the same time (while) negotiating with us." (Alternative partners)
Strategic objectives	"Our goals? We went to China to earn money, no question about that. We went there also to develop a significant market share in China, and to develop a low-cost sourcing base."
Initial contributions	"Most technology, about 80%, was imported from our American partner, but we contributed some equipment. Some of our equipment is still in use now."
Management structure	"Management of the firm will be two-tiered. The board of directors will have ten members with equal representation for each side... The chairman of the board will be from the PRC, and (the U.S. parent) will name the vice chairman. The second tier of management which will handle the day-to-day activities of the joint venture, also will be headed by the board chairman and vice chairman. The vice chairman, (the U.S. parent's) man, concurrently will hold the post of president of the joint venture."
Achievement of objective	(The U.S. firm) "now is one company who knows how to do business in China. I think this objective has been definitely achieved... We have established our credibility with the local people... Profitability? We are very profitable today. Profit margin is 49%."
Changes and dynamics	"In 1987, (the U.S. partner) shifted the production of this product to the joint venture, which significantly increased the joint venture's export and generated additional foreign exchange for us."
	"It takes much longer than we expected to transfer management to the Chinese... Though they have been pushing hard to cut the number of U.S. expatriates,... I would be reluctant to take any expatriates out in the first ten years of the joint venture."
	"Our first two objectives have been achieved. Low-cost sourcing (the third goal) has not... So, from an emphasis standpoint, probably the three objectives are now getting equal emphasis."

if inconsistency occurred between data collected from different sources, differences were reconciled either with additional sources of data or through verification by the original informants. For example, interview data on viable alternatives available to IndusCon's Chinese partner during the negotiation did not converge. We adopted the information provided by one of the informants, because support for this source was found in archival data contained in a published report by a third, independent source. Overall, as Table 4 shows, triangulation across different data sources revealed a high level of consistency.

Data coding was conducted by both researchers. We jointly developed the coding scheme and used the scheme to analyze one of the cases. Then, we divided the labor in coding the other three cases. One of the authors coded the data, while the other acted as an auditor (Lincoln and Guba 1985). The auditing role was performed by verifying both the process (the steps followed by the coder) and the product of data coding (maps and tables derived from the interview data).

Table 4. Triangulation of data.

Variables	Negotiation Context Factors	Strategic Objectives	Resource Contribution	Management Structure	Changes and Dynamics	Achievement of Objectives
Timing of assessment	Largely retrospective	Current and retrospective	Retrospective and current	Current and retrospective	Current with respect to past	Current
OfficeAid						
Data sources	Interviews (1, 2, 3, 4)	Interviews (1, 2, 3, 4) and archival	Interviews (1, 2, 3, 4) and archival	Interviews (1, 2, 3, 4) and archival	Interviews (1, 2, 3, 4)	Interviews (1, 2, 3, 4)
Cross-source agreement	Modestly high	High	Modestly high	High	High	Modestly high
IndusCon						
Data sources	Interviews (1, 3, 4) and archival	Interviews (1, 3, 4) and archival	Interviews (1, 3, 4) and archival	Interviews (1, 3, 4) and archival	Interviews (1, 3, 4)	Interviews (1, 3, 4) and archival
Cross-source agreement	Modestly high	High	High	High	High	High
DailyProduct						
Data sources	Interview (1, 3)	Interview (1, 3) and archival	Interview (1, 3) and archival	Interview (1, 3) and archival	Interview (1, 3)	Interview (1, 3) and archival
Cross-source agreement	*	High	High	High	*	High
BioTech Ltd.						
Data sources	Interviews (1, 2, 4) and archival	Interviews (1, 2, 4) and archival	Interviews (1, 2, 4) and archival	Interviews (1, 2, 4) and archival	Interviews (1, 2, 4)	Interviews (1, 2, 4)
Cross-source agreement	High	High	Modestly high	High	High	High

Informants representing: U.S. parent (1), Chinese parent (2), U.S. manager at the joint venture (3), Chinese manager at the joint venture (4).
*Data from single individual who was both a regional general manager of the U.S. parent and a general manager of the joint venture.
High: All sources of data are in agreement.
Modestly high: At least two sources are in agreement, while others are not.

2.4. Case analysis method

The method adopted in analyzing the cases is analytic induction (Znaniecki 1934; Robinson 1951; Glaser and Strauss 1967). In contrast to enumerative induction, which relies on statistical methods to generate simple, aggregate, and stable mental rules, analytic induction is a method for extending or refining existing theories by constantly comparing them with crucial instances or typical cases (Znaniecki 1934; Lindesmith 1947; Glaser and Strauss 1967). "The exceptional instance is the growing point of science... cumulative growth and progressive development of theory is obtained by formulating a generalization in such a way that negative cases force us either to reject the generalization or to revise it" (Lindesmith 1947, p. 12). Analytic induction involves the following steps:

> First, a rough definition of the phenomenon to be explained is formulated. Second, an hypothetical explanation of that phenomenon is formulated. Third, one case is studied... with the object of determining whether the hypothesis fits the facts in that case. Fourth, if the hypothesis does not fit the facts, either the hypothesis is reformulated or the phenomenon to be explained is re-defined, so that the case is excluded... Fifth, practical certainty may be attained after a small number of cases has been examined... Sixth, this procedure ... is continued until a universal relationship is established, each negative case calling for a redefinition or a reformulation. Seventh, for purposes of proof, cases outside the area circumscribed by the definition are examined to determine whether or not the final hypothesis applies to them. (Cressey, 1953, p. 16)

Following this procedure, we started with one case study and compared the findings with the theoretical model in Figure 1. Then, we modified the model based on the findings in the first case. This comparative process was repeated for each of the successive cases. Parkhe (1993a) has argued that the comparative case method is particularly appropriate for the study of joint ventures, given the need for rigorous theory development on the topic.

3. Findings

Although the logic of analytic induction was strictly followed (i.e., the cases were analyzed one by one in an incremental manner), because of the space limitations, we report only the final revision of the model. However, research findings on the relationships among the variables and the dynamic aspects of joint ventures will be presented case by case.

3.1. Bargaining power

Across the four cases, two components of negotiation context-based and seven of resource-based bargaining power were identified respectively (see Table 5). For each case, only those components that both partners acknowledged are listed.

Table 5. Relative bargaining power between the partners.

Components of Bargaining Power	OfficeAid	IndusCon	DailyProduct	BioTech Ltd.
	U.S. China	U.S. China	U.S. China	U.S. China
Context-based:				
Alternatives available	>>	<	=	=
Strategic importance	>	<	>	=
Resource-based:				
Technology	>>	>>	>	>
Management expertise	>	=	n.a.	=
Global service support	>>	n.a.	n.a.	n.a.
Local knowledge	<	<<	<	<
Product distribution	<	<	>>	<<
Material procurement	>	>	=	=
Equity	~=	~=	=	=
Overall bargaining power	>>	~=	>>	~=

>>: Higher level.
>: Moderately higher level.
=: Equal level.
~=: Approximately equal level.
n.a.: Not applicable (the item was not recognized by the partners).

3.1.1. Negotiation context-based. Evidence supporting the two components of context-based bargaining power (stakes and availability of alternatives) was present in all four cases. Stakes were reflected in the perceived strategic importance of the joint venture to the overall business of each parent. For example, BioTech was critically important to its U.S. parent, because this parent regarded China as one of its worldwide strategic markets. For the U.S. parent in DailyProduct, on the other hand, because the joint venture was nothing more than an experiment to test the Chinese market, the stakes were only marginally important.

Context-based bargaining power can also be derived from having alternatives, e.g., alternative partners with whom to negotiate and/or availability of existing channels through which to accomplish the same mission as the joint venture. For example, the Chinese partner in IndusCon was simultaneously engaged in negotiations with a Japanese firm and the U.S. partner. This enabled the Chinese to choose between two mutually competitive foreign firms, thereby increasing their bargaining power in negotiating with the U.S. company. In DailyProduct, because the local partner was "assigned" to the U.S. parent by the Chinese government, the U.S. firm had no alternatives. In another example, additional bargaining power accrued to the U.S. parent of OfficeAid, because they had existing business channels in China that could serve as alternative outlets. The U.S. firm's regional division in Hong Kong had previously exported to China, and this remained a viable alternative to the joint venture.

3.1.2. Resource-based. The components of resource-based bargaining power signify the resources and capabilities committed by the partners to the joint venture. These resource contributions are either explicitly specified in the joint-venture agreements (contracts, memorandums, or licenses) or verbally recognized by both partners during the negotiations. A consistent, complementary pattern is observed across all four cases with regard to the types of resource committed by the U.S. and by the Chinese partners, respectively. Predictably, the foreign firms contributed more heavily than did their local partners in technology (product design, manufacturing know-how, and special equipment) and global support (technical, marketing, and maintenance services), while the Chinese firms contributed more in knowledge about and skills to deal with the local government and other institutional infrastructures. IndusCon's U.S. parent's comments were illustrative:

> We have the technology and certain know-how. The Chinese partner knows how to make things happen in China. You put the two together right, it works.

In other areas, while both partners made contributions, apparent complementarity also existed. The U.S. partner tended to provide imported materials, channels for exporting the joint venture's product, and expertise in production management, while the Chinese partner contributed in areas of local sourcing, domestic distribution, and personnel management. In equity investment, both partners injected roughly the same amount of capital into all four joint ventures.

While both partners possessed bargaining power during the initial negotiations, the patterns of the relative bargaining power between the partners varied from one partnership to another. Since data is not available to assess the relative importance of each component in contributing to bargaining power, we assessed the relative bargaining power between the partners in each joint venture by assuming that all components contribute equally. In two of the four joint ventures (IndusCon and BioTech), bargaining power was balanced, or approximately equally shared between the partners. On the other hand, a significant imbalance in bargaining power occurred between the partners in the other two ventures (OfficeAid and DailyProduct), in which much higher bargaining power accrued to the U.S. partner. Overall patterns of the relative bargaining power between the partners are summarized at the bottom of Table 5.

3.2. Management control

Our data analysis revealed several unambiguous indicators of management control, which are congruent with the multidimensional notion of control (Geringer and Hebert 1989). Consistent with Schaan (1983, 1988), we found that nomination of the board of directors and of the joint venture's general manager were important control mechanisms. Both interview and archival data supported the important role played by the board of directors in making strategic decisions for the joint venture and solving critical problems regarding the partnership in general. The following quotes provide some evidence:

> We (the board) approve the annual budgets submitted by DailyProduct's management and decide everything important for its operation. When anything unexpected happens in China, I have to be there to talk to the Chinese chairman. (Vice-chairman of DailyProduct)

> The board of directors is empowered to discuss and take actions on all fundamental issues concerning the venture, namely, expansion projects, production and business programs, the budget, distribution of profits, plans concerning manpower and pay scales, the termination of business, the appointment or hiring of the president, the vice-president(s), the chief engineer, the treasurer and the auditors as well as their functions and powers and their remuneration, etc. (The Law of The People's Republic of China on Joint Ventures Using Chinese and Foreign Investment)

In each joint venture in this study, the board of directors meets at least twice a year to set annual goals, to review performance, and to approve operational plans for the venture.

Our data also suggest that substantial power is associated with the position of general manager in joint ventures. In each of the four ventures in this study, the general manager has always been a board member and served as the executive officer of the joint venture. General managers make important operating decisions for the ventures and act as the representatives of the respective parents to negotiate with the other partners on issues that arise unexpectedly. However, differences in decision power between the positions of general manager and deputy general manager (each is nominated by a different parent) vary significantly across our cases. In two joint ventures (OfficeAid and DailyProduct), the general manager exercised a higher level of control than did the deputy general manager, while in the other two ventures (IndusCon and BioTech), both positions were roughly equal in terms of control. For example, in OfficeAid,

> Eighty percent of the time he (the Chinese deputy general manager) would say "yes" when I made a decision... because I was the general manager, he was the deputy. If we didn't agree on anything, I made the decision. (The former U.S. general manager)

This is confirmed by a Chinese manager at OfficeAid who observed that "in the offices where there is an American manager, he will be in control though we have a deputy manager there." However, IndusCon and BioTech data suggest different stories, as revealed in the following quotes:

> The Chinese general manager and I were equals, co-managers. Mutual consulting between us continued throughout my term. This relationship was passed on to me from my predecessor. And it's true even today. (IndusCon's former deputy general manager from the U.S. parent)

> In organization design, our president (of the joint venture) should report to the Chinese chairman. However, in managing the joint venture, they are equally involved in making important decisions. (The U.S. parent of BioTech)

Another means through which the parents exercise control is associated with the way in which the joint venture is structured. We found that when the joint venture adopts a structure similar to one of its parent's with respect to its management system, decision process, and corporate policies, this parent exercises a higher level of control than its partner. In fact, the ability of this partner to replicate its way of managing in the joint venture reflects its level of control over the partnership, as the following quotes suggest:

> Three weeks after we hired the senior staff, we started training them in our corporate principles... We wanted to go through a process which is part of our management process, our management styles... I created a culture at the joint venture. (OfficeAid's first U.S. general manager)

> We structure the joint venture in China exactly the same way as we structure our organizations in other countries. In comparing with the Chinese state-run enterprises, we don't have the (Communist) party event and the union plays a very small role (DailyProduct's U.S. vice-chairman)

Our data also provide information about the overall control by each parent, as perceived by our interviewees. This indicator reflects both the scope and the extent of control (Geringer and Hebert 1989). Although relying on subjective judgments, the measure of perceived overall control may capture some aspects of control that cannot be covered by other, or more objective, measures. The following comments suggest that this indicator of control is important:

> (The U.S. company) always considers the joint venture as one of their own children and uses their own "standard model" to format it. They try to control it in great detail. (OfficeAid's Chinese deputy general manager)

> In making important decisions for BioTech, both sides make compromises. "Compromise" is the most appropriate word here. (BioTech's U.S. parent)

Table 6 summarizes the degree of control exercised by the partners in each case on the above four dimensions. On an overall basis, an imbalance in control favoring the U.S. parent occurred in OfficeAid and DailyProduct. In contrast, control in IndusCon and BioTech was approximately balanced between the parents.

Table 6. Management control between the partners.

Components of Management Control	OfficeAid		IndusCon		DailyProduct		BioTech Ltd.	
	U.S.	China	U.S.	China	U.S.	China	U.S.	China
Percent of board membership	=		<		=		=	
Nomination of key personnel	>>		~=		>>		<	
Similarity of management systems to parents'	>>		~=		>>		~=	
Perceived level of overall control	>>		~=		>>		~=	
Overall pattern of management control	>>		~=		>>		~=	

>>: Higher level.
>: Slightly higher level.
=: Equal level.
~=: Approximately equal level.

3.3. Venture performance

The four joint ventures exhibited considerable differences in the strategic objectives between the partners (see Table 7). The Chinese partners focused on upgrading technology and management and earning foreign exchange through export, while the U.S. partners aimed at penetrating the local market and earning a profit in China. These divergent, though potentially complementary, objectives imply that significant bias would occur if performance is assessed from only one partner's perspective or simply by using standard financial indicators if they were available. Moreover, in this study, we found that the joint-venture management did not provide performance assessment independent of those of the parents, because all the joint ventures operated under a close parent control. The joint venture's managers did not unitarily represent the partnership itself, but each acted as the representative of a respective parent. Therefore, it is inappropriate in this study to count the joint-venture managers' assessment of performance as independent of their parents', as previous researchers have suggested (Killing 1983; Anderson 1990).

The performance measure used in this study is the extent to which the partners have achieved their strategic objectives for initiating the joint venture. If an objective represents a long-term goal of a partner, we measure the extent to which satisfactory progress has

Table 7. Achievement of strategic objectives by the partners.

	Degree of Achievement			
Strategic Objectives	OfficeAid	IndusCon	DailyProduct	BioTech Ltd.
U.S.:				
Profit	Yes	Yes	Yes	Yes
Market share	Yes	Yes		Yes
Growth		Yes	Partially	
Local sourcing	No			
Learning			Yes	
Credibility with Chinese government			Yes	
U.S. partner's overall achievement	Largely achieved	All achieved	Largely achieved	All achieved
China:				
Technology	Partially	Mostly	Yes	Yes
Export	No		Yes	
Growth			Partially	Partially
Management				Yes
Import substitution		Yes		
Upstream technology		Yes		
Profit			Yes	
Chinese partner's overall achievement	Largely not achieved	Mostly achieved	Largely achieved	Largely achieved

been made by the venture toward the achievement of this goal. Using this measure fits well with the ways in which partners actually evaluate performance. The following comments by a U.S. firm are representative:

> The only appropriate criterion for performance evaluation is whether or not the partners and their stakeholders are happy with the joint venture's operation. The happiness for us is measured by its profitability and market share—the two most important goals we had... Our stakeholders are happy with what we have done in China.

Information about performance assessment for the joint ventures is presented in Table 7.

3.4. Relationship between bargaining power and management control

In the theoretical framework in Figure 1, the positive relationship between the relative bargaining power of the partners and the pattern of management control which they exercise was depicted. All four of our cases support this relationship. The relative bargaining power between the partners in two joint ventures (OfficeAid and DailyProduct) was uneven: the U.S. parent had higher bargaining power than did the local parent. Accordingly, in these two joint ventures, the U.S. partner exercised a higher level of management control than did its Chinese partners, for all indicators except the representation on the board, which was equally shared. For these two ventures, unevenly distributed bargaining power is associated with unbalanced management control. The partner who gained higher bargaining power during the negotiations exercised a higher level of management control in the venture. In the other two joint ventures (IndusCon and BioTech), both partners possessed roughly evenly matched bargaining power and exercised an equal level of management control over the venture. Overall, the pattern of relative bargaining power between the partners is consistent with, and positively related to, the pattern in which management control is shared between the partners (see Table 8).

Table 8. Overall patterns of bargaining power, management control, and performance.

	OfficeAid		IndusCon		DailyProduct		BioTech Ltd.	
Variables	U.S.	China	U.S.	China	U.S.	China	U.S.	China
Relative bargaining power	>		~=		>		~=	
Management control	>		~=		>		~=	
Venture performance	High	Low	Very high	Very high	High	High	Very high	High

>: Higher level.
~=: Approximately equal level.

3.5. Relationship between mangement control and performance

In the theoretical model in Figure 1, a direct, positive relationship is predicted between management control and performance. The bottom two rows in Table 7 depict the general patterns of management control and performance for each joint venture. Our findings suggest that the relationship between management control and performance was not as straightforward as predicted. To better understand how the cases deviate from the prediction, we focus on each individual case in the stepwise manner suggested by Cressey (1953).

3.5.1. OfficeAid. As discussed above, OfficeAid's U.S. parent exhibited a higher level of control than did the Chinese parent. With regard to performance, the U.S. parent has successfully achieved its two most important objectives, namely, profit and market share, respectively; though its objective to build a low-cost sourcing base in China has not yet been achieved. In contrast, the Chinese partner has only partially achieved one of its two equally important objectives (i.e., updating technology). Because the joint venture exported at a loss, the second Chinese objective of generating foreign exchange through export was not achieved. The significant imbalance at OfficeAid in achieving its parents' strategic expectations hindered the overall performance of the venture, which is the lowest among the four joint ventures.

The OfficeAid data seem to support the positive relationship between control and performance reported by previous studies (Killing 1983; Lecraw 1984). In other words, the partner who exercises a higher level of management control achieves a higher level of performance, judged from that partner's point of view.

3.5.2. IndusCon. In IndusCon the strategic objectives of both partners were realized (see Table 5). The U.S. partner has achieved its objectives of profitability and business expansion. IndusCon has been very profitable since its second year of operation. Because both partners reinvested all profit which the joint venture earned in the first five years, the venture grew rapidly. Regarding market penetration, the U.S. parent made the following assessment:

> Probably a couple of companies are bigger than we are in terms of volume per year. I think the market sees us as a quality company. . . We are definitely the leader in quality. We are high enough up there in volume. I think, on overall basis, if you ask the most potential customers in China who they consider as the quality leader company, they would probably say "IndusCon."

Nonetheless, the U.S. parent perceives that IndusCon still has room to grow, because its current market share is still below 10%, and the Chinese market is far from saturated.

The Chinese partner has also achieved its three objectives. First, by manufacturing locally, the joint venture has enabled the Chinese to reduce the level of imports of industrial control equipment—the principal objective of the Chinese partner. In the past ten years of operation, IndusCon has produced a variety of control systems which have been installed in many key Chinese industries. Second, regarding the objective of updating technology, the Chinese have been satisfied to the extent that IndusCon has become an important source of high-technology products in China. Third, IndusCon's efforts to upgrade the technical capacity of the local suppliers has increased localization of material sourcing, thus creating a "ripple" effect on the Chinese economy. As a result, IndusCon was twice selected as one of the "best run China–foreign joint ventures" in China in recent years. The Chinese partner is satisfied with the progress of technology transfer to date, though the key technology is still held by the U.S. partner. At an overall level, IndusCon stands as the best performer among the four ventures in this study, because it has achieved both of its parents' objectives.

In IndusCon, the partners exercise an equivalent level of management control, and both of them have achieved their strategic objectives. This finding contrasts with previous studies predicting inferior performance in joint ventures with shared management (Killing 1983), but it is consistent with Beamish's (1984, 1985, 1993) findings that shared or split control is superior for international joint ventures in developing countries. The inconsistencies between the OfficeAid and IndusCon data suggest that the previously proposed relationship between control and performance (e.g., proportional for each individual parent) underspecified the relationship. The inconsistencies can be reconciled, however, if we raise the level of analysis from the individual parent level to the level of that between parents. In OfficeAid, a relatively *unbalanced* level of management control (control was unequally shared) between the parents was associated with an *unbalanced* level of performance (high for the U.S. parent, while low for the Chinese parent). Similarly, in IndusCon, *balanced* or equally shared management control between the partners resulted in a *balanced* level of performance (both high in this case). To sum, then, the fact of whether the pattern of management control is balanced or unbalanced between the partners is associated with a similar pattern of performance in terms of the achievement of both partners' strategic objectives.

3.5.3. DailyProduct. Three out of the four strategic objectives of the U.S. partner, namely, learning how to do business in China, establishing credibility with the Chinese government, and earning a profit in operating the joint venture, have been completely achieved. The U.S. partner indicated that the joint venture achieved a 49% profit margin. With regard to the U.S. partner's third objective (expanding the business of personal hygiene products), some progress has been made (e.g., the venture's production has exceeded the planned capacity by 50%); however, their hope for market expansion was achieved to only a limited extent.

The Chinese partner has achieved its three most important objectives: earning a profit, exporting for foreign exchange, and updating the manufacturing technology at the joint venture. The Chinese objective of growth has been achieved only to the extent that the volume of the existing products has been increased beyond the original expectation. However, since the U.S. partner had some reservations about the transferring other products to the joint venture, the Chinese partner has not yet fulfilled the objective of expanding to its partner's other businesses. Nevertheless, DailyProduct has been successful in meeting most of its parents' expectations; its overall performance is much higher than OfficeAid, yet seems slightly lower than IndusCon.

DailyProduct displays an apparently different relationship between control and performance than what we found in the previous two ventures: Management control has been unequally shared between the parents, but performance has been balanced (both partners have achieved their most important strategic objectives). In other words, in DailyProduct, unbalanced control between the parents is associated with a balanced and moderately high level of performance. This forced us to reconsider the proposed direct relationship between balanced (unbalanced) control and high (low) performance.

Further examination suggests several factors that might have accounted for the relationship between control and performance revealed in DailyProduct. First, unlike the previous two ventures, in which the partners have radically different strategic goals, both partners in DailyProduct share some common objectives (e.g., profitability in hard currency). Thus, the achievement of one parent's objectives also means the achievement of the other parent's. Also, because both parents share a common destiny, conflict over how to operate the business is less likely to occur. Common goals may serve as an informal control mechanism which renders the pattern of formal management control less critical than in the case in which the partners' objectives radically diverge.

A second factor that might have accounted for the control-performance relationship in DailyProduct is that the most important objectives of the Chinese (the low-control partner) were incorporated in the partnership's operating plans, which is part of the joint-venture contract. Both parties agreed that within the first 18 months after start-up, the joint venture should (1) achieve an annual capacity of 50 million (for Product I) and 4 million (for Product II), (2) make a profit, (3) achieve surplus in foreign exchange, and (3) export 30% for Product I and 70% for Product II. These specific contractual stipulations probably have served as an alternative means of control for the weaker partner to ensure that its goals were reached.

A third, and probably the most important, factor is the high level of trust developed between the partners in DailyProduct. After the first 18 months of operation, when the joint venture's plan was alrady realized, the Chinese partner developed a very high level of trust with respect to its U.S. partner. After that period of time, "trust was no longer a problem. They trust us and leave the business to us," the U.S. partner observed. Therefore, mutual trust may be an important contingent or moderating factor of the control-performance relationship when management control between partners is unequally shared.

3.5.4. BioTech. The U.S. parent of BioTech has achieved both of its strategic objectives (market share and profit). BioTech has been very profitable, and acquired the highest market share among all international pharmaceutical joint ventures in China. The Chinese partner has achieved its first and second objectives: to update manufacturing technology and to gain the advanced Western management expertise needed for running a high-technology pharmaceutical enterprise. The Chinese are satisfied with the venture's business growth, because it has continuously added new pharmaceutical products. However, this objective has been achieved to only a limited extent, because the Chinese expectation of extending the business to the U.S. partner's other products (e.g., nutrition products) has not yet been achieved. Overall, similar to DailyProduct, BioTech demonstrates strong performance in achieving most of its parents' objectives.

The BioTech data provided confirmatory evidence for the relationship between management control and performance revealed in the previous cases: equally shared management control between the partners was associated with a balanced and relatively high performance for the partners. In fact, in regard to the control-performance relationships, BioTech is very similar to IndusCon.

3.6. Dynamic aspects of international joint ventures

The findings reported above are based on static analyses. But joint-venture arrangements do not necessarily remain static. In this study, we also secured information about how the joint venture had changed from its formation to date. We sought to identify sources of change that prompted shifts in partners' bargaining power since its initial configuration and that drove the joint venture toward structural reconfigurations. These changes are reflected in the feedback arrows in Figure 2. Next, we will first analyze the dynamic development of each joint venture and then summarize the cross-case effects.

3.6.1. OfficeAid. Since the joint venture's inception, the Chinese personnel in the venture have acquired some management expertise, operational techniques, and the production know-how associated with the existing products. At the same time, the Chinese engineers have become involved in the R&D process, thus making a technological contribution to the joint venture. These changes have had a positive effect on the Chinese partner's bargaining power.

On the other hand, changes have also occurred in the U.S. partner's bargaining power. First, the U.S. partner has gradually become experienced in operating in the Chinese system. The former American general manager indicated that he made friends with several important officials in the municipal government, including the mayor. Second, the U.S. partner has continuously provided new product designs for the venture, therefore firmly maintaining its position as a principal contributor in technology. Third, since the ten-year technology transfer agreement is subject to renegotiation, the U.S. partner has already begun using

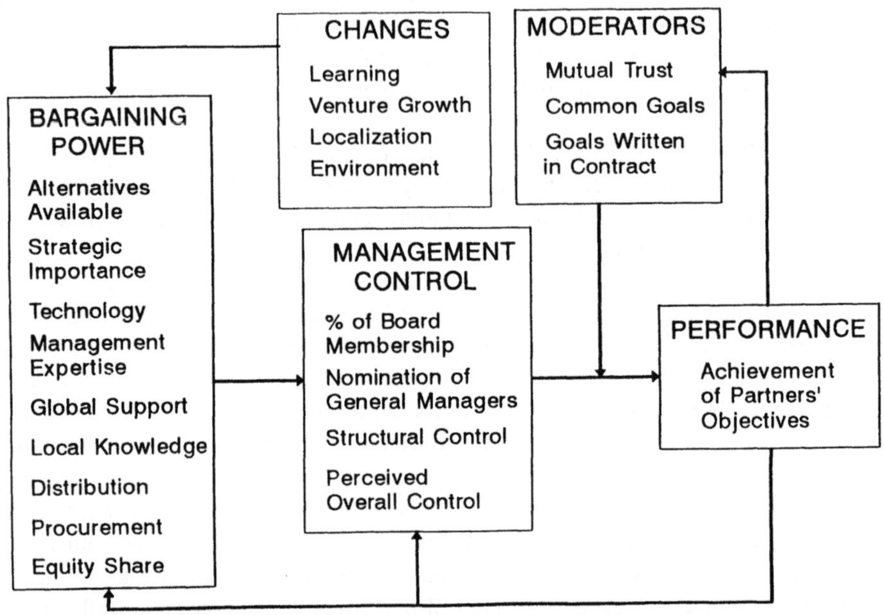

Figure 2. An integrative model of international joint ventures.

the renewal as leverage to gain additional bargaining power. All these factors have increased the bargaining power of the U.S. partner and offset the gains in the Chinese partner's bargaining power.

In addition, the growth of the partnership itself and changes in the local environment have altered the bargaining power of the partners. For example, the increase in local content and establishment of separate distribution channels have enabled the joint venture to become less dependent on its U.S. parent for imported materials and on its Chinese parent for marketing skills, respectively, thus, reducing the bargaining power of each parent. Additionally, because of the legalization of swap markets for obtaining foreign exchange, export has become less necessary. As a result, the U.S. partner's international distribution channels are less valuable to the joint venture now.

No significant changes have occurred in the initial pattern of control in OfficeAid. Despite the reduction in the number of the U.S. expatriates (from seven to five) in the past four years, the remaining five have the same extent of management responsibilities as their predecessors.

However, an undercurrent of struggle for control between the partners has persisted in OfficeAid. The Chinese have kept urging reductions in the number of U.S. expatriates and allocations of greater management responsibilities to the Chinese staff. For example, the Chinese partner has been expecting that the next general manager of the joint venture will be a Chinese. On the other hand, the U.S. partner has continuously made attempts to enhance its control. In 1988, the U.S. partner proposed to add a nonvoting U.S. observer to the board, but the Chinese countered with a similar request to keep the balance. Subsequently, the U.S. partner proposed restructuring the board:

> We have been hoping to go to a board of nine members instead of eight by adding a ninth from us. We were rejected, expectedly rejected. We may be able to throw in some sweeteners to make it more acceptable. (The U.S. partner)

With regard to potential shifts of management responsibilities to the locals:

> We are absolutely convinced if we let them manage the operations tomorrow, things will fail six months from now... I would be reluctant to take any expatriates out in the first ten years of the venture. (The U.S. partner)

Several changes in the partner's strategic objectives have been reported. First, because swap markets became available for foreign exchange, and the joint venture has been running at a loss in export, the Chinese partner modified their original objectives. At a board meeting in December 1991, the Chinese directors proposed that the venture abandon export as a channel for earning hard currency. Also, the Chinese partner added profit to its list of objectives, presumably as a result of the changes in government policies, which has empowered Chinese companies to keep a substantial portion of their operational gains. Since the U.S. parent's most important goals (profitability and market share) have been reached, low-cost sourcing has increased in importance. "From an emphasis standpoint, probably the three objectives are now getting equal emphasis" (the U.S. parent). Overall, OfficeAid's unbalanced record of performance has induced mistrust between the partners.

The Chinese partner attributed the loss in exports to the low internal transfer price set by the U.S. partner and perceived the U.S. partner's heavy intervention in the joint venture's operation as taking away the child from its Chinese parent. The U.S. partner acknowledged the issue of mistrust:

> I don't think we have, in all honesty, the level of trust between the parties that we should have... There always has been such a level of distrust, always a level of suspicion, specifically from the Chinese, that the foreigners are trying to take advantage of them.

3.6.2. IndusCon. The Chinese partner in IndusCon, like its counterpart in OfficeAid, has gained some bargaining power by learning about the management techniques and technological know-how over the past ten years. However, since technology in this industry is rapidly outdated and key production know-how is still kept at the U.S. partner's headquarters, the U.S. partner retains significant bargaining power, because the joint venture still heavily depends on it for up-to-date technology and new product designs. In 1987, the U.S. partner gained additional bargaining power by shifting production of a product marketed worldwide to China. This significantly increased the joint venture's exports and generated additional foreign exchange for the local partner.

Additional shifts in bargaining power were prompted by procurement and marketing changes. IndusCon now has its own procurement staff in the U.S., and no longer depends on its U.S parent for imported parts. Second, with the increase in local content, the joint venture has become more dependent on the Chinese sourcing channels, thus increasing the Chinese partner's bargaining power. Third, the Chinese partner's bargaining power diminished significantly when one of its wholly owned companies was acquired by the joint venture. This company was the exclusive distributor for the joint venture's products in the Chinese market.

The pattern of management control between the parents in IndusCon has not significantly shifted, because changes in bargaining power occurred simultaneously to both parents and in a relatively equal manner. More importantly, the superior performance of IndusCon has enhanced the level of trust between the partners and provided confirmatory evidence that the current control structure has worked well, therefore, no changes have been necessary. Because both parents' strategic objectives are long-term in nature, no changes in objectives were in evidence in IndusCon.

3.6.3. DailyProduct. As in previous cases, the local partner in DailyProduct has gained power by learning some technical know-how and management techniques. However, the U.S. partner's bargaining power has increased more significantly overall. Its contribution in management expertise, though initially not valued by the Chinese partner, is now acknowledged as a critical asset. Additionally, because the U.S. firm has achieved its strategic objectives (learning how to operate in China and building credibility with the Chinese), the strategic importance of the partnership to them has decreased significantly. These two changes, coupled with the more open foreign investment policy in China since 1984, have enabled the U.S. partner to launch negotiations for a majority joint venture in another Chinese city. Finally, high performance levels have satisfied the Chinese partner's most important objective, and thereby strengthened the U.S. parent's dominance. As the venture's U.S. vice chairman observed,

> Over time, the decision making process has changed. In the beginning we had to argue on some issues, but now, they would just let us make decisions though it is still a 50:50 joint venture... They absolutely trust us. They know that we can make money for them.

3.6.4. BioTech Ltd. The Chinese partner in BioTech gained bargaining power by learning the Western management techniques and technical know-how and through increased local content in the joint venture's products. However, the bargaining power of the U.S. partner increased substantially through its contribution in marketing expertise. When BioTech was formed, all its products were purchased and distributed by the local partner. As China was transforming its economic system from centrally planned to market oriented, the former distribution networks collapsed. In 1986 the U.S. partner was informed that its former Chinese partner was dismantled over night and that the local government would no longer buy any products from the joint venture. Since the local partner was not familiar with selling in a free market, the U.S. partner's contributions in building a distribution network and in training the venture's marketing staff increased its relative bargaining power.

These changes in the partners' bargaining power produced only a slight adjustment in control, namely, the nomination of one more expatriate manager responsible for marketing. As in IndusCon, a key factor that might have stabilized the pattern of control in BioTech is its superior performance. That is, if performance is good, the status quo is preserved.

3.6.5. Summary. Several factors that prompt shifts in the partner's relative bargaining power and trigger structural reconfigurations in joint ventures over time have been identified. They are summarized below.

(1) *Partner's learning*. Learning between joint-venture partners has been recognized by previous researchers. Vernon (1977) coined the term the "obsolescing bargain" to capture the impact of learning on bargaining power. More recently, Hamel (1991) argued that the effective learner in international joint ventures will raise the "price" for its continued participation in the partnership. This learning effect has been observed in all of our cases for both partners. However, our data suggest that the Chinese partners did not significantly gain bargaining power through learning. This is probably because the U.S. partners were cautious in transferring their technologies to their joint ventures and kept key technological secrets firmly in their own hands, or because these technologies are low in "transparency," so that there are high barriers to learning (Hamel 1991).

(2) *Growth of the joint venture's own capacity*. Over time, international joint ventures accumulate their own bases of knowledge and skills, thus becoming less dependent on their parents (Prahalad and Doz 1981). However, if this accumulation is accomplished in an unbalanced manner by acquiring knowledge or skills only from one parent, that parent's contribution will eventually be devalued. As a result, changes in the existing pattern of bargaining power between the parents will occur. OfficeAid exemplifies this type of change when it adopted the Chinese parent's distribution channels and developed the network for its own use.

(3) *Localization*. Our data suggest that material procurement channels for the joint venture constitute a source of bargaining power for the partner who provides these channels. Since both partners have inherent, though different, motivations for increasing local content (e.g., for the local partner to cultivate domestic suppliers, for the foreigner to reduce cost, and for both to save foreign exchange), this change can diminish the bargaining power of the partner, typically the foreign partner, on whom the joint venture depends for imported materials. Bargaining power changes resulting from localization were observed in all our case studies.

(4) *Environment changes*. Changes in the local environment, particularly in government policies can trigger structural reconfigurations in joint ventures. Relaxation of the prohibitions on direct foreign investment enabled IndusCon to acquire the sales and service company formerly owned by its Chinese parent. Similarly, this policy change afforded DailyProduct's U.S. parent the opportunity to form a new, majority joint venture, and thus to reduce the strategic importance of DailyProduct to that parent. More strikingly, the collapse of the state distribution network caused by the macro-system transformation induced the U.S. partner in BioTech to contribute its marketing expertise, and thereby to increase its bargaining power. These findings support the theoretical prediction that environmental changes can shift the original bargaining agreement between the partners (Harrigan and Newman 1990; Sharfman, Gray, and Yan 1991), therefore reconfiguring the venture's structure.

(5) *Performance*. The ongoing performance of joint ventures has an important feedback effect on the partners' relative bargaining power and the existing structure of control. While Killing (1983) noted that joint-venture parents enhance or loosen control over the venture as a response to its performance, our data suggest that performance also impacts the relative bargaining power and the pattern of management control *between* the parents. Superior performance creates an additional bargaining chip for the partner which is currently in control (e.g., in DailyProduct), or reinforces the extant control pattern (e.g., in the other three ventures). In addition, performance may also have a feedback effect on the moderating variables, especially on the mutual trust relationship between the partners. Superior performance enhances inter-partner trust over time (as exemplified in all the joint ventures except OfficeAid), while mediocre or poor performance (e.g., significantly unbalanced performance in OfficeAid) will cause distrust between the partners, which, in turn, can potentially deteriorate the venture's long-term performance (Killing 1983).

3.7. Toward an integrative model of bargaining power, control, and performance

Our findings regarding bargaining power, management control, performance, and the dynamic aspects of international joint ventures are summarized in an integrative model in Figure 2. The consistent evidence generated across all the case studies suggests a direct, positive relationship between bargaining power and management control. Though our data are not sufficient to test the relative importance of each component of bargaining power in shaping the joint venture's structure, they suggest that the overall pattern of the partner's relative bargaining power is highly related to how control is shared between parents. In addition, the pattern of management control in joint ventures is positively related to venture performance, although this relationship is not necessarily proportional. When the partners' control in the joint venture is evenly matched, an approximately equal level of performance from both partners' perspectives is expected. On the other hand, when control is unevenly shared between the partners, prediction of performance is less straightforward. The data suggest three alternative control mechanisms that moderate the relationship between formal management control and performance: the level of trust between the partners, the commonality of partners' strategic objectives, and the level of institutionalization of the partners' objectives, e.g., whether or not they are explicitly specified in contractual terms. When these moderating variables are present, management control is less predictive of performance. In addition, the relative bargaining power between the partners changes over time as a result of partners' learning, growth of the joint venture's own capacity, localization of the joint venture's operation, and environmental changes. The ongoing performance of the partnership exerts an important feedback effect on the partners' bargaining power, the existing pattern of management control, and the quality of the cooperative relationship between the partners. The relationships discussed above and depicted in Figure 2 are summarized in the following propositions:

Proposition 1. The relative bargaining power between potential joint venture partners will be positively related to the structure of management control that they exercise over the joint venture's operation.

Proposition 2. The structure of management control shared between the joint venture parents will be positively related to the pattern of venture performance.

Proposition 3. Relational characteristics of the joint venture partners (e.g., mutual trust, commonality of partner strategic objectives, and institutionalization of partner goals) will moderate the relationship between parent control and performance.

Proposition 4. Changes in the partners' bargaining power prompted by the environment, parents' strategies, and the joint venture's maturity will trigger reconfigurations of the venture's management control structure, which, in turn, will cause performance fluctuations.

Proposition 5. Performance changes in the joint venture will alter the existing balance of the partners' bargaining power, the current structure of control, and the trust relationship between the partners.

4. Discussion and conclusions

4.1. Ownership and management control

Our findings lead us to question the validity of treatment by previous studies that use ownership as a proxy for management control in joint ventures (Stopford and Wells 1972; Fagre and Wells 1982; Blodgett 1991). By and large, all four joint ventures in this study are equally shared ownership ventures.[2] However, while two of them showed balanced management control, the other two demonstrated an unbalanced, one-parent dominant pattern of control. Within each joint venture, we found that the ownership split is consistent with only one dimension of control (board membership). With respect to other dimensions, no consistent relationship was observed.

The results of our study also challenge the prevailing assumptions in the literature that all potential joint-venture partners prefer 100% ownership and that equity split between the partners is an outcome of negotiation as a representation of relative power between participating interests (Fagre and Wells 1982; Blodgett 1991). Our data tell a different story. In all four joint ventures in this study, ownership structure was voluntarily decided between the partners at the outset of the negotiations. As our interviewee at OfficeAid's U.S. parent noted,

> We could go wholly owned but I am against it. I don't see the end experiences in China with a wholly owned foreign enterprise. You go there as a foreign company and you really have nothing to work with.

Moreover, a mutually agreed ownership split for a prospective partnership is perceived by the partners as a "threshold" for seriously starting negotiations. As one of our interviewees noted; "You either accept it, at least in principle, to start the negotiation; or you reject it. Then, negotiations will never happen." This evidence is consistent with previous reports that the ownership pattern in international joint ventures in China has reflected both partners' needs and has not posed a major issue in joint-venture negotiations (Davidson 1987; Pearson 1991).

Overall, our findings provide additional evidence that the equity structure is not equivalent to management control. Rather, as a type of resource committed by the partners, equity investment constitutes a source of bargaining power, which, in turn, contributes to management control. Once the equity structure is agreed upon, it delineates the relative positions of the partners and sets a tone for the successive negotiations on control.

4.2. Each partner versus the partnership

This research provides consistent evidence across the four cases that the relative bargaining power between the partners is positively related to management control. It is important to note, however, that this positive relationship exists only at the inter-partner level when the patterns of bargaining power and control are examined from both partners' perspectives. That is, we are focussing on the interactive relationship between the partners as the unit of analysis. This finding helps to explain the conflicting results regarding the relationship between bargaining power and control in previous studies (e.g., between Lecraw 1984 and Beamish 1984), since the former examined this relationship from only one partner's perspective). Our data suggest that control in joint ventures is not unilaterally chosen by either partner, as suggested by previous research, but is a result of bargaining. Our approach also helps to reconcile the inconsistencies suggested by previous studies concerning the relationship between control and performance (Geringer and Hebert 1989). The positive control-performance relationship does not hold at each partner's level in our results. We suggest that the prevailing assumption that the higher the level of control by a partner, the higher the level of performance from that partner's point of view is incomplete at best. Instead, the positive relationship between control and performance exists only at the inter-partner level when the *patterns* of control between the partners and performance from *both* partners' point of view are examined.

Furthermore, our findings are consistent with those of pervious researchers who argue that the control-performance relationship is not always positive and direct (Geringer and Hebert 1989). However, the indirect effects identified in this study (inter-partner trust, the commonality of the goals between the partners, and institutionalization of partners' objectives) are different from those in the literature (e.g., the multinational parent's strategy, Franko 1971; strategy-structure fit, Janger 1980; Geringer and Hebert 1989), and fit between the areas of control and control mechanisms, Schaan 1983, 1988). The variation between our results and previous research, again, reflects the difference in the unit of analysis adopted in this study (i.e., inter-partner relationships instead of the multinational partner). Since previous studies, typically, did not even query the host-country partner, their arguments may be distorted or, at best, incomplete. One recent study, however, has provided evidence that cultural differences among the partners affects how they define trust and the relative importance it has in structuring performance assessment (Parkhe 1993b).

4.3. Shared versus dominant control

With respect to the impact of different control types (Killing 1983; Gray and Yan 1992), this study also differs from previous work. According to Killing (1983), shared control is the most problematic and often leads to inferior performance. Our data suggest the opposite: that the joint ventures with equally shared control (IndusCon and BioTech) demonstrated superior performance. This inconsistency may reflect differences in the sample of joint ventures studied (those between two developed countries versus those with a partner from a developing country). In developing-country joint ventures, management control exercised by the foreign and the local partners may be more differentiated and complementary, and thus less likely to prompt struggles and conflicts between the partners, than in ventures between developed-country partners. In this respect, our findings are consistent with Beamish (1988, 1993), who recommends shared management structure for international partnerships in less developed countries. However, our case data do not consistently support the negative relationship between foreign parent dominant control and performance that Beamish (1984) found. Rather, our findings suggest that such a relationship holds only when alternative means of control (reflected by the moderating variables) are absent. When a high level of mutual trust exists between the partners, or the partners share common objectives, or the partners' goals are highly institutionalized, foreign parent-dominant joint ventures can still satisfy both partners' needs. This finding supports Beamish's (1988) and Koenig and van Wijk's (1991) arguments that inter-partner trust is critical to venture success, and particularly, Thorelli's (1986) observations that trust may supplant contractual arrangements in Oriental cultures (see also Parkhe 1993b). The moderating variables revealed in this research suggest that both formal and informal means of control are necessary for predicting joint venture performance. These conclusions are suggestive at best, given our methodology, but they do offer insights that clarify the inconsistencies in previous research on the control-performance relationship.

4.4. *The imprinting effect*

The in-depth case studies also enabled us to explore the dynamic aspects of international joint ventures. We identified several factors that prompted changes in the relative bargaining power between the partners. However, structural reconfigurations in these four joint ventures were not observed. Significant shifts in management control between the partners did not occur. This structural stability seems to suggest the "imprinting" effect noted by organization theorists (Scott 1987). Since each organization requires a particular combination of economic, technical, and social resources during its formation stage, the building of such resource bases may set an organization on a course from which it becomes difficult to deviate (Stinchcombe 1965). Scott (1987) argues that once an organization is established, the basic characteristics present at its founding tend to be retained for a long period of time. While our data reveal no shifts in management-control patterns to date, changes in the components comprising the bargaining power of each partner have been observed in each joint venture. However, in none of the cases did the *relative* bargaining power between the parents shift significantly. In each venture, the foreign partner's resource contributions increased over time, but that partner did not experience a commensurate increase in control. This probably results from a diminishing of the initial bargaining power of the foreign partner over time (Dymsza 1988), particularly when the local partner is learning-oriented (Hamel 1991). This diminishing effect may also be attributable to the "sunk cost" or the fixed, highly specific investment made by the foreign partner as a "hostage" in the joint venture (Smith and Wells 1975; Williamson 1983). Therefore, the U.S. partner's increased resource contributions to the partnership simply replenish its naturally depreciated power or offset increases in bargaining power due to learning by the Chinese partner. Thus, an overall balance of bargaining power (and control) is preserved.

4.5. *Conclusions*

The findings of this comparative case study provide confirmative evidence that the relative bargaining power between the joint-venture partners has a significant impact on the pattern of parent control in the venture's management. By adopting a negotiations perspective that focuses on the partners' interdependence, we have been able to unpack some of the complexities of joint-venture formation, management, and performance, and to clarify the reasons for some of the conflicting or incomplete results of previous studies, which focused only on the multinational partner's perspective. By identifying factors that induce changes in the partner's bargaining power, our analyses also provide insight into the dynamic development of international joint ventures.

Are theories initiated in the West applicable in the Chinese setting? Our findings suggest yes. The key relationships in the theoretical model in Figure 1, which was primarily based on the works of the Western researchers, received significant support from our Chinese sample. In this respect, this study offers strong evidence that theories developed in the West are relevant and applicable to Chinese joint ventures. On the other hand, our findings on the nature of the relationships among the key variables, the moderating variables on the relationship between parent control and performance, and the dynamic evolution of international joint ventures enrich the current literature and provide new clues for future research on joint ventures in other countries, particularly on partnerships formed between developed- and developing-country sponsors.

Some special characteristics of Chinese joint ventures are noteworthy. First, significant differences exist in the strategic objectives between the foreign and local partners. Multinational firms form joint ventures in China primarily to penetrate the local market and to pursue financial goals. To them, market share and profitability are important measures of venture performance. In contrast, the Chinese partner is more technology-oriented. The overwhelming motivation for cooperating with the West is to learn the more advanced Western technology. The strong contrast of objectives between the partners, though they may be complementary, provides both partners with strong incentives to exercise managment control over the venture's operation, because control is perceived as the most critical means of fulfilling their strategic intentions. Second, in the interest of learning, the Chinese expect, from the outset, that management will be shifted from the foreigners to the locals over time. As a result, in order to maintain control, the foreign partner will have to make continuing commitments of resources in order to maintain the original balance of bargaining power. Therefore, in Chinese joint ventures, management control is a long-term issue, about which continuing renegotiations between the partners should be expected.

4.5.1. Limitations. Several limitations of the study should be acknowledged. First, the empirical research reported here was based on data from U.S.–China joint ventures. Characteristics idiosyncratic to Chinese joint ventures, such as government influence and seemingly strong complementarity of partner objectives, might have impacted the research results. Therefore, generalization of our findings to other joint ventures should be made with caution. The resultant model of this study needs further testing on a larger sample of Chinese joint ventures, as well as on joint ventures in other countries. Second, since Chinese joint ventures necessarily have short histories, our analysis of the dynamic evolution of international alliances is limited by the longevity of the partnerships. Additional research using longitudinal data is needed to learn how joint-venture structural reconfigurations prompt changes in venture performance over time. A third limitation of the study is associated with the homogeneity of the sample—most of the joint ventures in the sample were relatively high-performing ventures. Although they may be representative, because joint ventures in China in general are more successful than their counterparts in other countries (Beamish 1993), our performance variable may not have enough variance to ensure that we have captured all of the potential factors affecting venture performance. Fourth, the analyses conducted in this study were partially based on retrospective data, which might have introduced an additional source of bias, as a result of faulty memory or retrospective sense making on the part of our informants. This problem, however, is not critical, because, in most cases and for most variables, multiple sources of data were available, and data triangulation among these sources has revealed a high level of consistency. A final limitation may be related to sampling. This study is restricted to manufacturing joint ventures. Future work on Chinese joint ventures needs to investigate the applicability of the model to international partnerships in service industries.

4.5.2. Future research directions. Finally, we offer several suggestions for future research which will extend this study and overcome several of its limitations. (1) Regarding international joint ventures in countries like China, in which the local government plays a role, greater specification of the functions performed by the government and the local company is needed. Additional research should investigate whether the achievement of the individual Chinese partner's objectives supersedes those of the Chinese government in newly formed joint ventures. (2) This study suggests that formal and informal control mechanisms interact and jointly impact venture performance. Future research should pay more attention to the informal aspects of control (particularly, the inter-partner trust relationship, partner's long-term commitment, and joint development of partner competence) and their impact on performance. (3) Valuable insights into the dynamic relationship between bargaining power and management control can be gained from studies that trace the formation processes on a real-time basis. This may further clarify the causal relationships between the two phenomena and the relative importance of contextual power and resource-based power possessed by the partners. It would also shed light on the intriguing question of whether characteristics of joint venture formation imprinted at birth ultimately determine the success and failure rates of international partnerships. (4) The model derived from this research needs to be tested by using larger samples and with joint ventures created by partners from different countries. In order to capture the dynamic characteristics of joint ventures, investigations using longitudinal, repeated-measures designs are needed.

Notes

1. Yin's (1989) position that case studies should start with a priori theoretical propositions obviously contrasts with Eisenhardt's (1989) argument that case study should start with a clean theoretical slate, so that the researchers are less likely to be bound by preconceived theoretical notions. However, an ideal of a clean theoretical slate is virtually impossible to achieve (Parkhe 1993a), given the accumulative nature of scientific inquiry (Kuhn 1970), the education which the researcher has received from prior theories, and the potentially infinite number of variables affecting a phenomenon under study.
2. Most international joint ventures formed in early 1980s in China adopted a relatively equal ownership structure or foreign minority ownership, though this pattern has been changing in recent years as a result of the more open attitude of the Chinese government toward foreign investment in China. However, legislatively, the Chinese Joint Venture Law (both July 1, 1979 and April, 7. 1990 versions) specifies only a lower limit (25%) but not upper constraints with respect to the levels of foreign ownership in joint ventures. In fact, foreign majority partnerships and even wholly owned foreign subsidiaries were possible even in years prior to 1985 (Pearson 1991), though only a limited number of such ventures were actually formed.

References

Anderson, E. (1990). "Two Firms, One Frontier: On Assessing Joint Venture Performance," *Sloan Management Review* (Winter), 19–30.
Arrow, K.J. (1974). *The Limits of Organization*. New York: W.W. Norton & Co., Inc.

Bacharach, S.B., and J.L. Lawler. (1984). *Bargaining: Power, Tactics, and Outcomes*. San Francisco, CA: Jossey-Bass.

Bartlett, C.A., and S. Ghoshal. (1986). "Tap Your Subsidiaries for Global Reach," *Harvard Business Review* 6, 87–94.

Beamish, P.W. (1984). "Joint Venture Performance in Developing Countries." Unpublished doctoral disseration, University of Western Ontario.

Beamish, P.W. (1985). "The Characteristics of Joint Ventures in Developed and Developing Countries," *Columbia Journal of World Business* 20(3), 13–19.

Beamish, P.W. (1988). *Multinational Joint Ventures in Developing Countries*. New York: Routledge.

Beamish, P.W. (1993). "Characteristics of Joint Ventures in the People's Republic of China," *Journal of International Marketing* 1, 29–48.

Blodgett, L.L. (1991). "Partner Contributions as Predictors of Equity Share in International Joint Ventures," *Journal of International Business Studies* (First Quarter), 63–78.

Campbell, N. (1988). *A Strategic Guide to Equity Joint Ventures in China*. New York: Pergamon.

Child, J. (1991). "Managerial Adaptation in Reforming Economies: The Case of Joint Ventures." Presented at the Academy of Management Meetings, Miami Beach, FL (August 13, 1991).

Chowdhury, M.A.J. (1988). "International Joint Ventures: Some Interfirm Organization-Specific Determinants of Success and Failure—A Factor Analytic Exploration." Unpublished doctoral dissertation, Temple University.

Contractor, F.J. (1990). "Ownership Patterns of U.S. Joint Ventures Abroad and the Liberalization of Foreign Government Regulations in the 1980s: Evidence from the Benchmark Surveys," *Journal of International Business Studies* 21(1), 55–73.

Cressey, D.R. (1953). *Other People's Money*. Glencoe, IL: The Free Press.

Daniels, J.D., J. Krug, and D. Nigh. (1985). "U.S. Joint Ventures in China: Motivation and Managment of Political Risk," *California Management Review* (Summer), 46–58.

Davidson, W.H. (1982). *Global Strategic Management*. New York: John Wiley & Sons.

Davidson, W.H. (1987). "Creating and Managing Joint Ventures in China," *California Management Review* (Summer), 77–94.

Diesing, P. (1972). *Patterns of Discovery in the Social Sciences*. London: Routledge & Kegan Paul.

Dwyer, R.F., and O.C. Walker. (1981). "Bargaining in an Asymmetrical Power Structure," *Journal of Marketing* (Winter), 104–115.

Dymsza, W.A. (1988). "Successes and Failures of Joint Ventures in Developing Countries: Lessons from Experience." In F.J. Contractor and P. Lorange (eds.), *Cooperative Strategies in International Business*. Lexington, MA: Lexington Books, 403–424.

Eisenhardt, K.M. (1989). "Building Theories from Case Study Research," *Academy of Management Review* 14, 532–550.

Eiteman, D.K. (1990). "American Executives' Perceptions of Negotiating Joint Ventures with the People's Republic of China: Lessons Learned," *Columbia Journal of World Business* (Winter), 59–67.

Fagre, N., and L.T. Wells, Jr. (1982). "Bargaining Power of Multinationals and Host Governments," *Journal of International Business Studies* (Fall) 3, 9–23.

Fayerweather, J. (1982). *International Business Strategy and Administration*. Cambridge, MA: Ballinger.

Fisher, R., and W. Ury. (1981). *Getting to YES: Negotiating Agreement without Giving In*. New York: Penguin Books.

Flamholtz, E.G., T.K. Das, and A.S. Tsui. (1985). "Toward an Integrative Framework of Organizational Control," *Accounting, Organizations and Society* 10(1), 35–50.

Franko, L.G. (1971). *Joint Venture Survival in Multinational Corporations*. New York: Praeger Publishers.

Geringer, J.M. (1986). "Criteria for Selecting Partners for Joint Ventures in Industrialized Market Economies." Doctoral dissertation, University of Washington.

Geringer, J.M., and I. Hebert. (1989). "Control and Performance of International Joint Ventures," *Journal of International Business Studies* (Summer), 235–254.

Geringer, J.M., and L. Hebert. (1991). "Measuring Performance of International Joint Ventures," *Journal of International Business Studies* (Summer), 235–254.

Glaser, B., and A. Strauss. (1967). *The Discovery of Grounded Theory*. Chicago: Aldine.

Goodman, P., and J. Pennings. (1980). "Critical Issues in Assessing Organizational Effectiveness." In E. Lawler, D. Nadler, and C. Cammann (eds.), *Organizational Assessment*. New York: Wiley-Interscience, 185–215.

Gray, B., and A. Yan. (1992). "A Negotiations Model of Joint Venture Formation, Structure and Performance: Implications for Global Management, In S.B. Prasad (ed.), *Advances in International Comparative Management*, Vol. 7. Greenwich, CT: JAI Press, 41–75.

Hamel, G. (1991). "Competition for Competence and Inter-Partner Learning within International Strategic Alliances," *Strategic Management Journal* (12), 83–103.

Hamel, G., Y. Doz, and C.K. Prahalad. (1989). "Collaborate with Your Competitors and Win," *Harvard Business Review* (January).

Hamilton, W.F., and H. Singh. (1991). "Strategic Alliances in Technological Innovation: Cooperation in Biotechnology," *Journal of High Technology Management Research* 2(2), 211–221.

Harrigan, K.R. (1986). *Managing for Joint Venture Success*. Lexington, MA: Lexington Books.

Harrigan, K.R., and W.H. Newman. (1990). "Bases of Interorganization Cooperation: Propensity, Power, Persistence," *Journal of Management Studies* 27(4), 417–434.

Hendryx, S.R. (1986). "Implementation of a Technology Transfer Joint Venture in the People's Republic of China: A Management Perspective," *Columbia Journal of World Business* (Spring), 57–66.

Ho, A.K. (1990). *Joint Ventures in the People's Republic of China*. New York: Praeger.

Janger, A.R. (1980). *Organization of International Joint Venture*. New York: Conference Board.

Killing, J.P. (1983). *Strategies for Joint Venture Success*. New York: Praeger.

Koenig,. C., and G. van Wijk. (1991). "Interfirm Alliances: The Role of Trust." In R.A. Thietart, and J. Thepob (eds.), *Microeconomic Contribution to Strategic Management*, Chapter 9. North-Holland Elsevier: Advanced Series in Management, pp. 1–16.

Kogut, B. (1989). "The Stability of Joint Ventures: Reciprocity and Competitive Rivalry," *Journal of Industrial Economics* (2), 183–198.

Kuhn, T.S. (1970). *The Structure of Scientific Revolutions*, 2nd ed. Chicago: The University of Chicago Press.

Lax, D.A., and J.K. Sebenius. (1986). *The Manager as Negotiator*. New York: Free Press.

Lecraw, D.J. (1984). "Bargaining Power, Ownership, and Profitability of Transnational Corporations in Developing Countries," *Journal of International Business Studies* (Spring–Summer), 27–43.

Levin, J.B., and J.A. Byrne. (1986). "Corporate Odd Couples," *Business Week* (July 21), 100–106.

Lewin, A., and J. Minton. (1986). "Determining Organizational Effectiveness: Another Look and an Agenda for Research," *Management Science* 32, 514–538.

Lincoln, Y., and E. Guba. (1985). *Naturalistic Inquiry*. Beverly Hills, CA: Sage.

Lindesmith, A.R. (1947). *Opiate Addiction*. Bloomington, IN: Principia Press, Inc.

Lo, T.W. (1989). "New Developments in China Trade: Industrial Cooperation with the West." Unpublished doctoral disseration, City University, London, U.K.

Mann, J. (1989). *Beijing Jeep*. New York: Simon and Schuster.

Mathur, I., and J.S. Chen. (1987). *Strategies for Joint Ventures in the People's Republic of China*. New York: Praeger.

Newman, W.H. (1992). "Focused Joint Ventures in Transforming Economics," *Academy of Management Executive* 6(1), 67–75.

O'Reilly, A.J. (1988). "Establishing Successful Joint Ventures in Developing Nations: A CEO's Perspective," *Columbia Journal of World Business* (Spring), 65–71.

Ouchi, W.G. (1977). "The Relationship between Organizational Structure and Organizational Control," *Administrative Science Quarterly* 20, 559–569.

Parkhe, A. (1993a). " 'Messy' Research, Methodological Predispositions, and Theory Development in International Joint Ventures," *Academy of Management Review* 18(2), 227–268.

Parkhe, A. (1993b). "Partner Nationality and the Structure-Performance Relationship in Strategic Alliances," *Organizational Science* 4(2), 301–314.

Parkhe, A., and R. Shin. (1991). "The Case Study Method in International Joint Ventures Research: A Critical Assessment and a Program of Application." Paper presented at the Academy of International Business meetings, Miami, FL.

Pearson, M.M. (1991). *Joint Ventures in the People's Republic of China: The Control of Foreign Direct Investment under Socialism*. Princeton, NJ: Princeton University Press.

Pfeffer, J., and G.R. Salancick. (1978). *The External Control of Organizations*. New York: Harper & Row.

Pomfret, R. (1991). *Investing in China: Ten Years of the Open Door Policy*. Ames, IA: Iowa State University Press.

Porter, M.E. (1990). *The Competitive Advantage of Nations*. New York: Free Press.

Prahalad, C.K., and Y.L. Doz. (1981). "An Approach to Strategic Control in MNC's," *Sloan Management Review* (Summer), 5-13.

Robinson, W.S. (1951). "The Logical Structure of Analytic Induction," *American Sociological Review* 16, 812-818.

Root, F.R. (1988). "Some Taxonomies of International Cooperative Arrangements." In F.J. Contractor, and P. Lorange (eds.), *Cooperative Strategies in International Business*. Lexington, MA: Lexington Books, pp. 69-80.

Schaan, J.L. (1983). "Parent Control and Joint Venture Success: The Case of Mexico." Unpublished doctoral disseration, University of Western Ontario.

Schaan, J.L. (1988). "How to Control a Joint Venture Even as a Minority Partner," *Journal of General Management* 14(1), 4-16.

Schnepp, O., M.A. Von Glinow, and A. Bhambri. (1990). *United States-China Technology Transfer*. Englewood Cliffs, NJ: Prentice-Hall.

Schelling, T. (1956). "An Essay on Bargaining," *American Economic Review* 46, 281-306.

Scott, W.R. (1987). *Organizations: Rational, Natural, and Open Systems*. Englewood Cliffs, NJ: Prentice-Hall.

Shan, W. (1991). "Environmental Risks and Joint Venture Sharing Arrangements," *Journal of International Business Studies* 22(4), 555-578.

Sharfman, M., B. Gray, and A. Yan. (1991). "The Context of Interorganizational Collaboration in the Garment Industry: An Institutional Perspective," *Journal of Applied Behaviroal Science* 27(2), 181-208.

Smith, D.N., and L.T. Wells, Jr. (1975). *Negotiating Third World Mineral Agreements*. Cambridge, MA: Ballinger.

Stinchcombe, A.L. (1965). "Social Structure and Organizations." In J.G. March (ed.), *Handbook of Organizations*. Chicago: Rand McNally, pp. 142-193.

Stopford, J.M., and L.T. Wells, Jr. (1972). *Managing the Multinational Enterprise*. New York: McGraw-Hill.

Strauss, A. (1987). *Qualitative Analysis for Social Scientists*. New York: Cambridge University Press.

Taylor, S.J., and R. Bogdan. (1984). *Introduction to Qualitative Research Methods*, 2nd ed. New York: John Wiley & Sons.

Teagarden, M.B., and M.A. Von Glinow. (1990). "Sino-Foreign Strategic Alliance Types and Related Operating Characteristics," *International Studies of Management and Organization* 20(1-2), 99-108.

The U.S.-China Business Council. (1990). *Special Report on U.S. Investment in China*. Washington, DC: China Business Forum.

Thorelli, H. (1986). "Networks: Between Markets and Hierarchies," *Strategic Management Journal* 7, 37-51.

Tung, R.L. (1982). *U.S.-China Trade Negotiations*. New York: Pergamon Press.

Tung, R.L. (1988). "Toward a Conceptual Paradigm of International Business Negotiations," *Advances in International Comparative Management* 3, 203-219.

Van de Ven, A.H., and M.S. Poole. (1990). "Methods to Develop a Grounded Theory of Innovation Processes in the Minnesota Innovation Research Program," *Organization Science* 1(3), 313-335.

Vernon, R. (1977). *Storm over Multinationals*. Cambridge, MA: Harvard University Press.

Williamson, O.E. (1983). "Credible Commitments: Using Hostages to Support Exchange," *American Economic Review* 73, 519-540.

Yan, A., and B. Gray. (1995). "Reconceptualizing the Determinants and Measurement of Joint Venture Performance." In L.R. Gomez-Mejia, and M.W. Lawless (eds.) *Strategic Alliances in High Technology* Vol. 5. Greenwich, CT: JAI Press, 87-113.

Yin, R.K. (1989). *Case Study Research: Design and Methods* rev. ed. Newbury Park, CA: Sage.

Znaniecki, F. (1934). *The Method of Sociology*. New York: Farrar & Rinehart, Inc.

Barriers to International Joint Ventures and Strategic Alliances: A Commentary

KATHRYN RUDIE HARRIGAN
Henry R. Kravis Professor of Business Leadership, Columbia Business School

The inexorable drive towards corporate alliances may represent a new chapter in the development of capitalism. Many industries that were not so when the original "rules of competition" were being written have become *international* in scope—pharmaceuticals, biotechnology, electronics, information-processing, telecommunications, petrochemicals, and many others. Meanwhile economic maturity in the home markets of key players within these global industries has forced these firms' managers to balance their entrepreneurial orientations with strategies for survival amidst economic downsizings and changes in their nations' industrial bases.

Managers now acknowledge their firms' new motivations for taking partners. Although risk aversion—the desire to take a little piece of everyone's action to minimize the risk of guessing wrong—is still a strong motivation (as is the financial need to share the costs and risks of new capital outlays), new economic realities are beginning to influence alliance strategies. Recognition of these forces (and a better understanding of what corporate alliances can accomplish through horizontal and vertical partnerships) is augmenting firms' uses of cooperative strategies.

1. Using alliances to cope with new competitive realities

Managers are seeking international counterparts who can help their respective firms to rationalize productive assets and share their surviving capacity within nations where demand is maturing, even as their firms establish footholds elsewhere in nations where industry cycles are just beginning. Critical to the success of such international product life cycle schemes are manager's abilities to candidly assess each partner's strengths and perform their strategic triage free from exit barriers in a world where postindustrial governments are becoming ever more protectionist and the factors of production no longer flow frictionlessly to their best uses.

1.1. The international vision

Even if managers can honestly assess the merits of each partner's resource contributions to devise optimal retirements of redundant assets, many impediments prevent the integration of partners' operations in a seamless fashion. Briefly, corporate alliances for global strategy must ensure that where customers' needs and wants are becoming homogeneous across countries served, the standardized products of their families of alliances can be delivered to these increasingly homogeneous customers using centrally coordinated marketing campaigns (with regional customizations) to sell outputs from plants making the same, nearly interchangeable components from remote locations, using knowledge which may be created anywhere in the global alliance system and will be transferred without prejudice to anywhere else within cooperating firms' organizations as needed (and that its adoption will be encouraged through sponsoring firms' cross-fertilization policies) using personnel who are interchangeable for specified job descriptions within their global family of alliances' operating sites to improve their value to the cooperating firms. Organizational boundaries become blurred across spider's webs of alliances where international competitive advantage is the prize.

International partnerships will fuel the transfer of technologies and operations to regions where the best balance of cost reduction, productivity improvements, and responsive service can be maintained. Capacity expansions to capture technological leaps will be accompanied by facility closings and downsizings. Corporate alliances will become the focal point for resource arbitrage where firms bring parallel capabilites and assets to their joint operations. They will be the engine for exploiting virgin resources within awakening markets and the major vehicle for transferring best management practices to new populations of employees.

1.2. The nightmare of autarky

This scenario of worldwide rationalizations raises many public policy questions for governments whose competitive policies are out of synch with the realities of global competition. Answers affecting living standards adversely will not be well received in nations where economic regulation policies are inherently populist.

As corporate alliances to achieve global strategies redistribute the "greasy jobs" that provide the widest platforms for jobs in supporting industry sectors, what impediments to transnational cooperation can be anticipated? How will "local content" policies be interpreted in environments where "greasy jobs" are exported? How will governments' rising demands for greater proportions of "knowledge workers" affect managers' prerogatives to transfer employees and manage training programs? How will corporate expatriate policies affect host governments' respective development objectives? Although the vision of a transnational global village is a tempting one for managers and scholars (and progress has been made towards devising systems of global networks for cooperation), the trend towards greater recognition of ethnic differences in political entities reduces the likelihood of the vision being realized soon.

How long is the reach of U.S. antitrust? Mature markets require horizontally related competitors to pool resources in order to survive, yet market divisions have long been regarded as illegal under American interpretations of competitive markets. The very decision among alliance partners to specialize by product (or value-adding processing step) is like a tacit decision not to enter certain parts of the total market that highly integrated firms might enter. Clearly policies of the 1890s—both antitrust laws and internal preferences for vertical integration—must be reconsidered in light of international competition. Managers of firms within failing industries need breathing space from policies of social welfare guarantees, job protection, and simple nose-count measures of competitive industry structures to do what they must to restructure and regroup into viable organizational entities.

Nobody wants to dance with a frog, and it is illogical for firms possessing the wherewithal to forge families of international alliances willingly to choose failing firms when contemplating viable alliances. Yet the benefits of being on a winning international team are withheld from "ugly" firms and their stakeholders. How can governments help local firms to become more attractive as dancing partners? What changes must be endured to ensure that local firms get a piece of the international action? Which bargaining chips can make local firms be more readily accepted as partners? How can the frog turn into a prince?

Changes in governing administrations are an especially sensitive time for managers of international networks. They want to know the rules that their firm must play by within each venue so as to assess the future value of each facility to their transnational goals. Corporate alliances can take on a myriad of forms yet still attain their purpose. Because managers excel at inventing ways around the letter of badly forged laws, their firms will continue to disseminate best demonstrated practices to worldwide affiliates—regardless of information impediments—until censorship and autarky are the norm.

2. Using virtual organizations to focus on core competencies

Although they may be horizontally related, corporate alliance partners embraced for international core competency enhancements need not possess capabilities that parallel each other's expertise. Forging networks with outsiders to offset in-house specialization in activities important to the firm's "core" would be the logical way to use corporate alliances (if the public policy nightmare sketched above could be avoided). Managerial breakthroughs in systems of organizational communication and governance now enable firms to de-integrate from structures where virtually all steps in the value-adding chain—from ultra raw materials to serving ultimate consumers—were once performed entirely in-house. Although pursuit of international strategy requires greater vertical integration than domestic-only operations, the key managerial innovation of the twenty-first century is the development of ways for coordinating vertically related activities within partially owned affiliates with stand-alone organizational capabilities. These new, virtual *forms* of vertical ownership—corporate alliances, long-term contractual ties, distributorships, and many other quasi-integrated arrangements—allow international firms quickly to reconfigure their value-adding chain of activities to specialize in what they do best while outsourcing tasks of lesser importance to a particular firm's core competency development to affiliates with different (but complementary) specializations.

2.1. Selective investments

Managers are still learning how to achieve their purpose through corporate alliances. They are cautious in using cooperative strategies, because delegating responsibility to outsiders for steps in their firm's value chain raises managerial issues and risks. The rewards can be high; if managers choose effectively where to develop their firm's sources of competitive advantage, their international family of alliances can avoid duplication of capabilities, enjoy lower unit costs (through higher scale economies in capacity utilization), and accelerate their firm's pace of technological innovation (by reaching the breakeven needed for recovering seed capital investments faster). But the specter of atrophied capabilities deters managers from relying too quickly on partners with asymmetrical value systems, experiences, and skills.

Organizational barriers prevent managers from relying too heavily on allies. Rather than relinquish all germane knowledge to the shared responsibilities of their corporate alliance, managers keep some resources in reserve (to rebuild outsourced functions if alliances sour). Parallel, in-house replenishment of innovation capabilities also provides future "bargaining chips" to keep their attractiveness lively to partners.

2.2. *The need for flexibility*

As timeliness becomes an ever more important basis for competitive advantage, managers must wrestle with new ways to streamline the process of working within a shared decision-making milieu while enhancing in-house strengths. Until their firms devise a shorthand for cooperative coordination of international networks, the "millstone" effect of corporate alliances undermines potential first-mover advantages. Firms must concentrate on ways of managing intra-organizational as well as interorganizational synergies if they intend to get the shared learning of their alliances back to their firm's core organization.

It is clear that the market for innovation is becoming global and that knowledge is diffusing rapidly. Managers recognize that the greatest benefit goes to the team that is first to exploit innovations. Because skillful copy-cat competitors can push down profit margins for innovations faster than pioneers can recover their costs, flexibility in governing networks of international alliances will determine their survival in the years ahead.

Transnational Partners in Commercial Class Aircraft Manufacturing: Why and How

VICKI L. GOLICH
Associate Professor Political Science, College of Arts and Sciences, California State University, San Marcos and Faculty Associate, Center for Research in Conflict and Negotiation, The Pennsylvania State University

Abstract.

This article identifies variables that have impelled the creation of transnational joint ventures in commercial-class aircraft manufacturing despite the latter's strategic value to individual nations. It demonstrates that policy-maker choices are influenced by a complex combination of international and domestic-level political, economic, and technology factors. Finally, it describes four alliance structures which firms have adopted—namely, vertical, horizontal, vertical-horizontal combination, and supplier-driven.

Key Words: commercial class aircraft manufacturers, economic factors, horizontal allilance model, political factor, prime manufacturer, supplier driven alliance model, technology factor, transnational production arrangements, vertical alliance model, vertical-horizontal combination alliance model

1. Introduction

In the early 1900s, young scientists, engineers, and entrepreneurs transformed the airplane from a tool of military intelligence and circus feats to a new mode of travel which would revolutionize global transportation and communication networks. These aviation pioneers shared ideas and aircraft production under license during the Golden Age of Aviation, 1927–1932. By the mid-1930s, corporate and government policymakers, sensitive to aviation's increasing military value, decided to protect the industry so that competitors could not access new and improved aircraft. Thus began an era of government-encouraged industry rationalization via domestically bounded merger and acquisition, each state seeking to dominate the critical sector. This approach continued until the mid-1960s, when a renewed interest in transnational joint production emerged. The purposes of this article are to identify the factors that impelled this shift and the range of models available to firms considering transnational joint ventures.

An analysis of commercial-class aircraft manufacturing offers significant insights into the trend toward global alliances among firms, precisely because it has transitioned from a sector characterized by a large number of competitive firms which often participated in joint production efforts and sometimes shared technology, to a set of oligopolistic domestic firms which jealously guarded it, to the recent trend toward global alliances. It is also a powerful case, because it has been considered strategic—critical to national security, prestigious, and capable of generating special benefits for the rest of the economy (Tyson 1988)—since World War I. Hence, governmental efforts to protect and dominate it are especially compelling (Golich 1989). The following analysis is consciously historical and evolutionary. It is intended to tell the story of changes in production structures by reference to a fluctuating combination of international and domestic-level political, economic, and technological factors (see Figure 1).

The distribution of power among relevant actors and their ability to use that power to achieve specified goals constitute *political factors*. Globally, power is distributed among states and firms and includes military or market-share dominance, as well as the ability to influence other states or firms to comply with policy preferences. Domestic-level power distribution refers to corporate market share and access to decision makers (Lindblom 1977). At each level, choices will be affected by prevailing ideas about accepteable state-market relationships (Reich 1989), the consequences of previous policy implementation (Golich 1989; Krasner 1983), policymaker perceptions about what goals are feasible and how they can best be achieved (Maxfield and Nolt 1990; Strange 1988), and the behavior of others (Axelrod and Keohane 1985).

The policy outcomes of the political game essentially define the framework of economic activity by affecting the size and operating rules of the marketplace. Market characteristics are not only affected by sector-specific policies, but can also be influenced by seemingly unrelated domestic and foreign-policy decisions perceived at the moment to be of higher priority. Economic behavior, manifested in corporate policies shaped by the market, can redistribute resources, thus transforming the political configuration and redefining markets in a glacial, but nevertheless, dramatic and continuing process (Gilpin 1975; Maxfield and Nolt 1990; Webb 1990). Global and domestic *economic factors* include degree of market openness, size, location, participants, capital availability, and product value.

Technology factors include advances in aircraft performance—range, capacity, and environmental operations—and can affect industry dynamics such as developmental lead time, launch costs, marketing, and return on investment cycles.

The reciprocal and simultaneous interplay of these factors explains the transformation in global civil-aircraft production strategies. At different points in time, some factors have

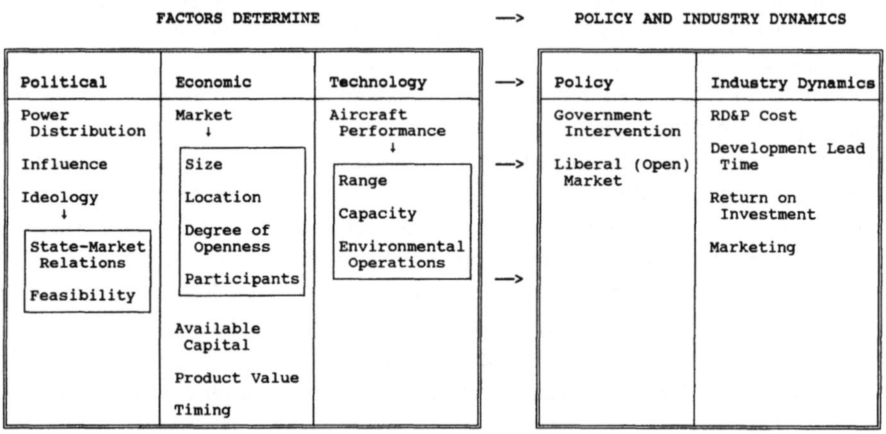

Figure 1. Factors shaping evolution of commercial class aircraft manufacturing production structures.

played more important roles than others *and* their character has changed over time. For example, capital availability has been constrained at times by currency valuations and by decreased government spending at others.

1. Industry evolution

Prior to World War I, aviation had little value beyond military intelligence and circus feats. Commercial air transport service and government involvement in aircraft manufacturing were minimal. Technological advances cost little, but they dramatically improved aircraft performance. The world seemed comfortable with a political structure dominated by Great Britain and Western Europe largely through a series of colonial empires which generally served to demarcate markets for limited trade. Aircraft production was a relatiely cheap proposition and took place in a variety of small competitive firms whose owners and engineers often shared technology and production through licensing. Toward the end of the 1930s, however, states and firms, suspicious of Germany's intentions, began to retrench their aircraft production to protect national interests.

At the end of World War II, the United States emerged as an undeniable superpower, while Europe was devastated politically and economically. Its manufacturers confronted a moribund capacity to build commercial-class aircraft: Many of their factories had been destroyed; their technological expertise focused on tactical military aircraft, whereas their primary competitors, U.S. manufacturers, had continued to build transports throughout the war.

Industry dynamics had also changed radically. Technological innovation, financed by governments, dramatically improved aircraft performance such that aviation clearly had strategic value: It was prestigious; its military potential had been proven; it promised to improve transportation significantly and to generate substantial revenues.

Although the war was over, American and European governments continued to provide direct and indirect support to the aviation industry. In the United States, firms earned high rates of return on military programs and used the profits to initiate risky commercial aircraft projects in GOCO (Government Owned, Contractor Operated) facilities. They also enjoyed favorable depreciation allowances, tax credits, low-interest Eximbank loans to foreign airlines for American aircraft purchases, and government-financed research. Finally, U.S. firms benefitted from the pivotal role of the dollar in determining prices, which added an exchange rate risk burden to European firms (see, e.g., Hayward 1986; Mowery and Rosenberg 1989). Despite rhetorical support for collaborative production efforts (Morrocco 1987), U.S. corporate and government policy makers preferred perpetuating a mostly domestic industry. This preference was supported by its superpower status, which included the overwhelming dominance of its aircraft manufacturers in the global market.

In contrast, Europeans decided that successful participation in commercial-class aircraft manufacturing would require collaboration with foreign firms. Europe's leaders initially hoped to regain unilateral dominance for national producers by encouraging domestically bounded industry rationalization and linking state-owned, airline-fleet purchases to local manufacturers. However, by the 1960s, heeding Jean-Jacques Servan-Schreiber's advice, French officials initiated a successful call for continental collaboration (1968).

The primary political factor impelling the decision to collaborate was European concern about U.S. dominance. Believing that the development and exploitation of technology could alter power relations (Williams 1984), Europeans were determined to resist and to match American technological dominance (Nau 1974; Ruggie 1975) and to prevent the presence "of an American monopoly in a major sector" (Hayward 1986). European concerns were fueled by several aborted efforts to collaborate with U.S. firms in the production of military and commercial aircraft. As U.S. dominance of commercial-class manufacturing increased, Europeans sought to avoid a situation in which their manufacturers would be relegated to the production of components (Hayward 1986).

The primary economic factor impelling European collaboration was market size. Whereas the U.S. market was unified and huge, both geographically and in terms of air travel demand, European national markets were compartmentalized, and air transport competed with very efficient rail transport networks. The United Kingdom, France, and Germany each had at least two major aircraft manufacturers, which were smaller than the leading U.S. firms (Hochmuth 1974a). European aircraft manufacturers were compelled to design aircraft to the specifications of captive national champion airlines, leading to limited appeal globally and a very long list of unsuccessful commercial aircraft.

Europeans viewed collaboration as a way to reverse this trend by reducing research, development, and production (RD&P) risks and by expanding market access. Three other factors worked to make decisions to collaborate relatively easy in Europe. First, Europe was no stranger to transnational aircraft production; it had been fairly common prior to World War II. Second, economic cooperation, manifested in projects such as the European Coal and Steel Community and the emerging Common Market, were proving viable, overcoming many initial fears related to the potential vulnerability associated with such interdependency. Third, Europeans were more comfortable than Americans with the direct involvement of their governments in shaping market dynamics (Chapman 1991; Reich 1989).

2. The 1970s and beyond: explanations of change

Today no aircraft is launched without careful attention to choosing production partners from around the world. As the 1970s progressed, global politics were increasingly characterized by transnational interdependencies among a variety of actors across a wide range of issue areas (Keohane and Nye 1977). Mutual dependencies, which were particularly prevalent in trade relations, were accompanied by a more equal, if still asymmetrical, distribution of power among states. Several industrialized countries now participated in many highly competitive market sectors, while most former colonies had become independent sovereign states. Though still not strong enough to influence major decision outcomes, the new states began to assert themselves by demanding participation in industries which they believed would facilitate economic modernization. In aircraft production, a proliferation of offset agreements, initiated in 1972 with a planes-for-hams swap between McDonnell-Douglas and Yugoslavia and evolving into a guarantee for production participation, reflect this change (Schaufele 1988).

At the domestic level, declining military budgets hurt the commercial sector. Between 1968 and 1971, industry sales to the U.S. Department of Defense dropped 24%, and jet transport sales dropped 68%. Support was further undermined in the U.S. by decisions to end the development of a supersonic transport and the B-70 manned bomber, and to significantly reduce B-1 bomber funding. Most recently, the collapse of the Soviet Union precipitated further and even more significant cuts in defense spending, with new orders for aerospace products and services falling an estimated 23% in 1993 to less than half the new business received in 1989 (Napier 1994). The decrease in direct and indirect government finance began to strain corporate budgets just as RD&P in high technology industry sectors began to skyrocket. Likewise, the U.S. airline response to domestic economic deregulation added to aircraft manufacturer trouble by glutting the market with capacity: rationalization via merger, acquisition and bankruptcy often decreased the *need* for new aircraft purchases, while adding old or fleet-incompatible aircraft to the burgeoning pool. Fare wars aimed at increasing market share led to historically low profit margins and significant losses, decreasing airlines' *ability* to buy aircraft.

Meanwhile, technological advances dramatically enhanced aircraft performance and launch costs. In the 1940s, when Douglas developed the DC6, the launch cost to equity ratio was 42%: when the DC10 was developed in 1970, it had skyrocketed to 155% (Taneja 1980). Likewise, a four- to five-year return on investment cycle during the 1940s and 1950s was common, whereas today it can take that long just to develop a new airframe or engine, while the return on investment has stretched to 10 to 15 years. At the same time, commercially valuable technological advances resulting from government-financed military R&D decreased throughout the 1980s, as civil and military aircraft performance requirements diverged (Mowery and Rosenberg 1989).

Higher RD&P costs increase manufacturer cash-flow needs and multiply the number of planes which have to be sold to earn a return on investment, while raising airframe prices (see Figure 2), thus decreasing the ability of airlines to replace or increase their fleets. In recent years, this phenomenon has been exacerbated by the abysmal profit performance of the U.S. airlines, which have lost more than $10 billion between 1990 and 1993 ("Panel. . ." 1993), and by surplus capacity in all civil-aircraft market segments (Lopez and Yager 1987). Perhaps, ironically, technological advances increased the potential life span of an aircraft from 25 to 50 years, lengthening the replacement cycle and aggravating surplus capacity. Frustrated manufacturers, in order to get rid of "white tails"—complete aircraft with no buyer—initiated long-term lease arrangements. As leases ran out, these aircraft were added to the pool of relatively cheap transports.

Despite complications wrought by advancing technology and surplus capacity, aircraft manufacturers were still pressured by the airlines to meet strict on-time delivery schedules so that they could exploit economic efficiencies and marketing advantages associated with operating new equipment. By the 1970s, as little as a "six-month delay in introducing a new generation of equipment [could] cost a manufacturer sixty percent or more of the total market" (Bluestone et al. 1981). This is critical, since it is increasingly difficult for a firm missing out on one generation of aircraft to challenge for success in the next (Hayward 1983, 1986).

This shift in industry dynamics was accompanied by a restructuring of the market size and shape from a series of distinct national markets linked by trade to a single market where regulation variation is often only marginally more significant than that which exists between any two U.S. states. The customer base for commercial transports, though global

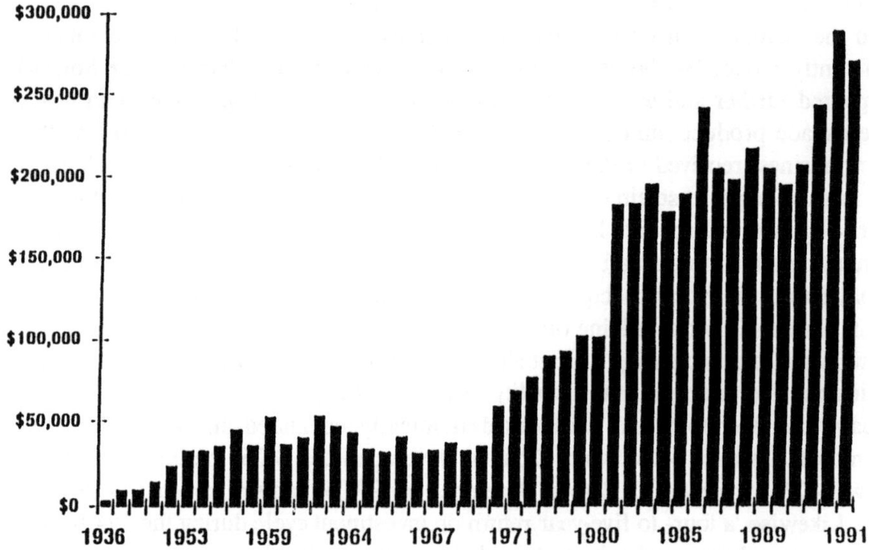

Figure 2. Summary of aircraft prices per seat, 1936–1991 (current U.S. dollars). (Source: Shenton, 1991).

in scope, is small in number: 25 major air carriers account for more than 70% of the world travel market, with approximately two-thirds of the commercial transport market located outside the United States, a trend that is likely to continue for some time to come (Clarkson 1992; Taneja 1994). Despite the current trend toward liberalizing global air transport, foreign airlines are often government owned or supported, hence state participation in aircraft sales negotiations is common.[1] Historically, state policy makers have actively encouraged airlines to contract with domestic manufacturers (Hayward 1986; Gidwitz 1980). However, this logic may not prevail over the variety of current considerations which determine aircraft purchases.

Today Boeing, McDonnell-Douglas, and Airbus Industries are the only surviving large commercial transport primes, the manufacturers responsible for final assembly and delivery of the final product. With barriers to entry at an all time high, this oligopolistic structure makes the loss of a single firm very costly to a national economy. Hence, all governments, anxious to maintain a presence in this industry sector, assist firms in financial arrangements needed to facilitate aircraft sales. This has triggered intense debates about how much and what type of state involvement is appropriate, issues which have proved difficult to resolve. At the Tokyo Round of the General Agreement on Tariffs and Trade negotiations, a code of conduct and a complex formula delineating acceptable aircraft financing terms were established. Nevertheless, public subsidies of this industry sector were back on the bargaining table at the recently concluded Uruguay Round, and yet another tentative agreement was reached.

Finally, the strategic value of commercial-class aircraft manufacturing now rests more than ever on its potential to contribute significantly to the domestic economy. Military and commercial aircraft manufacturers have always shared the same production base—namely, a complex infrastructure of firms supplying sophisticated components, materials, and equipment including electronics, communications equipment, and scientific instruments. However, civil aircraft have accounted for 80% of the total aircraft production weight during times of peace.

The economic benefits generated by the industry are both tangible and intangible. Since the late 1950s, aerospace has been the leading industrial contributor to United States' export earnings. Since 1982, aerospace exports have increased at an average annual rate of $1 billion per year; in 1990, commercial aircraft contributed a positive balance of $16 billion, with 80% of total aerospace exports (Napier 1991) and supported approximately $25,000 for each $1 billion exported (Lopez and Yager 1987). Despite significant decreases in domestic and foreign sales through 1993, overall aerospace profitability has remained high—approximately 6% operating profit (Napier 1994).

Manufacturers not only purchase a significant number of goods and services to build their airframes, but they also produce an essential good for the vital air transport service sector. Any business which depends on air transport benefits from more efficient provision of the service afforded by up-to-date equipment. Thus, the "linkage externality" is positive—both the private returns to aircraft manufacturers and the social and private returns to downstream users is increasing (Krugman 1986). Finally, its technological innovations positively affect core technologies, those which lead to the development of many products, have a significant impact on production processes, and affect many sectors of the economy (Van Tulder and Junne 1988). The constant pursuit of further advances helps to maintain a strong knowledge base, while the early application and use leads to decreased costs and more rapid diffusion to other industries, all of which are thought to be critical to maintaining a competitive position in today's economy (The Committee... 1988; Tyson 1988).

With domestic economic health now considered a fundamental aspect of national security, and with the jet transport market projected to be worth $600 billion in 2005 (Clarkson 1992), policy makers want to ensure that a healthy domestic civil aerospace industry sector is able to take advantage of the continuing expansion of this potentially lucrative global market.

3. Benefits of internationalization

At first, it may seem odd that the strategic value of an industry would impel the proliferation of transnational production strategies among firms. States have clearly demonstrated their preference to maintain or increase national participation in this industry sector through a variety of intervention tools (Golich 1989). The definition of what constitutions *participation* has changed over time. It no longer implies dominance or the active presence of a prime manufacturer, a critical component producer may well suffice. Industry dynamics as shaped by political, economic, and technology changes are key to understanding how strategic value can lead to industry globalization.

By the 1980s, U.S. manufacturers recognized what European firms had discovered in the late 1960s: Several potential benefits can be derived from participation in transnational production arrangements (Clarkson 1992; Eden 1991; Hoffman and Kaplinsky 1988). First, risks are reduced by pooling resources and talent, and no single entity bears market failure costs. Second, suppliers of specialized goods and services can market to prime manufacturers in different countries and achieve economies of scale associated with increased sales volume, thus driving down costs. Third, though domestic aircraft production no longer ensures domestic airline purchase, potential market size is increased and some production arrangements, such as offsets or turnkey, can be linked to aircraft purchase. Fourth, critical financial support can be obtained from program participant governments. Even the new rules restricting heavy subsidies allow some support on both the RD&P and the sales sides of the equation. Fifth, denying a potential foreign partner's access to a production market may encourage it to form a competitive production alliance; alternatively it may invite costly retaliation (Mowery 1987). Sixth, learning to manage transnational projects is important in an era of proliferating cross-border arrangements; Airbus's success has been attributed, in part, to the management lessons learned from the Concorde project (Lawler 1985; Raphael 1993).

No doubt, technology transfer is the most contentious potential benefit. Virtually everyone agrees that transnational production, particularly if it involves joint R&D work, will transfer technology. Some argue that controls should be avoided except in clearly defined and unusual circumstances, noting that the technology transferred may not undermine the competitive position of production partners (Fuqua 1989; Julius 1990), that it can be a source of revenues via royalties and fees, and that the most sensitive technologies can be protected (Williams 1991). Moreover, sharing technology may strengthen relations with foreign production and trade partners and, based on the principle of reciprocity, help ensure access to critical technology bases. Others argue that it is better to control technology transfer, even for a limited time, because, in a dynamic environment, a small lead can be turned into a large lead over time (Krasner 1990; Tucker 1991).

4. Transnational partnering in commercial-class aircraft manufacturing

Global strategic alliances can, have, and will continue to fail. The number of obstacles impeding success are formidable, including excessive nationalism, policy or legal barriers such as antitrust legislation or variances in safety or environmental standards, political infighting among corporate participants, poor communications regarding rights and responsibilities, insensitivity to cultural differences, disagreement about costs and benefits distribution, compensation for technology transfer, the high cost of changing corporate operations, and lack of sector compatibility with global production structures (Perlmutter and Heenan 1986; Hochmuth 1974b). Despite these potential pitfalls, commercial aircraft manufacturers are pursuing a variety of global production arrangements which fall roughly into four models: vertical, horizontal, a vertical-horizontal combination, and supplier-driven (see Figure 3).

The vertical model is characterized by a hierarchical arrangement among participant firms in which one member, usually a prime manufacturer, assumes a "senior partner" role and is supported by a global network of firms in other categories. The senior partner exercises control over critical production decisions—project and design choices, marketing and distribution, technology transfer, and final assembly plans.

Boeing has preferred this model of globalization as demonstrated by its evolving relationship with Japanese producers (Clarkson 1992). In 1969, Mitsubishi Heavy Industries

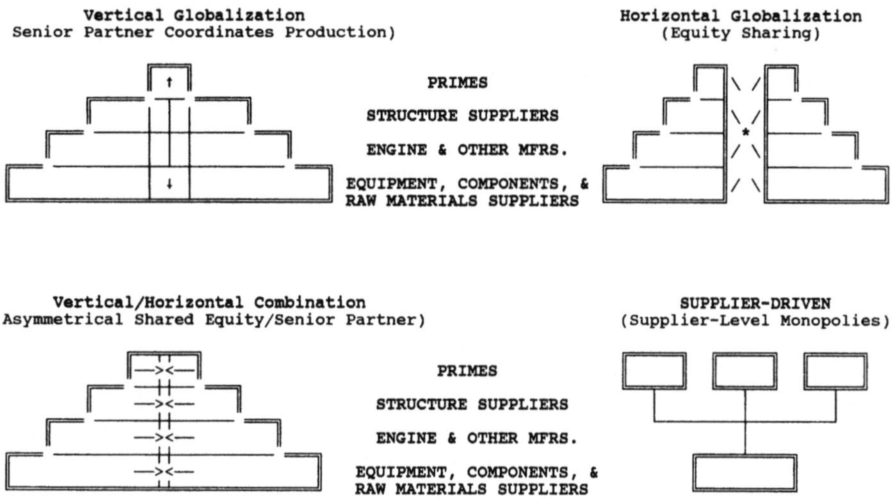

Figure 3. Industry globalization structures.

built relatively simple engine carriage kits for Boeing's 747 aircraft under contract. Within a few years, Japanese firms participated in "build per drawing" work, Boeing supplying the blueprints, and the Japanese building the product. By 1978, Japanese and Boeing engineers worked together to design B-767 airliner components. Currently, several firms—namely, Fuji Heavy Industries, Mitsubishi Heavy Industries, and Kawasaki Heavy Industries—produce nearly 15% of the value of each airframe. Japanese firms are expected to build 20% of the B-777 twinjet due to enter service in 1995. These firms do not hold an equity position, but are referred to as program partners, because each shares some risk via heavy investment in the development costs paid by the Japanese Aircraft Development Corporation, a subsidiary of the Ministry of International Trade and Industry.

Horizontal global production is characterized by equity-sharing arrangements among participant firms. Project members can be drawn from within the same or closely related categories or include corporations from the entire range of component manufacturers. Partners participate jointly in critical decisions about all phases of research, development, production, and sales. Horizontal arrangements need not preclude members from holding a junior partner position in a transnational vertical structure, participating in supplier-driven arrangements with both domestic and foreign partners, or contracting for parts with nonmember firms.

Airbus Industries best represents this model of global production. It was officially born on December 18, 1970 as a *Groupement d'Intérêt Économique* (GIE), following nearly a decade of negotiations initiated in the early 1960s between the British and the French about the joint production of a short/medium range, wide-bodied aircraft. By 1967, Germany had joined the talks, and the three governments signed a Memorandum of Understanding which committed them to the RD&P of the A300, to the purchase of at least 25 A300s by the three national airlines, and to refrain from supporting a competitive project (Hayward 1986). The *groupement* is a French industrial organization structure in which members maintain their autonomy, "their own fixed capital, production facilities, research laboratories, and administrative services" (Chapman 1991). The legal framework (see Figure 4) allows participants to cooperate on individual projects without having to merge or sacrifice individual identities. For the production of Airbus aircraft,

> Airbus Industrie coordinates design, development and production, and each Airbus type has a project manager with a small team to liaise with the partners and with the government. But sales and product support are the only functions it performs on behalf of the members (Hayward 1986).

U.S. prime manufacturer McDonnell-Douglas (MDD) is pursuing a combination of the vertical and horizontal production models. Since the early 1980s, MDD has supervised the coproduction of MD80 aircraft with Shanghai Aviation Industry Corporation. In November 1991, McDonnell-Douglas signed a memorandum of understanding with the Taiwan Aerospace Corp. (TAC), which called for MDD and TAC to form a new company to launch the MD12. TAC would acquire up to a 40% equity stake valued at $2 billion, and other Asian investors would buy another 9% equity interest. While the final outcome of this negotiation remains uncertain, the preferred structure still places MDD in a senior partner position with 51% equity. However, the minimal majority position represents a significantly constrained senior partner role, as compared to that preferred by Boeing (Velocci 1992; Smith 1992).

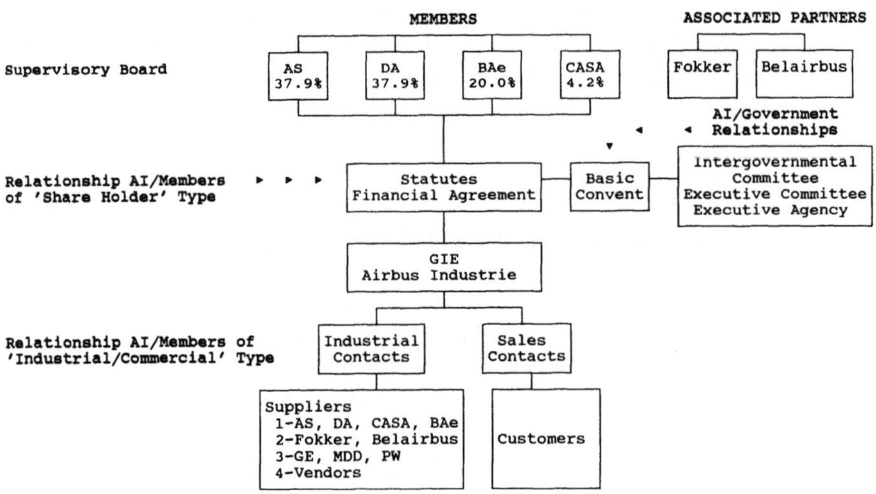

Note: AS = Aerospatiale; A = Deutsche Airbus; BAe = British Aerospace; CASA = Construcciones Aeronauticas S.A.; AI = Airbus Industries; GIE = Groupement d'Interêt Économique; GE = General Electric; MDD = McDonnell-Douglas; PW = Pratt & Whitney.

Figure 4. Airbus Industrie legal structure. (Source: Hayward, 1986)

Supplier firms have initiated another global production structure. Lynn Mytelka notes that the smaller supplier firms may seek a strategic partner or an equity sharing arrangement with a prime as a means of preserving their independence, but prime manufacturers have resisted this approach (1990). Hence, supplier firms have diversified customers and have become intermediate level monopolists so as to avoid the vulnerability associated with the absence of equity-sharing arrangements. Here, prime manufacturers remain in control of key decisions; however, suppliers sell components to more than one prime. Honeywell, which supplies components for virtually every aircraft that currently flies, represents the model sought by intermediate-level producers.

5. Conclusions

Impelled by a number of political, economic, and technology factors, the volume and variety of transnational arrangements is increasing at a rapid pace. While no definitive structure seems to be emerging, several conditions can be identified which should contribute to their success. First, participants must perceive that the partnerships are founded upon mutual trust and respect (Koenig and van Wijk 1992), that they will generate a "win-win" outcome over the long term, that each partner will contribute something critical to goal achievement, and that each will be relatively equal in its ability to influence critical decisions (Tucker 1991).

The European approach embodied in the Airbus Industrie horizontal internationalization model ultimately requires a mutual perception that these conditions apply. The *groupement* structure facilitates participation by otherwise autonomous members, ensures clear lines of authority and communication via a unitary (not a parallel-track) management system to handle daily operational decision making, and encourages compromise so as to take advantage of cultural strengths. It also creates a "positive vulnerability," since partners recognize that each contributes a unique and critical part of the whole.

Europeans have not progressed along a learning curve of international collaboration because they have great propensity to cooperate. Rather the combination of political, economic, and technology changes following World War II, along with their long history of state-firm and firm-firm cooperation, favored cooperation over autarky. European collaboration has been impelled by both a defensive motivation—to resist U.S. hegemony—and offensive motivations—to build on past experience of joint production of aircraft in the 1920s as well as modern successes associated with European Community progress, and to respond to changes in industry dynamics.

U.S. participation in transnational production arrangements reflects a different reality. The preferred structure for U.S. primes is still predominantly a vertical arrangement. This is true for both Boeing and McDonnell-Douglas. Boeing's recently announced participation with several Airbus partners to study the development of a super jumbo transport capable of carrying 600–800 passengers with a range of 10,000 miles supports consistent claims that it has "no intention of relinquishing control of the program" ("Boeing..." 1985; "Now..." 1993). MDD is willing to yield more decision making authority in exchange for R&D capital and future market access (Velocci 1992; Smith 1992). Nevertheless, it has not yet sacrificed its senior partner position. Their structures suggest a lingering suspicion related to the compromise required for successful global collaboration.

Their motivations for pursuing transnational production appear to be more defensive in nature—avoiding tariff barriers, nullifying or diluting competition, avoiding antitrust restrictions, and responding to demands for industrial offsets in exchange for aircraft purchases (Hayward 1986; Reynolds 1988). This likely reflects the history of independence and hegemony experienced by U.S. firms and reinforced by U.S. political and economic global hegemony. Only recently have changes in political, economic, and technology realities favored collaboration over autarky for U.S. firms.

New market realities—global scope, small customer base, high RD&P costs—are probably permanent. Less certain is the potential for several even more recent changes—the collapse of the Soviet Union, the lull in further European Community union, and the advent of cheap and sophisticated telecommunications technology—to reinforce or undermine the trend toward strategic alliances among aircraft manufacturers.

While the trend toward some kind of transnational production is probably here to stay, the permanence of equity-sharing, strategic alliances may be less certain. Firms may prefer more flexible partnering arrangements in the future. Even the Airbus Industries organization—the tightest alliance among foreign production partners in the aircraft industry—links independent firms which are legally free to leave the partnership. For now, multiple forces hold them together, but in a politically, economically, and technologically volatile world this glue may not be so super.

Notes

1. To date, liberalization has only affected the North American and North Atlantic markets—the United Kingdom and Canada are among the very few which have pursued strategies of privatizing state-owned airlines. Even if airlines are privatized, most states are more actively involved in supporting private actors than is the United States (Gidwitz 1980; Golich 1990).

References

Axelrod, Robert, and Robert Keohane. (1985). "Achieving Cooperation Under Anarchy: Strategies and Insitutions," *World Politics* 38 (October), 226–254.

Bluestone, Barry, Peter Jordan, and Mark Sullivan. (1981). *Aircraft Industry Dynamics: An Analysis of Competition, Capital, and Labor.* Boston, MA: Auburn House Publishing Company.

"Boeing Plans Substantial Foreign Involvement in 7-7 Development," *Aviation Week and Space Technology* (June 3, 1985), 212.

Chapman, Herrick. (1991). *State Capitalism and Working-Class Radicalism in the French Aircraft Industry.* Berkeley, CA: University of California Press.

Clarkson, L.W. (1992). "Challenges & Opportunities: Civil Aviation in the Asia Pacific Region." Presentation at the Kyushu International Aerospace Exhibition, Kyushu, Japan (January 23).

The Committee on Technology Issues that Impact International Competitiveness. (1988). *The Technological Dimensions of International Competitiveness*. Washington, DC: Council for the National Academy of Engineering.

Eden, Lorraine. (1991). "Multinational Responses to Trade and Technology Changes: Implications for Canada." In Donald McFetridge (ed.), *Foreign Investment, Technology and Growth.* Toronto: Investment Canada.

Fuqua, Donald. (1989). "The FSX: Looking Backward, Look Forward," *Aerospace Industries Association Newsletter* 2(4) (October), 3.

Gidwitz, Betsey. (1980). *The Politics of International Air Transport*. Lexington, MA: Lexington Books.

Gilpin, Robert. (1975). *U.S. Power and the Multinational Corporation.* New York: Basic Books.
Golich, Vicki L. (1989). *The Political Economy of International Air Safety: Design for Disaster?* London: Macmillan.
Golich, Vicki L. (1990). "Liberalizing International Air Transport Services." In Dennis J. Gayle and Jonathan N. Goodrich (eds.), *Privatization and Deregulation in Global Perspective.* New York: Quorum Books, pp. 156–176.
Golich, Vicki L. (1992). "From Competition to Collaboration: The Challenge of Commercial-Class Aircraft Manufacturing," *International Organization* 46(4) (Autumn), 899–934.
Hayward, Kieth. (1983). *Government and British Civil Aerospace: A Case Study in Post-War Technology Policy* Manchester, UK: Manchester University Press.
Hayward, Kieth. (1986). *International Collaboration in Civil Aerospace.* New York, St. Martin's Press.
Hochmuth, Milton. (1974a). "Aerospace." In Raymond Vernon (ed.), *Big Business and the State: Changing Relations in Western Europe.* Cambridge, MA: Harvard University Press, pp. 145–169.
Hochmuth, Milton. (1974b). *Organizing the Transnational: The Experience with Transnational Enterprise in Advanced Technology.* Cambridge, MA: Harvard University Press.
Hoffman, Kurt, and Raphael Kaplinsky. (1988). *Driving Force: The Global Restructuring of Technology, Labour and Investment in the Automobile and Components Industries.* Boulder, CO: Westview Press.
Julius, DeAnne. (1990). *Global Companies & Public Policy: The Growing Challenge of Foreign Direct Investment.* New York: Council on Foreign Relations Press.
Keohane, Robert O., and Joseph Nye. (1977). *Power and Interdependence: World Politics in Transition.* Boston: Little, Brown & Co.
Koenig, C., and G. van Wijk. (1992). "Inter-firm Alliances: The Role of Trust." Paper presented at the International Conference on Joint Ventures and Strategic Alliances, The Pennsylvania State University, University Park, PA, (April 6–8).
Krasner, Stephen D. (1983). *International Regimes.* Ithaca, NY: Cornell University Press.
Krugman, Paul, ed. (1986). *Strategic Trade Policy and the New International Economics.* Cambridge, MA: MIT Press.
Lawler, Anthony. (1985). "Presentation to the Air Transportation Research International Forum." Indianapolis, IN (June 12).
Lindblom, Charles E. (1977). *Politics and Markets: The World's Political-Economic Systems.* New York: Basic Books.
Lopez, Virginia, and Loren Yager. (1987). "An Aerospace Profile: The Industry's Role in the Economy, The Importance of R&D," *Facts and Perspectives* (April) (Aerospace Research Center, Washington, DC).
Maxfield, Sylvia, and James H. Nolt. (1990). "Protectionism and the Internationalization of Capital: U.S. Sponsorship of Import Substitution Industrialization in the Philippines, Turkey and Argentina," *International Studies Quarterly* 34(1) (March), 49–81.
Morrocco, John D. (1987). "Pentagon Reviews Trade Pacts," *Aviation Week and Space Technology* (October 19), 45.
Mowery, David C. (1987). *Alliance Politics and Economics: Multinational Joint Ventures in Commercial Aircraft.* Cambridge, MA: Ballinger Publishing Company.
Mowery, David, and Nathan Rosenberg. (1989). *Technology and the Pursuit of Economic Growth.* Cambridge, UK: Cambridge University Press.
Mytelka, Lynn K. (1987). "Knowledge-Intensive Production and the Changing Internationalization Strategies of Multinational Firms." In James Caporaso (ed.), *A Changing International Division of Labour.* Boulder, CO: Lynne Reiner Publishers, pp. 43–70.
Napier, David H. (1994). "1993 Year-End Review and Forecast: An Analysis.'' Aerospace Industries Association, Washington, D.C. (January).
Napier, David H. (1991). "1990 Year-End Review and Forecast: An Analysis." Aerospace Industries Association, Washington, D.C. (January).
Nau, Henry. (1974). *International Politics and International Technology.* Baltimore: Johns Hopkins University Press.
"Now for the Really Big One." (1993). *The Economist* (January 9), 57–58.
"Panel Suggests Lower Taxes for Ailing Airline Industry." (1993), *Los Angeles Times* (July 20), D1, 17.
Perlmutter, Howard V., and David A. Heenan. (1986). "Cooperate to Compete Globally," *Harvard Business Review* (March–April), 136–52.
Raphael, David. (1993). "Aviation Alliances: The Market for Airline Services Industry Restructuring." Presentation for the Transportation Research Board Annual Meeting, Washington, D.C. (January 12).

Reich, Simon. (1989). "Roads to Follow: Regulating Direct Foreign Investment," *International Organization* 43(4) (Autumn), 543–584.
Ruggie, John G. (1975). "International Responses to Technology," *International Organization* (Summer), 557–584.
Servan-Schreiber, Jean-Jacques. (1968). *The American Challenge.* New York: Atheneum.
Smith, Bruce A. (1992). "McDonnell Douglas, Taiwanese to Start New Round of Transport Talks Next Month," *Aviation Week and Space Technology* (March 13), 31.
Strange, Susan. (1988). *States and Markets.* New York: Basil Blackwell.
Taneja, Nawal K. (1994). "Significant Trends." Presentation for the Transportation Research Board Annual Meeting, Washington, D.C. (January 10).
Taneja, Nawal K. (1980). *U.S. International Aviation Policy.* Lexington Books, MA: Lexington Books.
Tucker, Jonathan, (1991). "Partners and Rivals: A Model of International Collaboration in Advanced Technology," *International Organization* 45(1) (Winter), 83–120.
Tyson, Laura. (1988). "Competitiveness: An Analysis of the Problem and a Perspective on Future Policy." In Martin K. Starr (ed.), *Global Competitiveness: Getting the U.S. Back on Track.* New York: W.W. Norton & Co., pp. 95–120.
Van Tulder, R., and G. Junne. (1988). *European Multinationals in Core Technologies.* New York: John Wiley.
Velocci, Anthony L. (1992). "Taiwan Aerospace Waffling on Taking Stake in MD-12," *Aviation Week and Space Technology* (May 25), 26–27.
Webb, Michael. (1991). "International Economic Structures, Government Interests, and International Coordination of Macroeconomic Adjustment Policies," *International Organization* 45(3) (Summer), 309–342.
Williams, Roger. (1984). "The International Political Economy of Technology." In Susan Strange (ed.), *Paths to International Political Economy.* London, George Allen & Unwin, pp. 70–90.

Interviews and Correspondence

Krasner, Stephen D., Editor, *International Organization* (August 6, 1990).
Reynolds, Robert, Former Negotiator for McDonnell-Douglas foreign aircraft purchases (July 7, 1988).
Schaufele, Roger D., Vice-President & General Manager of Commerical Advanced Products for Douglas Aircraft Company (July 7, 1988).
Shenton, Harold, Aviation Specialist, AVMARK Inc., Arlington, VA (January 12, 1991).
Williams, David L., Director of Program Development and Marketing, McDonnell-Douglas Corporation (June 4, 1991).

Antitrust Analysis of Joint Ventures: An Overview

DENNIS A. YAO
Commissioner, U.S. Federal Trade Commission, and Associate Professor of Public Policy and Management, Wharton School, University of Pennsylvania

Abstract.

As businesses become more active in global markets, many are considering strategic alliances with other companies as a means of becoming more efficient and more vigorous competitors. Companies are also becoming more creative in the types of alliances which they are forming. The purpose of this article is to present an overview of the impact of government antitrust policy on business choices regarding joint ventures and other strategic alliances. The article will provide an overview of how U.S. antitrust enforcement agencies assess the competitive impact of such alliances and will highlight the antitrust issues that businesses face when considering such options.

Key Words: strategic alliances, joint ventures, antitrust, regulation

1. Introduction: Why antitrust analysis is important when considering alliances[1]

While the vast majority of proposed joint ventures pose no anticompetitive problem, some will. Which joint ventures are proposed, of course, partially depends on anticipated legal problems, so the legal constraint is more binding than the numbers alone would suggest.[2]

Looser forms of strategic alliances (such as limited licensing arrangements) generally involve lesser antitrust scrutiny. Simple licensing agreements typically involve little, if any, integration or coordination between the contracting firms, and thus antitrust concerns are less likely.[3] That is not to say, however, that such licensing agreements will not attract antitrust scrutiny, especially if the agreement contemplates significant interaction or sharing of information during the term of the license. For example, even a simple royalty formula can be used, in theory, to achieve anticompetitive outcomes such as reductions in output. Consequently, firms considering such agreements should also proceed cautiously.

Some observers and practitioners have argued that American antitrust laws have restricted the formation of potentially beneficial joint ventures,[4] and, consequently, reduced the competitiveness of U.S. firms in global markets. This concern led to the passage of the National Cooperative Research Act of 1984 and the National Cooperative Production Amendments of 1993.[5] These acts limited antitrust exposure from treble damage penalties to actual damage penalties if the participants notify the enforcement agencies of their intent to create the venture. Nevertheless, critics still argue that joint ventures in the United States are being inhibited by its antitrust policies, even with the existence of these statutes.[6] Ordover and

The views expressed in this article are the author's and do not represent those of the FTC or any other Commissioner. Joseph Krauss provided able assistance, and Mark Whitener provided helpful comments on this article.

Baumol, as well as Jorde and Teece, argue for a more permissive antitrust policy in favor of joint ventures, so that society can realize the social benefits of such arrangements.[7]

On the other hand, some argue that this criticism is misguided[8] or that the antitrust laws should be enforced vigorously. For example, Porter argues for a strong antitrust enforcement policy in order to gain the advantages of securing vigorous domestic rivalry, which in turn leads to worldwide competitive industries. He comments:

> Few roles of government are more important to upgrading of an economy than ensuring vigorous domestic rivalry... The importance of domestic rivalry for national advantage has strong implications for antitrust policy, particularly policy toward mergers and alliances. Yet the need for antitrust has been questioned because of the globalization of industries and the view that domestic firms must merge to gain economies of scale... In fact, creating a dominant domestic competitor rarely results in international competitive advantage.[9]

These ongoing concerns and the increased use of joint ventures and other strategic alliances in the global marketplace have made antitrust treatment of these organizational arrangements more salient. Thus, it is important for businesses to be cognizant of the constraints imposed by law on the types of alliances available.

2. Legal framework for analyzing strategic alliances

The antitrust enforcement agencies can challenge an existing strategic alliance as an unlawful restraint of trade, or, as in the case of mergers and acquisitions, attempt to enjoin a proposed alliance before it is consummated. The former authority is found in the Sherman Act.[10] which generally condemns unreasonable restraints of trade, and in the Federal Trade Commission Act,[11] which prohibits unfair methods of competition and unfair acts or practices. The latter authority is found in the Clayton Act,[12] which prohibits transactions that may substantially lessen competition or tend to create a monopoly. In practice, it is often more difficult to find effective remedies after the alliance has been fully implemented, and so the agencies would much prefer to block anticompetitive alliances before they are formed. As is the case in most potentially troubling merger cases, many of the potential anticompetitive effects can be remedied without blocking the alliance in its entirety.

Where some form of integrative efficiencies is created, joint ventures are analyzed under the rule of reason.[13] On the other hand, a "sham" joint venture where there is no meaningful economic integration between the participants is subject to per se condemnation.[14] Courts have looked to integrative efficiencies such as pooling capital and "sharing the risks of loss as well as the opportunities for profit."[15] If such integration is found, the rule of reason applies, and the joint venture's effect is analyzed after determining the relevant product and geographic markets, as well as the relevant market conditions, including market shares and the existence of entry barriers.

Although strategic alliances can take many forms, to provide some idea of how alliances would be analyzed, I will use the example of the analysis of a joint venture.

3. Potential antitrust concerns with joint ventures

Although joint ventures are often limited in their scope and are therefore less troubling on average than mergers, they often pose unique competitive problems that must be examined carefully.[16] For example, some joint ventures involve the creation of a new entity that competes in the same market as either or both of the parents to the venture. Thus, the venture creates a new horizontal competitor. In such cases, competition may decrease as the parent companies no longer find it in their best interests to compete vigorously head-to-head. Furthermore, the participants might find it in their best interests to coordinate their own activities with that of the venture. Consequently, although the purpose of the venture might have been originally to create a new competitor, its effect may be to dampen existing competition.

Such concerns underlay the Federal Trade Commission's 1984 consent order governing the GM–Toyota NUMMI joint venture where the Commission was concerned (among other things) that the NUMMI joint venture might lead GM to limit or altogether eliminate its production of small cars.[17] To guard against this, the consent order limited the venture's output and duration.[18]

Along these same lines, it is possible that a joint venture in a market in which the parents are not currently competing may deter a future entry by the parents that might otherwise have occurred. The threat that a new competitor might enter a concentrated market may induce existing competitors to behave competitively. If a joint venture between two potential entrants (or between a potential entrant and an incumbent firm) removes that threat, higher prices or reduced output could occur or remain unchecked.[19] This lessening of potential competition is an important element in the analysis of joint ventures.[20]

Another major concern in analyzing joint ventures is that such entities present the possibility of coordination of the parents' actions through the joint venture. This is what the antitrust literature refers to as the "spillover" effect to other markets. The joint venture could provide an opportunity for the participating firms to exchange marketing plans, pricing data, or production statistics. In markets characterized by high innovation, a joint venture could allow the participants to monitor each other's research and development efforts. Additionally, the joint venture could serve as a vehicle through which one participant could "punish" the other for cheating on an independent collusive agreement.[21]

Finally, another potential concern is that a joint venture or alliance that creates or forecloses an essential input to a downstream product may inadvertently (or perhaps intentionally) produce a barrier to entry into the downstream market. For example, a joint venture between pulmonologists for the provision of oxygen delivery systems to patients in their homes was recently challenged by the FTC as, among other things, creating a barrier to entry into the oxygen supply business.[22]

4. Antitrust analysis of joint ventures

The analysis that is used to examine joint ventures is substantially the same as that used to examine horizontal mergers set out in the 1992 Horizontal Merger Guidelines.[23] The basic assumption of the 1992 Guidelines is that mergers (or joint ventures) should not be permitted to create or enhance market power or to facilitate its exercise in any relevant market. This analysis requires a thorough examination of market conditions, including determining the relevant product and geographic markets, market shares, conditions of entry, and likelihood of anticompetitve effects.

Joint ventures can be challenged either before or after their creation.[24] Pre-creation challenges avoid remedy problems that will sometimes exist because of the difficulty of "unscrambling the eggs"[25] and, therefore, are likely to impose less costs on the joint venture participants relative to post-creation remedies. Post-creation challenges afford the enforcement agencies the benefit of seeing the effect of any ancillary restraints between the joint venture participants that the joint venture might produce, in addition to seing the effect of the whole joint venture itself. It is usually more difficult to determine what effect these restraints might have before the venture is begun. Consequently, the enforcement agencies have more avenues to explore after the joint venture is created to determine whether the joint venture (or some part of it) is anticompetitive.

The analysis of joint ventures after they are created is much the same as that used prior to their creation—examining the structural conditions in the market to determine if the restraints are likely to lead to anticompetitive effects.[26] However, the FTC has modified slightly how the ancillary restraints between the joint venture participants are analyzed under its *Mass. Board* approach.[27] This approach does not explicitly incorporate a market power analysis, but instead concentrates on an analysis of whether the restraint is "inherently suspect"—that is, it is a restraint that, absent an efficiency justification, would tend to restrict output. Such agreements are condemned unless the respondent can proffer a valid efficiency justification.

Although certain joint ventures might pose competitive problems, the majority are competitively innocuous and, indeed, produce significant efficiencies that ultimately benefit consumers. Furthermore, the characteristics of joint ventures should temper, in most cases, any competitive concern that is posed. In light of this, enforcement agencies have shown some propensity to challenge joint ventures less frequently than they do mergers.[28]

Joint ventures usually result in an increase in the number of competing organizations in a product market, a procompetitive effect. Furthermore, many have a limited life by design and many more survive for only a limited period of time. Thus, to the extent that competitive concerns are ambiguous, the time limitation should work to alleviate those concerns.

In addition, most joint ventures are structured with a very narrow purpose, and require little integration between the participating firms. Furthermore, many times the participants come to the joint venture with differing objectives, thus making it harder to coordinate effectively through a joint venture.[29] The resulting decision-making structure or "constitution" of many joint ventures will often make tight parental control difficult. Where these characteristics exist they should further lessen any competitive concern that a particular joint venture might produce.

On the other hand, a joint-venture analysis might also be deficient if the analysis examines a joint venture without regard to other alliances in which the participants might be engaged. A particular joint venture might only be one part of a "web of alliances" that either or both of the participants might have structured in an industry that might allow either to control price or restrict output.[30] In such a case, enforcement agencies might erroneously conclude that a particular joint venture poses no competitive threat.

5. R&D joint ventures

Many joint ventures involve research and development relating to future generations of a particular product or completely new products. Research joint ventures will increasingly introduce the difficult topic of innovation, and its spillover issues, to antitrust analysis.[31] For example, research jvs will often entail interaction with patent rights, bringing the difficult issue of patent "monopoly" property rights incentives into the analysis. Such joint ventures also may produce as yet unknown changes in the structure of the market, changes that are even difficult for the joint-venture participants to predict. This creates uncertainties among the participants and may imply that collusion may be more difficult. Uncertain outcomes reduce the ability to show a likelihood of competitive harm, and, practically speaking, make it difficult to prevail in court.[32]

When the evidence of anticompetitive effects tips only slight in the favor of an enforcement action, one issue that often carries weight with enforcement agencies is whether less restrictive alternatives to the joint venture (e.g., a more limited joint venture that would accomplish the same basic efficiency goals) are available. Also, the agencies may concentrate solely on any ancillary restraints that may exist within the joint venture. Both approaches allow decision makers to make easier judgments (e.g., a relative versus an absolute assessment of competitive harm).[33]

Notes

1. Antitrust laws differ from country to country. For example, although the principal goal of U.S. antitrust laws is to maximize consumer welfare, EC antitrust laws seek to preserve undistorted competition (Treaty of Rome of 1957, 298 U.N.T.S. 11, (March 25, 1957, Article 3(f)). Although these goals are similar, in practice they sometimes lead to different results.
2. Considerable guidance is provided to the business and legal communities concerning mergers and joint ventures. For example, the U.S. Department of Justice and the FTC make guidelines available and provide advisory opinions and business review letters. (See, e.g., U.S. Department of Justice and Federal Trade Commission Horizontal Merger Guidelines (1992), reprinted in 4 Trade Reg. Rep. (CCH) ¶ 13,104 ("1992 Horizontal Merger Guidelines"); U.S. Department of Justice and Federal Trade Commission Statements of Enforcement Policy and Analytical Principles Relating to Health Care and Antitrust (1994), U.S. Department of Justice Antitrust Division Release No. 94-554 ("1994 Health Care Policy Statements"); U.S. Department of Justice Antitrust Enforcement Guidelines for International Operations (1988), reprinted in 4 Trade Reg. Rep. (CCH) ¶ 13,109 ("1988 International Guidelines").
3. In fact, the FTC often employs licensing agreements to remedy potential anticompetitive effects of mergers.
4. See, e.g., Thomas Piriano, *Beyond Per Se, Rule of Reason or Merger Analysis: A New Antitrust Standard for Joint Ventures*, 76 Minn. L. Rev. 1, 23 (1991).
5. 15 U.S.C. § 4301, et seq.
6. See Thomas Campbell, Commentary, 58 Antitrust L.J. 591, 603-7 (1989). (He notes that by 1989, although 130 filings had been made since the passage of the National Cooperative Research Act, 1,300 joint venture filings had been made under the European system for joint ventures during that same time period.)
7. J. Ordover and W. Baumol, Antitrust Policy and High-Technology Industries, 4 Oxford Review of Economic Policy 13-34 (1988); T. Jorde and D. Teece, "Innovation, Cooperation, and Antitrust," *Antitrust, Innovation, and Competitiveness* (1992), pp. 47–81.
8. See Diane Wood, Commentary, 58 Antitrust L.J. 591, 592–603 (1989). (She believes it is misguided to blame the antitrust laws for any lack of competitiveness of U.S. firms in international markets.)

9. Michael Porter, *The Competitive Advantage of Nations* (1990) p. 662. Porter favors vigorous antitrust enforcement on horizontal relationships, but less vigorous enforcement on vertical relationships. See p. 636 for discussion of his limited enthusiasm for cooperative research efforts.
10. 15 U.S.C. § 1.
11. 15 U.S.C. § 41, et seq.
12. 15 U.S.C. § 12, et seq.
13. In contrast to the per se standard where the existence of circumscribed behavior is sufficient to find liability, the rule of reason standard involves an examination of the overall impact of the venture before liability can be found.
14. See, e.g., Southbank IPA, Inc., 56 Fed. Reg. 50, 912 (1991).
15. *Arizona v. Maricopa County Medical Society*, 457 U.S. 332, 356 (1982).
16. See, generally, ABA Antitrust Section, *Antitrust Law Developments* (3d ed., 1992), for a summary of the law in this area.
17. *General Motors Corp.*, 103 F.T.C. 374 (1984). For a general discussion of the GM–Toyota joint venture, see James Langenfeld and David Scheffman, Innovation and U.S. Competition Policy, 34 Antitrust Bull. 1 (1989).
18. Recently, the Commmission decided to set aside the consent order. See General Motors Corp. and Toyota Motor Corp., Docket No. C-3132 (Nov. 2, 1993). The Commimssion said that GM and Toyota had shown that changed conditions in the industry eliminated the need for the order and made its continued application inequitable and harmful to competition.
19. The 1984 Merger Guidelines discuss the potential competition theory. U.S. Department of Justice Merger Guidelines (1984), reprinted in 4 Trade Reg. Rep. (CCH) ¶ 13,1003, at § 4.1.
20. See, e.g., *Institut Merieux*, Docket No. C-3301, 55 Fed. Reg. 38,854 (1990), and *Roche Holding, Ltd.*, Docket No. C-3315 (1990), both of which were grounded on potential competition concerns.
21. This was also a concern to the Commission in the GM–Toyota NUMMI joint venture. To address this concern, the consent order imposed procedural safeguards to minimize the risk to competition from unnecessary exchange of price, cost, and planning data.
22. Home Oxygen & Medical Equipment Co., FTC File No. 901-0109, and Homecare Oxygen & Medical Equipment Co., FTC File No. 911-0020 (consent orders issued for public comment November 2, 1993).
23. 1992 Horizontal Merger Guidelines. See also 1988 International Guidelines.
24. Some argue that this leads to an antitrust enforcement bias in favor of mergers and against joint ventures, since joint ventures are continually open to attack. Joseph Brodley, Antitrust and Innovation Cooperation, 4 J. Econ. Persp. 97, 108 (1990).
25. *Federal Trade Commission v. Rhinechem Corp.*, 459 F. Supp. 785, 790 (N.D. Ill. 1978).
26. See, e.g., 1988 International Guidelines § 3.4.
27. *Massachusetts Board of Registration in Optometry*, 110 F.T.C. 549, 604 (1988).
28. An example is the joint venture between General Motors and Toyota which was approved by the FTC, even though, as then Chairman Miller stated, a merger between those two automobile companies would surely have been challenged. See James Miller, Research Joint Ventures, Antitrust, and Industrial Innovation, Prepared Remarks Before the Berlin Cartel Conference 6 (July 2, 1984) at 10.
29. Jorde and Teece note the problems of coordinating across international joint ventures. See n. 7, supra.
30. See Joseph F. Brodley, Joint Ventures and Antitrust Policy, 95 Harvard Law Review 1521, 1584 (1982) (dealing with interlocking joint ventures).
31. See, generally, Joseph Kattan, Antitrust Analysis of Technology Joint Ventures: Allocative Efficiency and the Rewards of Innovation, 6 Antitrust L.J. 937 (1993).
32. Brodley argues that there may be less competitive concern with joint ventures the earlier such ventures are in the value chain of the relevant product (e.g., research is earlier than marketing). See Brodley, 95 Harvard Law Review at 1570-73. The level of likely antitrust concern can also be characterized over other dimensions. For example, purchasing joint ventures may be less problematic than selling joint ventures. Unless the value of the purchases under the joint venture accounts for a large percent of the total sales of the purchased product and a large percent of the final price of the products sold by the participants, it is unlikely that such arrangements could force prices of the purchased products below competitive levels. See, for example, 1994 Health Care Policy Statements (Policy Statement No. 5, which provides an "antitrust safety zone" for certain joint purchasing arrangements among health care providers).

33. Analyses of joint ventures by the enforcement agencies are sometimes encumbered by information availability problems. For example, the prospect of efficiencies plays a critical role in a company's decision to enter into a joint venture, yet solid evidence of the existence and the size of these efficiencies is often lacking. This evidence can be important to the analyses of the ultimate impact to the consumer. See Dennis A. Yao and Thomas N. Dahdouh, Information Problems in Merger Decison Making and Their Impact on Development of an Efficiencies Defense, 62 Antitrust L.J. 23 (1993), for a discussion of information requirements and efficiencies in the context of mergers. The same information problems might also exist in determining future anticompetitive effects of joint ventures in innovative markets where the future parameters of the product market are still in doubt.

Appendix: International Symposium on Joint Ventures and Strategic Alliances

April 6–8, 1992, Nittany Lion Inn
Sponsored by: Center for Research in Conflict and Negotiation (CRCN) Penn State
The Smeal College of Business Administration
Fuji-Xerox
Institute for Policy Research and Evaluation, Penn State

Monday, April 6, 1992

1:30–1:45 p.m.	**Welcome and Introduction** *J.D. Hammond*, Dean, The Smeal College of Business Administration, Penn State	Ballroom C
1:45–2:00 p.m.	**Introduction of Participants**	Ballroom C
2:00–2:45 p.m.	**Opening Address** **"Joining Forces: Reflections from Fuji-Xerox"** *Hideki Kaihatsu*—Senior Managing Director Fuji-Xerox Co. Ltd.	Ballroom C
2:45–3:30 p.m.	**"Strategic Alliances in Telecommunications"** *Alan G. Chynoweth*—Vice President for Applied Research, Bellcore	Ballroom C
3:30–3:45 p.m.	**Break**	Atrium
3:45–5:00 p.m.	**"Strategic Alliances: Key Organizational and Policy Issues"** Panel participants: *Janusz A. Ordover*—Deputy Assistant Attorney General, Antitrust Division, U.S. Department of Justice *Dennis Yao*—Federal Trade Commissioner, United States Federal Trade Commission *Kathryn Harrigan*—Professor of Strategic Management and Director, Strategy Research Center Columbia University *Michael L. Katz*—Professor of Business Administration University of California at Berkeley	Ballroom C

6:30–7:00 p.m.	**Reception**	Ballroom C
7:00–9:00 p.m.	**Dinner**	Ballroom C

Tuesday, April 7, 1992

7:30–8:30 a.m.	**Breakfast**	Ballroom C

Morning Sessions—"Comparing Strategic Alliances in Different Industries"

8:30–9:15 a.m.	**"A Case Study of Successful GE/SNEMCA Joint Venture"** *Arthur O. Kohn*—Technical Director, Emeritus, CFM International, General Electric Company	Ballroom A
9:15–10:00 a.m.	**"Strategic Alliances in Commercial Biotechnology"** *Stephen Barley*—Associate Professor of Organizational Behavior, Cornell University	Ballroom A
10:00–10:30 a.m.	**Break**	Atrium
10:30–11:15 a.m.	**"The Political Economy of International Collaboration in Commerical Class Aircraft Manufacturing"** *Vicki L. Golich*—Assistant Professor of Political Science and Faculty Associate, CRCN, Penn State	Ballroom A
11:15–12:00 noon	**Discussion** *Amitabha Sen*—Member of Technical Staff, Corporate Research and Development, Motorola, Inc.	Ballroom A
12:00–1:15 p.m.	**Lunch**	Ballroom C

Afternoon Sessions—"Strategic Alliances: Perspectives from Executives"

1:15–2:00 p.m.	**"Joint Ventures...Some Thoughts on Why to Create Them and What Factors Can Influence Their Success"** *Vivian L. Gernand*—Director of New Business Development, Corning Inc.	Ballroom A
2:00–2:45 p.m.	**"Corporate Strategies and Joint Ventures"** *Wayne A. Hinman*—Vice President for Corporate Planning, Air Products and Chemicals, Inc.	Ballroom A
2:45–3:00 p.m.	**Break**	Atrium
3:00–3:45 p.m.	**"Joint Ventures in Newly Emerging Economies"** *Frans Ryckebosch*—Manager, Business Strategy, Latin America and China, Xerox	Ballroom A

3:45–4:30 p.m.	**"Organizational Learning—The Differential Advantage"** *Robert Radway*—President, Radway and Associates	Ballroom A
4:30–5:30 p.m.	**"Toward a Research Agenda: Roundtable Discussion"**	Ballroom A
6:30–7:30 p.m.	**Reception**	Ballroom C
7:30 p.m.	**Dinner** (Local Restaurants)	

Wednesday, April 8 1992

7:30–8:30 a.m.	**Breakfast**	Ballroom C

Morning Concurrent Sessions

8:30–9:15 a.m.		
Track A	**"Antitrust Policy, the Breadth of Patent Protection and the Incentive to Develop New Products"** *Suzanne Scotchmer*—Professor of Public Policy, University of California at Berkeley	Ballroom A
Track B	**"The Perpetuating Partnership: The Management of Long-Term Multi-Purpose Alliances"** *Michael Rubin*—President, Molinaro/Rubin Associates, Inc.	Ballroom B
9:15–10:00 a.m.		
Track A	**"Research Models of Joint Ventures: The Choice of Contract and Organizational Form for R&D Cooperation** *Michael L. Katz*—Professor of Business Administration University of California at Berkeley	Ballroom A
Track B	**"Industry Type, Autonomy and Performance of International Joint Ventures"** *J. Michael Geringer*—Assistant Professor of Policy and International Business, University of Western Ontario	Ballroom B
10:00–10:30 a.m.	**Break**	Atrium
10:30–11:30 a.m.		
Track A	**"Competing Joint Ventures** *Morton Kamien*—Joseph and Carole Levy Professor of Entrepreneurship, Northwestern University	Ballroom A

Track B	**"Organizing and Reconfiguring Joint Ventures: A Negotiations Model"** *Barbara Gray*—Professor of Organizational Behavior and Associate Director, CRCN, Penn State *Aimin Yan*—Ph.D. Candidate, Management and Organization, Penn State	Ballroom B
11:30–12:00 noon		
Track A	**Discussion** *Kalyan Chatterjee*—Professor of Management Science and Director, CRCN, Penn State *Keith Crocker*—Associate Professor of Economics and Faculty Associate, CRCN, Penn State	Ballroom A
Track B	**Discussion** *Kathryn Harrigan*—Professor of Strategic Management and Director, Strategy Research Center, Columbia University	Ballroom B
12:00–1:15 p.m.	**Lunch**	Ballroom C

Afternoon Concurrent Sessions

1:15–2:00 p.m.		
Track A	**"Endogenous Structures of Association in Oligopolies"** *Francis Bloch*—Assistant Professor of Economics, Brown University	Ballroom A
Track B	**"Interfirm Alliances—The Role of Trust"** *Christian Koenig*—Associate Professor of Strategy Managment, ESSEC (France) *Gilles Van Wijk*—ESSEC (France)	Ballroom B
2:00–2:45 p.m.		
Track A	**"Noncooperative, Cooperative and Delegative R&D"** *Sugata Marjit*—Associate Professor of Economics, Jadavpur University, India, and University of Rochester	Ballroom A
Track B	**"Back in the Box: Negotiating Collaborative Potential in International Joint Ventures"** *Kurt H. Loess*—Ph.D. Candidate, Case Western Reserve University *Paul F. Salipante*—Associate Professor of Labor and Human Resource Policy, Case Western Reserve University	Ballroom B

2:45–3:00 p.m.	**Break**	Atrium
3:00–3:45 p.m.		
Track A	**"Coalitions of Innovators: The Case of Canadian Patents"** *Stéphane Gauvin*—Assistant Professor of Marketing, Laval Université	Ballroom A
Track B	**"Negotiating Across Cultures: Some Potential Pitfalls"** *Rajesh Kumar*—Assistant Professor of International Business, Penn State, and Visiting Professor, Rennes University, France	Ballroom B
3:45–4:30 p.m.		
Track A	**Discussion** *Dennis Yao*—Federal Trade Commissioner, Federal Trade Commmission	Ballroom A
Track B	**Discussion** *Barbara Gray*—Professor of Organizational Behavior and Associate Director, CRCN, Penn State *Victor Israelian*—Fulbright Visiting Professor, Penn State and Ambassador U.S.S.R.	Ballroom B
4:30 p.m.	**Closing Comments**	Ballroom C

MIX
Papier aus verantwortungsvollen Quellen
Paper from responsible sources
FSC® C105338

If you have any concerns about our products,
you can contact us on
ProductSafety@springernature.com

In case Publisher is established outside the EU,
the EU authorized representative is:
Springer Nature Customer Service Center GmbH
Europaplatz 3, 69115 Heidelberg, Germany

Printed by Libri Plureos GmbH
in Hamburg, Germany